Concepts and Cases in Economic Analysis

Under the General Editorship of
Albert Gailord Hart
COLUMBIA UNIVERSITY

Concepts and Cases

in Economic Analysis

AARON W. WARNER
COLUMBIA UNIVERSITY

VICTOR R. FUCHS
COLUMBIA UNIVERSITY

WITHDRAWN

HARCOURT, BRACE AND COMPANY · NEW YORK

[b · 5 · 59]

Library of Congress Catalog Card Number: 58-9446

Printed in the United States of America

EDITOR'S FOREWORD

Economics aims to explain reality. But one of the standing problems of the teacher is to give the student a sense of reality without unduly sacrificing explanatory principles to mere description. How often have we all wished for a book which builds a body of teaching materials out of interesting happenings in the real world, but so grouped and presented that the details will not block the student's view of the analysis!

Here is such a book. It is designed to present economic analysis as a procedure for understanding and solving real problems. Constantly relating theory to the evidence, it unobtrusively keeps in focus both the sources and the limitations of economic knowledge. It nudges the student out of the groove of "passive learning," and gives him a basis for confidence that he is acquiring a useful set of tools, without encouraging him to try to make his economics prove too much.

This body of materials should prove invaluable both to instructors who want to supplement the treatment of a single standard text and to those who prefer to draw on a number of sources and points of view in introducing the student to economics. The case material is so rich that the instructor can assign few or many cases on any one of the topics covered; and there is ample range in the level of difficulty they present. The analytic introductions to which successive groups of cases are tied are sufficiently detailed to provide a framework for a course not based upon a standard text. At the same time they are brief enough not to involve undue duplication in a course that is based on such a text: the student who has worked through in a topic in a standard textbook chapter will be able to set himself a rapid reading pace, and will value the introductions as a safeguard against the ambiguities which can arise from divergencies in the use of economic terms. These introductions thus provide a frame of reference without overshadowing that testing of theory in the light of cases which is the book's unique contribution.

ALBERT GAILORD HART

New York, April 1958

PREFACE

This book represents a new approach to the study of basic economic theory. Although some conventional textbook material is included, the major effort is to teach the subject matter through source materials of various kinds. Our own teaching experience has convinced us that the use of such materials can arouse greater interest and stimulate more thoughtful consideration of economic problems than is possible within the limits of the standard textbook approach.

The emphasis throughout is on the proper use of the *concepts* and *tools* of economic analysis in specific and for the most part real situations, rather than on the discussion of broad policy questions. In our view, conceptual tools must be mastered before the student can be expected to think fruitfully about policy.

This text therefore differs in organization from many standard texts. Instead of organizing the course around a series of broad problems such as unemployment and inflation or monopoly and competition, the text adopts an approach which emphasizes the use of tools and concepts: demand, supply, equilibrium, elasticity, maximization and marginal analysis, and finally the essential concepts of macroeconomic analysis.

This is not to say that descriptive and applied economics have been disregarded. The student will find in the cases ample opportunity to grapple with problems in agriculture, labor, international trade, money and banking, fiscal policy, and the like. (An index of cases arranged by the topics in descriptive and applied economics to which they relate appears at the end of the book.) It should be noted, however, that some of the cases do presuppose an acquaintance with such economic institutions as the banking system, the elements of business organization and trade unionism, and national income accounting. If the student has not already acquired this background through a social science survey course, a previous course in economics, or perhaps business experience, he will want to acquire it through concurrent reading in a standard text or other sources.

Considerable attention has been given to the order in which the materials are presented. Our basic objective has been to allow the student to build logically upon what he has previously learned. Each analytic topic is therefore introduced by a concise statement of the basic theory or the nature of the analytic tool being presented. The topic is then developed through the use of illustrative case materials followed by questions for each case designed to raise the pertinent issues and to enable the student to apply the tools or concepts he has learned. The cases are drawn from a variety of sources ranging from current newspaper items and government publications to articles from professional economic journals and quotations from classic economic literature. The knowledge the student acquires is thus cumulative; by building upon what has gone before, and testing his knowledge in increasingly complex situations, he acquires a firm foundation for dealing with economic questions wherever he may encounter them.

Although the cases are primarily drawn from existing published sources, this is by no means a collection of "readings." The cases are frequently summaries or extracts from larger articles and are intended to illustrate a particular concept rather than to represent the views of the author. Where suitable materials did not appear to be available, we have in some instances included fictitious "cases" or problems.

We have designed the book to be used either as a basic text in economic analysis or as a supplement to be used with other readings. At Columbia University these materials have been used as the basic text in the second semester of a one-year principles course following a first semester which emphasizes descriptive and institutional background. Alternatively, the book can be used as the core around which the one-or-two semester course in principles of economics is organized, with supplementary material from a standard text or other sources being introduced as needed. Where it is used primarily to supplement a standard text, the book should offer a high degree of flexibility. Students can read the text material for a methodical and concise review of theoretical concepts. The instructor can select particular cases to illustrate key points and to enliven classroom discussions. Other cases may serve as the basis for outside assignments or for periodic quizzes.

We are indebted to Albert G. Hart for his many helpful criticisms and suggestions. Thanks to him and to others who have generously offered editorial assistance, our writing chores have been substantially lightened; any errors that remain are of course our own. We are also extremely grateful to the many authors and publishers who have cooperated so generously in granting permission to use portions of their work. We invite and will welcome the comments, criticisms, and suggestions of our teaching colleagues everywhere. It is to them that we dedicate this book.

AARON W. WARNER
VICTOR R. FUCHS

New York, April 1958

CONTENTS

TWO • Demand

FIVE • Elasticity, Part I

S I X • Elasticity, Part II

INCOME ELASTICITY OF DEMAND, 158

CROSS ELASTICITY OF DEMAND, 169

ELASTICITY OF SUPPLY, 173

S E V E N • Maximization and Marginal Analysis

MAXIMIZATION, 183

THE MARGIN, 185

MARGINAL REVENUE, 186

Marginal Revenue and Total Revenue as Related to Price Elasticity of Demand, 193

MARGINAL COST, 195

Marginal Cost and the Firm's Supply Curve, 196
Marginal and Other Costs, 199

MARGINAL PRODUCT, 215

The Concept of Marginal Product, 215
Marginal Revenue Product, 217

MARGINAL UTILITY, 221

EIGHT • Aggregative Analysis: Monetary Concepts

MONETARY CONCEPTS, 226

The Quantity Theory of Money, 226
The Equation of Exchange, 226

NINE • Aggregative Analysis: Keynesian Concepts

THE MULTIPLIER AND THE ACCELERATOR, 267

The Multiplier, 267
The Accelerator, 268

USE OF KEYNESIAN CONCEPTS FOR PUBLIC POLICY, 273

CHAPTER ONE

The Nature of
Economic Analysis

ECONOMICS AND ECONOMIC ANALYSIS

What Is Economics?

It is both customary and appropriate to begin the study of a subject by attempting to define it. Broadly speaking, economics may be defined as that branch of the social sciences which studies the production and exchange of commodities and services that are scarce in relation to human wants. In this definition we may notice several important elements.

First, it should be observed that we are studying human behavior. When we speak of economic activity, we refer to the actions of people. Moreover, we are primarily concerned with human activity in a social context. Sometimes, in seeking a point of departure for theorizing, economists begin by describing the behavior of Robinson Crusoe alone on a desert island. This may be suitable as an introduction, but the subject would quickly lose significance if it stopped there. Sooner or later, if we are dealing with economics, Robinson Crusoe rejoins his fellow men in a more complex society.

Second, the definition of economics assumes that we are dealing with scarcity. This is a relative term describing a relationship between wants or desires and the means available to satisfy them. Scarcity, of course, is not confined to economics. Wherever scarcity exists, there may be a problem of having to ration whatever it is that is scarce among the various uses to which it may be put. This process of choosing among alternative uses is sometimes referred to in a general way as "economizing." Thus, we may speak of "economizing" in the use of time, in the use of physical strength, and so on. Economists, however, are concerned with a specific kind of scarcity—the situation that exists when the desire for commodities and services exceeds the amount that is produced and exchanged at any given time. This scarcity of commodities and services is primarily the result of scarcity of the resources used to produce them: land, labor, and capital equipment. If scarcity did not exist—that is, if productive resources were so abundant that all commodities and services were freely available, and there were no unsatisfied needs or wants—there would be no economic problems and economics would cease to be of use or importance.

Finally, we assume that the processes of production and exchange that men engage in are intended to enhance their material well-being. Implicit in the study of economics is the idea that scarce resources should be used efficiently to satisfy material wants through the production and exchange of commodities and services. Economics would be of little help in explaining social behavior if the activities of production and exchange were merely part of some tribal custom or religious ritual.

The Study of Economics

We study economics primarily because we want to be able to understand and offer explanations and predictions about those aspects of man's behavior which may be referred to as economic. Interest in making predictions about economics is nearly universal; we all wish to improve our material well-being. In our private capacities as consumers, workers, businessmen, and investors, we are all called upon to make decisions concerning prices, employment, income, interest rates, and the like. Implicit in these decisions are attempts to predict future changes in these economic phenomena. Furthermore, as members of a social group acting through the institution we call government, we want to understand and control the forces which cause changes in the volume and the content of the nation's economic activity.

The study of economics falls naturally into three separate but closely interrelated categories: descriptive economics, applied economics, and economic analysis. In *descriptive economics*, we seek to ascertain the facts which are essential to our understanding of economic behavior. Thus, we may investigate the extent to which productive resources are available, the size and composition of the federal budget, or the organization of the Federal Reserve System. *Applied economics* deals with the realm of economic policy: the making of economic decisions or the solving of economic problems. The economic decisions and predictions that we make as individuals or private groups may be designated matters of private policy, while those which must be made collectively through government may be termed matters of public policy. We may also distinguish between economic policy that deals with specific aspects of economic activity, such as the prices of particular commodities or wages for particular occupations, and economic policy that is concerned with aggregate levels of economic activity, such as the level of employment or unemployment or the average level of prices or wages. *Economic analysis* provides the link between descriptive and applied economics; it is the bridge between fact and policy.

The Functions of Economic Analysis

Economic analysis may be described as the battery of tools, concepts, and techniques which are useful in finding solutions to economic problems. Analysis in itself does not arrive at decisions; but the policymaker may use analysis to simplify his task. Specifically, he will find analysis useful in defining his problem, in arranging his factual materials, and in deciding the extent to which relevant questions can be answered by the materials that are available. Analysis provides the investigator with a method of approach to his problems and a means of ascertaining the extent of his knowledge. In short, analysis provides "not a body of truth, but a means for discovering the truth."

This book is devoted to the task of introducing the student to economic analysis. It assumes that the student already has, or is currently acquiring, some factual knowledge about the nation's economy, and consequently it is not concerned with descriptive economics as such. Nor is it concerned with the systematic discussion of policy problems in the various fields of economic activity. Its purpose is to equip the student so that when he does encounter problems of economic policy, he will be able to deal with them with the tools of the economist.

Economic analysis may be applied both to problems of private policy and problems of public policy. While many students who study economics tend to think of its usefulness primarily in private terms, it must be emphasized that most of the great economists have been concerned with the problems of society as a whole. In the broad sweep of economic literature, the student will find that the overwhelming emphasis is on the problems of public policy, not on those of private policy. (In recent years, however, there has been a notable increase in the number of professional economists employed by business firms and trade associations on questions of private policy.) The tools of analysis which the student will encounter in this book may be applied to both types of economic problems.

Is Economics a Science?

Because economics is concerned with human behavior, there are some who question whether it can be regarded as a science. How, they ask, can reliable predictions be made when such predictions depend upon the behavior of millions of consumers, workers, businessmen, and investors who cannot themselves know what their future actions will be? This question highlights some of the difficulties involved in attempting to understand the economic world, but it does not negate the fact that economics, and especially economic analysis, does have many of the attributes of a science.

The test of any science is the extent to which it makes prediction possible. It is generally conceded that the social sciences, of which economics is one, offer less basis for prediction than the more exact sciences, such as physics. However, every science has areas of uncertainty, and even the "laws" of the most exact sciences are now being restated in terms of probability. Moreover, economics offers greater predictability than some of the criticisms would imply. In spite of the uncertainties involved in human behavior, there is still a sufficient degree of uniformity in the way people respond to permit the formulation of economic "laws" (or probabilities). The economist can also pursue scientific methods to give greater certainty to his findings. These include the maintenance of an objective attitude, the methodical collection of data, the use of this data in formulating generalizations or theories, and the testing of these theories by observing their application in new situations. By concentrating on phenomena which can be expressed and analyzed in quantitative terms, economics conforms to one famous definition that "science is measurement."

In spite of these scientific attributes, however, economics remains an inexact science, and students must be wary of its pitfalls. Whereas the natural sciences work with variables whose characteristics remain fairly stable over time, economic variables tend to undergo constant change. For this reason it is difficult in economics to duplicate, for purposes of study, any situation that has occurred in the past. The historian, E. H. Carr, suggested some of the difficulties facing social scientists when he compared science with history, saying: "In science the drama repeats itself over and over again because the *dramatis personae* are creatures unconscious of the past or inanimate objects. In history the drama cannot repeat itself because the *dramatis personae* at the second performance are already conscious of the prospective *dénouement;* the essential conditions of the first performance can never be reconstituted." [1] As a result, the economist must constantly accumulate new data and re-examine old theories.

Another pitfall which besets economists is the intrusion of value judgments. It is often difficult to draw a line between scientific analysis

[1] E. H. Carr, *The New Society*, Macmillan, London, 1951, p. 5.

and personal judgments as to what "should be." This is particularly true when economists are asked to make analyses and recommend policies in areas where they have (perhaps inescapably) formed judgments of what is right or wrong, good or bad, from an ethical point of view.

It is largely for this reason that competent economists may often differ among themselves. They may agree in an analysis of the relationship between policies and goals, and still disagree about the choice of policy or of goal. It is essential, therefore, to keep in mind the distinction between economic analysis and economic policy-making. Analysis requires no value judgments; in dealing with policy it is difficult to escape them. Both aspects of economics are of equal importance, but they cannot lay equal claim to being scientific.

CASE 1-1   What is economics?

Below are two of the best-known answers to the question: "What is economics?"

"Political economy or economics is a study of mankind in the ordinary business of life; it examines that part of individual and social action which is most closely connected with the attainment and with the use of the material requisites of well-being." [2]

"Economics is the science which studies human behavior as a relationship between ends and scarce means which have alternative uses." [3]

Questions

(Note that in this and succeeding cases, some questions may require you to refer back to the preceding text for a complete answer.)

1. How would you distinguish economics from other branches of study?
2. In what ways are the two definitions similar? In what respects do they differ?

CASE 1-2   Economic questions

The questions below are intended to illustrate the difference between problems of *private* and problems of *public* economic policy. You will note that some of these questions, although they have the appearance of being economic, cannot be answered only in economic terms. Identify those prob-

---

[2] Alfred Marshall, *Principles of Economics*, 8th ed., p. 1. Copyright, 1920 by The Macmillan Company, N.Y. Reprinted by permission.
[3] Lionel Robbins, *Essays on the Nature and Significance of Economic Science*, Macmillan, London, 1946, p. 16.

lems that are (a) primarily problems of private policy, (b) primarily problems of public policy, (c) problems of both private and public policy, (d) problems that cannot be answered only in economic terms. (Warning: You are not expected to provide substantive answers to these questions.)

1. Which industries and firms have the best profit potential for next year?

2. Are my inventories too high?

3. What fare should the city-owned subways charge to obtain the largest net revenue?

4. What is going to happen to wheat prices?

5. How can we get more schoolteachers?

6. What are the causes of the wave of corporate mergers? What are its effects?

7. How can we solve unemployment?

8. How will a storage loan price-support program for farmers and a direct production subsidy program differ in their effect upon consumers and taxpayers?

9. Would English exports rise if the pound were to be devalued?

10. What is a fair distribution of income?

11. What are the effects of minimum wage legislation?

12. Will my money be worth more or less next year?

13. Should the Federal Reserve raise the discount rate?

14. How do changes in the distribution of income affect the demand for my product?

15. Is "creeping socialism" bad?

16. Should I cut the price of my product?

17. What would happen if the United States abolished tariffs?

18. Should trade unions be abolished?

19. Should I increase my firm's rate of output?

20. How much advertising would be best?

21. Should the federal government try to balance the budget?

CASE 1-3   Kinds of economic problems

The following list of items is suggestive of some of the problems faced in economics. Determine for each item whether it suggests a problem *primarily* involving (a) the specific aspects, (b) the aggregate level of economic activity, or (c) both aspects.

1. Inflation	5. Economic growth	8. Builders' profits
2. Price of coffee	6. Level of interest	9. Antitrust laws
3. Tariffs	rates	10. Taxes
4. Unemployment	7. Sugar rationing	11. Value of money

| 12. Dividend rates | 14. The price of elec- | 15. Subsidies |
| 13. Market potentials | tricity | 16. Strikes |

CASE 1-4 What is an economist?

One popular definition of economics tells us that "economics is what economists do." In the following exchange, which took place during the Senate Committee hearings on the nomination of Arthur F. Burns to be a member of the Council of Economic Advisers,[4] a leading economist attempts to answer the question: "What is an economist?"

"*Senator Frear.* Mr. Chairman, Mr. Burns, are you an economist?

Mr. Burns. Yes.

Senator Frear. What is an economist?

Mr. Burns. Well, Senator, I think that is a very fair question. It is one I haven't been asked to answer for close to 30 years, but one that I keep asking of my students. I think justice does catch up with one.

Turning to your question, Senator, I think an economist is a person who has devoted himself seriously to the study of how goods and services are produced, how income is distributed among the people, what are the forces that make for changes in the volume and in the specific content of economic activity.

Senator Frear. Is it purely a study?

Mr. Burns. Well, I mention the study because that has been the activity that I have been engaged in. I like to think of it as a branch of knowledge that is approaching very slowly, very gradually, the status of a science."

Questions

1. Explain the difference between changes in the *volume* and changes in the *specific content* of economic activity.
2. What factors would determine whether economics is a science or not?
3. What considerations enter into the making of economic policy which are not present if economics is "purely a study"?

CASE 1-5 Economics and economic analysis

The following quotation sheds some additional light on the problem of the definition of economics, and also attempts to answer the question: "What is economic analysis?"

"The purpose of this paper is to determine the meaning that can be attached with consistency to the term 'economic' in the social sciences. . . .

---

[4] Hearing before the Committee on Banking and Currency, U.S. Senate, 83rd Congress, 1st Session, March 11, 1953, p. 10.

The simple recognition from which all such attempts must start is the fact that in referring to human activities, the term economic is a compound of two meanings that have independent roots. We will call them the substantive and the formal meanings.

The substantive meaning of economic derives from man's dependence for his livelihood upon nature and his fellows. It refers to the interaction with his natural and social environment, insofar as this results in supplying him with the means of material-want satisfaction.

The formal meaning of economic derives from the logical character of the means-end relationship, as apparent in such words as 'economical' or 'economizing.' It refers to a definite situation of choice, namely, that between the different uses of means induced by an insufficiency of the means. If we call the rules governing choice of means the logic of rational action, then we may denote this variant of logic, with an improvised term, as formal economics.

The two root meanings of economic, the substantive and the formal, have nothing in common. . . .

This combination of terms sprang from logically adventitious circumstances. The last two centuries produced in Western Europe and North America an organization of man's livelihood to which the rules of choice happened to be singularly applicable. This form of the economy consisted in a system of price-making markets. Since the acts of exchange, as practised under such a system, of necessity involve the participants in choices induced by an insufficiency of their means, the system could be reduced to a pattern that lent itself to the application of methods based on the formal meaning of economic. . . .

Last but not least economic analysis. This discipline results from the application of formal economics to an economy of a definite type, namely a market system. The economy is here embodied in institutions that cause individual choices to give rise to interdependent movements of objects and activities. This is achieved by generalizing the use of price-making markets. All goods and services, including the use of labor, land, and capital, are available for purchase in markets and have, therefore, a price; all forms of income derive from the sale of goods and services—wages, rent, and interest, respectively, appearing only as different instances of price according to the items sold. Since money is useless unless it is scarce, the general introduction of purchasing power as the means of acquisition converts the process of meeting requirements into an allocation of scarce means, namely, money. It follows that both the conditions of choice and its results are quantifiable in the form of prices. It can, therefore, be asserted that by concentrating on price as the economic fact *par excellence,* the formal method of approach offers a total description of the economy as determined by choices induced by an insufficiency of means. The conceptual tools by which this is performed constitute the discipline of economic analysis." [5]

Questions

1. What is the essence of the distinction that is made here between "substantive" and "formal"?
2. Is there more to economics than economic analysis? If so, how does it relate to analysis?
3. According to the view expressed in the above case, would economic analysis be meaningful in the absence of a market economy? Why or why not?

CASE 1-6 Descriptive economics, applied economics, and economic analysis

Fact, analysis, and policy are usually closely interwoven in the real world. As an exercise, the student should read the following discussion of the relation between reserve banking and currency and try to identify those passages which are good examples of descriptive economics, applied economics, and economic analysis. Also explain the basis for your choices.

1. "Currency shortages, together with other related developments, caused several financial crises or panics. One of the tasks of the Federal Reserve is to prevent such crises by providing a kind of currency that responds in volume to the needs of the country. The Federal Reserve note is such a currency.

Federal Reserve notes are paid out by a Federal Reserve Bank to a member bank on request and the amount so paid out is charged to the member bank's reserve account. Any Federal Reserve Bank, in turn, can obtain the needed notes from its Federal Reserve Agent, the representative of the government. The Federal Reserve Agent is located at the Federal Reserve Bank and has custody of all unissued notes. The Reserve Bank obtaining notes must pledge with the Federal Reserve Agent an amount of collateral at least equal to the amount of notes issued. This collateral may consist of gold certificates, United States Government securities, and eligible short-term paper discounted or purchased by the Reserve Bank. The amount of notes which may be issued is subject to an outside limit in that a Reserve Bank must have gold certificate reserves of not less than 25 per cent of its Federal Reserve notes in actual circulation. Gold certificates pledged as collateral with the Federal Reserve Agent and gold certificates deposited by the Reserve Bank with the Treas-

[5] Karl Polanyi, *Semantics of General Economic History* (revised). unpublished mimeographed paper, pp. 1–5.

ury of the United States as a redemption fund against Federal Reserve notes both count as such reserves."

2. "It has already been stated that the amount of currency in circulation now changes in response to changes in the public's needs. These changes are substantial and frequent. The demand varies for different days of the week, for different days of the month, and for different seasons. It increases before holidays such as Independence Day, Labor Day, and Thanksgiving, when many people take trips and need more pocket cash. There is an extraordinary increase in the demand before Christmas, when cash is used for Christmas shopping and as gifts. After the holidays, excess currency is promptly deposited in the banks by the merchants, hotelkeepers, and others with whom it has been spent, and the banks in turn send it to the Federal Reserve Banks. The effect of holiday movements of currency, when they occur at a week-end or month-end, is sometimes offset by other influences.

In addition to seasonal changes in the demand for currency, there are changes that reflect variations in business conditions. When business activity rises, the demand for currency increases, and when business activity declines, the demand also declines. . . .

During the war the amount of currency in circulation increased greatly in response to a variety of influences: the growth of payrolls, retail trade, and travel; many and widespread changes in places of residence; payments to members of the armed forces; larger incomes of people not in the habit of using banks; and, no doubt, hoarding of currency for various reasons. The demand for additional currency subsided after the war, but the volume in circulation remained extraordinarily large. . . ."

3. "If the banking system had no excess reserves, it would have to obtain additional reserves. The Federal Reserve could supply the reserves by lending to member banks, or it could buy an equivalent amount of government securities in the open market if this were considered desirable. Whichever procedure was followed, the demand for Federal Reserve credit and Reserve Bank holdings of discounts and securities would increase. The increase, however, would be only $200 in the case of the demand for $1,000 of checking deposits, while it would be $1,000 in the case of demand for an equal amount of currency. Because the increase in the demand for Federal Reserve credit is so much greater when the public withdraws its funds from banks in currency than when it leaves them on deposit, the volume of discounts and securities held by the Federal Reserve Banks is greatly influenced by changes in the demand for currency. As noted before, the changes in this demand are both frequent and substantial."

4. "Federal Reserve policy with respect to the expansion or contrac-

tion of Reserve Bank credit must always be alert to the character of the demand for such credit and, in the interests of economic stability, must be adapted to it. It is principally because of the large growth in currency in circulation during the war that the Federal Reserve Banks' ratio of reserves to combined note and deposit liabilities declined to a point where in 1945 it threatened to impinge upon the Federal Reserve's freedom of policy action. In these circumstances, Congress deemed it wise to reduce the reserve requirements of the Reserve Banks from 40 per cent for Federal Reserve notes and 35 per cent for deposits to 25 per cent for each kind of liability.

While the Federal Reserve pays out currency in response to the demand of the public and absorbs currency that the public does not need, it should not be concluded that currency demand is free of influence by the Federal Reserve. The policies pursued by the Federal Reserve affect this demand, as they also do the community's use of bank deposits. The main task of the Federal Reserve in providing an elastic currency, however, is to see that the total of the two forms of money is appropriately related to the volume of trade and production and does not itself tend to make the total demand for goods excessive or deficient." [6]

ECONOMIC RELATIONSHIPS

Meaning of Variables

"The object of all inquiry," wrote the philosophers Cohen and Nagel, "is the discovery of significant relations within the subject matter studied." [7] Before we can hope to find significant relations in any field, however, we must first identify the variables which are related; that is, we must decide what is the "subject matter" to be "studied."

What is a variable? Most simply defined, it is anything that is capable of change or of being changed. It may be something physical, or it may be in the nature of an "event" or "phenomenon" which undergoes change. Different fields of interest have their own sets of variables. In chemistry, for example, some of the important variables are temperature, pressure, and volume. Physicists are concerned with distances, velocity, and forces. Biologists ponder over cells, reproduction rates, and mutational changes.

Economists study "economic" variables, i.e., those events or phenomena connected with the production and exchange of commodities

---

[6] Board of Governors of the Federal Reserve System, *The Federal Reserve System*, Washington, D.C., 1954, pp. 89–90, 92–96.

[7] Morris R. Cohen and Ernest Nagel, *An Introduction to Logic and Scientific Method*, Harcourt, Brace, N.Y., 1934, p. 312.

and services. Examples of economic variables include the size and distribution of the national income, the price of wheat, the rate of interest, and the number of automobiles produced each month. There are many variables which are part of economics which are also of interest to other disciplines. Examples include the birth rate (sociology), tax rates (political science), extent of competition (jurisprudence), and productivity (industrial engineering).

Related Variables

When there is a relationship between two variables in the sense that the value of one depends upon the value of the other, we say that one variable is a *function* of the other. This statement can also be written in the form of an equation as follows:

$$y = f(x)$$

which simply says that the variable represented by the letter y is a function of (is related to) the variable represented by the letter x.

Most of us are already familiar with many functional relationships: perhaps that between the weight of a parcel-post package and the postage required, or that between the speed of a falling body and the distance it has fallen, or that between the salary of an outfielder and his batting average. Economists speak about such functional relationships among economic variables as those between spending and income, between the rate of interest and the size of the money supply, or between the foreign exchange rate and the volume of imports. Economists say, for example, that the number of cans of beer that people buy each month is a function of the price of beer.

Although the equation $y = f(x)$ tells us that there is a relation between two variables, the exact nature of the relationship is not revealed. In some cases, where we have additional information concerning the nature of the relationship between variables, we are able to "define" the function more specifically. Thus, if we know that one variable will always be twice as large as a related variable, we may indicate this relation by the equation $y = 2x$. Similarly, the equation $yx = 18$ tells us that the variables are related in such a way that their product always will equal 18.

Quite often in economics we have some information about the relationship between variables, but cannot be as precise as the examples above. We may know, for example, that variable y decreases as x increases and vice versa (that is, y increases as x decreases); in this case we can say that the variable y is a decreasing function of the variable x. In some cases, the variable y may remain constant for certain values of x. Even such limited knowledge may be of considerable help in explaining or predicting changes in economic variables. The knowledge that a decrease in price will increase sales, or that an increase in the tariff will cut down the domestic imports of a commodity, is obviously of use even though the precise degree of the change may be unknown.

At this point we must sound two warning notes about functional relationships. First, the fact that two variables are functionally related does not mean that one *causes* the other. In chemistry, for example, we can say that the temperature of a gas is a function of the velocity of its molecules. This does not imply that the velocity is the cause and the temperature the effect; we could just as easily say that the velocity is a function of the temperature. The important consideration is that the variables in a functional relationship are mutually dependent; that is, the statement that y is functionally related to x implies that x is also functionally related to y. Thus, $y = f(x)$ implies $x = g(y)$, where g merely indicates another functional relationship. For example, if $y = 2x$, then $x = \frac{1}{2}y$. In the second place, the fact that a variable is said to be a function of another does not mean that it may not also be a function of a third, a fourth, or even more variables. For example, although we say that the number of cans of beer that you buy is a function of the price of beer, it is probably also a function of other variables such as your income, the price of Pepsi-Cola, and the number of baseball games you attend.

Where we are dealing with multiple relationships of this sort, we will often find it useful in economics to analyze the relationships between one variable and another, ignoring for the moment the influence of changes in the other variables. This procedure is known as "assuming other things being equal," or "holding other things constant," or *ceteris paribus*. The justification for this analytical device is twofold; sometimes the influence of the "other things" is very small relative to the variable we are studying, and even when this is not the case, our best analytical procedure may be to study the influence of the several variables one at a time.

Tautologies and Theories

In the study of economic analysis the student will find it useful to distinguish clearly between tautologies and theories. Both are often stated in the form of functional relationships, and both are important to the progress of a science, but they have entirely different meanings and uses.

A tautology is a statement about variables which is always "true" because its terms are defined to make it so. (Indeed, tautologies are sometimes referred to as identities or truisms.) Thus when we say, "A ton of coal weighs 2,000 pounds," we are making a statement which is logically correct, always holds true, and cannot be argued. Perhaps the most famous tautology is the statement that 2 plus 2 equals 4. Tautologies are frequently useful; much human knowledge depends upon statements of identity, such as the two preceding statements. But tautologies can neither be confirmed nor denied by experience; their "truth" is a matter of definition and the rules of logic.

A theory is a statement about variables which may be either true or false. By examining the phenomena of the real world, we can determine whether the relationship posited by the theory does in fact hold, i.e., whether or not it corresponds to reality. If it does, then we may continue to work with and make use of the theory, always keeping in mind that a new look at the facts may some day reveal that the theory is false or incomplete. Theories are sometimes referred to as hypotheses, especially when they have yet to undergo rigorous testing. When a theory has been subjected to repeated tests and never found to be false, we tend to speak of it as a law, e.g., "the law of gravity." But even such "laws" offer us only probability, never absolute certainty.

An example may help to sharpen the distinction between the two types of statements as applied to economic variables. If we write $M = D$, meaning that the quantity of money in the economy is equal to the volume of demand deposits, we have offered a tautology. We define M and D in such a way that the statement can never be false. On the other hand, if we write $GNP = 4D$, meaning that the gross national product in any year will be equal to four times the volume of demand deposits, we have offered a theory or a hypothesis. By comparing GNP and D for various years we can test whether the theory is valid or not.

CASE 1-7   Selecting relevant variables

Make a list of variables you would be most likely to consider when studying each of the following policy problems:

1. The housing problem in New York City.
2. The advisability of tariff reduction for the United States.
3. Whether the Federal Reserve should tighten or ease the money supply.
4. Whether corporate income taxes should be lowered.

CASE 1-8   "Other things being equal"

The following quotation is one of the clearest expositions of the use of the concept of *ceteris paribus*.

"The forces to be dealt with are, however, so numerous that it is best to take a few at a time, and to work out a number of partial solutions as auxiliaries to our main study. . . . We reduce to inaction all other forces by the phrase 'other things being equal': we do not suppose that they are inert, but for the time being we ignore their activity. This scientific device is a great deal older than science; it is the method by which, consciously or unconsciously, sensible men have dealt from time immemorial with every difficult problem of ordinary life." [8]

Questions

1. Give examples of this device in fields other than economics.
2. What is the advantage of using this device? Can you think of any disadvantages?

CASE 1-9   On cause and effect

In the following extract, a well-known mathematically oriented economist discusses in nonmathematical terms the nature of the relationship between two variables.

"In nonmathematical language, the independent variable x in an algebraic equation corresponds to a *cause*. Sometimes that is an admissible translation; sometimes it is not. For *cause*, colloquially speaking, must necessarily come before its effect. Thus, you can consider the price of something as the *effect* and the cost of its production as the *cause*, or you can turn it about and consider the cost of production as the *effect* and the selling price to be the *cause*. For in that case there are a series of actions and reactions which permit you to suppose either that the supply of the product precedes the demand or that the demand precedes the supply on the market. In fact, there is a mutual dependence between supply and demand, and this mutual dependence can theoretically be expressed by an equation. You could not, in colloquial language, invert similarly the relation in which you call the freezing of water the cause, and the breaking of a pipe its effect, and say that the break caused the water to freeze. But, leaving terminology aside, if you are concerned only with the experimental relation between these two facts, isolating them from all others, you could easily deduce the existence of a break in a pipe from the freezing of the water in it and vice versa. For, in fact, there is

[8] Alfred Marshall, *op. cit.*, p. 14.

a mutual dependence between the change of temperature which turns the water into ice and the resistance of the pipe containing it. Thermodynamics, thanks to the language of mathematics, expresses this mutual dependence in a rigorous way; colloquial language expresses the same thing, but imperfectly.

Suppose we have two quantities, x and y, in a state of mutual dependence. In mathematical terms, we say that there is an equation between these two variables, and it is unnecessary to say more. But if we speak colloquially, we shall say that x is determined by y, which at once reacts on x, and so y finds itself depending on the new x. You can invert the terms and equally well say that y is determined by x, but that y reacts on x, and so x finds itself also dependent on y. Sometimes this method gives the same results as the mathematical equations; sometimes it does not. So we can substitute the colloquial method only with a good deal of circumspection." [9]

Questions

1. If we eliminate any consideration of cause and effect, of what value is a functional relationship?
2. If change in one variable in a functional relationship is not the cause of change in the other, what accounts for the continuing relationship?

CASE 1-10   Economic and noneconomic variables

1. The general price level
2. Movie admissions
3. Amount of unemployment
4. Average July temperature
5. Personal income
6. Size of West German army
7. Divorce rate
8. Price of TV sets
9. Democratic vote in Illinois
10. Volume of imports
11. Steel output
12. Quantity of money
13. Wage rates
14. Cigarette smoking
15. Human blood types
16. Ratio of men to women
17. Calories consumed per day
18. Extent of urbanization
19. Incidence of tuberculosis
20. The rediscount rate
21. Corporate profits
22. Number of farmers
23. Foreign exchange rates
24. Stock prices
25. Number of hurricanes
26. Volume of investment
27. Government deficit or surplus
28. Union membership

---

[9] Vilfredo Pareto, quoted in *The Practical Cogitator, or The Thinker's Anthology*, ed. by C. P. Curtis, Jr., and F. Greenslet, Houghton Mifflin, Boston, 1945, pp. 235–36.

Questions

1. From the list given on page 16, pick out those variables that are primarily "economic."
2. Pick out pairs of variables which you believe may be functionally related.
3. Put this information down in the form of equations using symbols to represent the variables.
4. Indicate any other variables (including, if necessary, variables not on this list) which might also enter into these functional relationships.

CASE 1-11   The goal of economics

"The ultimate goal of a positive science is the development of a 'theory' or 'hypothesis' that yields valid and meaningful (i.e., not truistic) predictions about phenomena not yet observed." [10]

Questions

1. Why is it necessary to distinguish between a theory that yields "valid and meaningful" predictions and "truistic" statements?
2. How would you go about forming valid and meaningful theories?

CASE 1-12   Branch Rickey's baseball equation

Branch Rickey, considered by many to be the smartest man in baseball, was asked by *Life* magazine to develop an equation for analyzing the strength or weakness of a baseball team.

Rickey divided baseball into two parts, offense and defense. Offense could be measured by the number of runs a team scored, defense by the number of runs scored against it. Thus, his first equation was:

$$G = O - D$$

where G equals game or victory; O equals runs scored by the offense; and D equals runs scored by the defense.

The next step was to find out what determined O and D. Rickey enlisted the aid of statisticians, and using his basic knowledge of baseball as a guide, they analyzed past statistics to find variables which were closely correlated with O and D. The equation which they finally developed was as follows:

$$G = \left[\frac{H + BB + HP}{AB + BB + HP} + \frac{3(TB - H)}{4AB} + \frac{R}{H + BB + HP}\right] -$$
$$\left[\frac{H}{AB} + \frac{BB + HB}{AB + BB + HB} + \frac{ER}{H + BB + HB} - \frac{SO}{8(AB + BB + HB)} - F\right]$$

---

[10] Milton Friedman, *Essays in Positive Economics*, U. of Chicago Press, Chicago, 1953, p. 7. © 1953 by the University of Chicago.

where H equals	hits	R equals	runs
BB	bases on balls	HB	hit batsman
HP	hit by pitcher	ER	earned runs
AB	times at bat	SO	strike outs
TB	total bases	F	fielding

Rickey states that the equation fits very well with past results, but he concludes: "Although the formula gives a comprehensive diagnosis of teams and players, it has limitations. It cannot predict the performance of a team on any given day or in any brief series because players have good and bad days. Nor can it foresee with accuracy the outcome of a pennant race because players do not always live up to past performance. But the formula is a valuable tool for analysis. . . ." [11]

Questions

1. Is the equation $G = O - D$ a hypothesis or a tautology? Explain.
2. Is the second equation a hypothesis or a tautology? Explain.
3. Is the fact that the second equation fits very well with past results a good test of its accuracy as a tool for prediction? If not, how would you test the validity of the equation?
4. In view of the second and third sentences in the Rickey quotation in the last paragraph above, how can he justify his statement that "the formula is a valuable tool for analysis"?

USE OF CHARTS IN ECONOMIC ANALYSIS

Graphical Representation of Related Variables

We have defined variables as events or phenomena which undergo change. We may now observe that change may either be *continuous* (that is, it may take place through a connected series of infinitely small changes), or *discontinuous* (that is, the intervals of change may be finite and perhaps irregular). Thus, a rise in temperature may be said to be continuous, while a change in price may be regarded as discontinuous.

Changes in economic variables are not normally continuous. This is due in part to the fact that measurement in economics usually takes place in finite, rather than in infinitely small, units. The price of wheat, for example, may be quoted in tenths of a cent per bushel, but not in hundredths or thousandths of a cent. The national income may be estimated in millions of dollars, but is certainly not measured down to the

---

[11] Branch Rickey, "Good-bye to Some Old Baseball Ideas," *Life*, August 2, 1954, p. 79. © 1954 by Time, Inc.

last penny. The result is that changes in these variables appear to be discontinuous in nature. Nevertheless, it is customary to treat changes in economic variables as continuous for analytical purposes, regardless of the fact that they are generally set forth in discontinuous terms. The justification for this is twofold: first, the assumption of continuity usually will not noticeably affect our results; and second, the ease and convenience of this treatment make it highly desirable. In cases where the assumption of continuity would have an adverse effect on our conclusions, we can allow for this separately without destroying the usefulness of the assumption in other situations.

The assumption of continuity is particularly useful because of the widespread use of graphs or charts in economic analysis. Graphs are an easy way of representing or portraying functional relationships between variables. The student will find them of great help in gaining an understanding and working knowledge of the concepts discussed in the following chapters.

If we are dealing with one variable and wish to represent it graphically we can do so on a single straight line. By arbitrarily selecting one point on the line as representing zero, we can show that for any possible value of the variable there is a corresponding point on the line. If the line is horizontal, we usually adopt the convention of having the positive (plus) values of the variable increase as we move to the right from zero, and the negative (minus) values increase as we move to the left from zero (see Fig. 1-1).

FIG. 1-1
$$-20 \quad -15 \quad -10 \quad -5 \quad 0 \quad +5 \quad +10 \quad +15 \quad +20 \quad \text{Variable } x$$

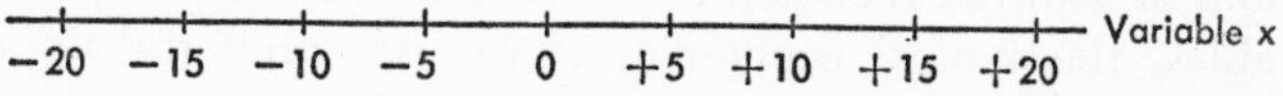

If we wish to represent two related variables on the same chart, we need two dimensions. These are usually depicted by horizontal and vertical lines which intersect at zero. On the horizontal line, the positive (plus) values increase as we move to the right from the intersection, while the negative (minus) values increase as we move to the left from the intersection. On the vertical line, the positive (plus) values increase as we move up from the point of intersection, while the negative (minus) values increase as we move down from that point. The horizontal and vertical lines, or base lines, are called the axes of the chart. The point where the axes cross, i.e., the point of zero value for each variable, is known as the "origin." Each axis has its own scale of values, and it should be noted that the scale on one axis need not be the same as the others (see Fig. 1-2).

FIG. 1-2

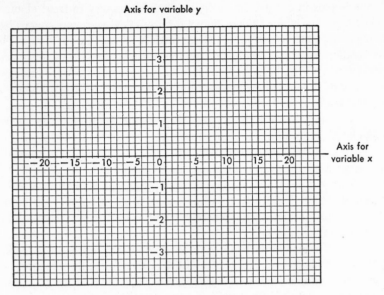

The chart is divided into four quarters by the two axes. If we limit ourselves to the upper right-hand quarter of the chart, both variables have positive values. If we are in the lower left-hand quarter, both variables have negative values. In the other two quarters of the chart, one of the variables will be negative, and the other positive. Since we are almost always concerned in economics with the positive values of variables, the typical economics chart uses only the upper right-hand corner and looks like the one in Fig. 1-3.

Now let us suppose that we have two variables y and x, that are functionally related as follows:

$$y = 3x$$

How may we represent this function on a graph? First, we would prepare a table showing the various values of y which correspond to certain values of x, as:

y	x
3	1
6	2
9	3
12	4

etc.

Next, we draw our two-dimensional chart and measure x along one axis and y along the other. The following step is to take any pair of values, e.g., $y = 3$, $x = 1$, and find a *point* on our chart which will correspond to these values. To do this, we move up three from zero in the vertical direction and then right one from the origin in the horizontal direction (see Fig. 1-3). We may plot several such points, each one representing a pair of values for our variables y and x. Finally, we may connect these points with a *line*, which represents our functional relationship or equation. Inspection will show that any point on the line we have drawn will satisfy the terms of the equation.

FIG. 1-3   Plotting a Functional Relationship

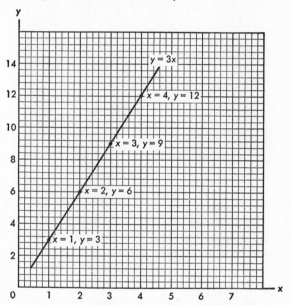

The equation in our example is represented by a straight line. Other equations may yield lines of many different shapes. The whole family of lines used to represent functional relationships will be referred to as *curves*, regardless of shape.

Graphical Solutions of Problems Involving Related Variables

One of the great conveniences of charts is that they make it relatively easy to solve problems involving sets of related variables. For example, if we have two different pieces of information about the relationship between two variables, such as $y = 2x + 4$ and $y = 13 - x$, we could, using algebra, find the only values of x and y that will hold true for both statements.[12] We can do the same thing graphically by drawing the two curves and then finding the point which is common to both curves. This can occur only where the two curves cross. The values of x and y at that point constitute the solution to the problem (see Fig. 1-4). Even if the equations were much more complicated in form, the graphical solution would still be relatively easy.

FIG. 1-4 Graphical Solution of a Problem Involving Two Functional Relationships

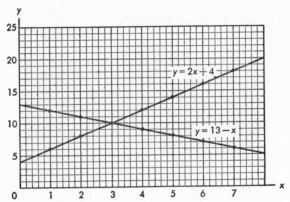

In economics we usually do not have precise information about the functional relationships, and therefore we cannot write out equations in as simple and well-defined form as in the above. We may be able to sketch in curves, however, which give a rough approximation of what we know about the variables, and in this way obtain an approximate solution. Identifying the variables, discovering as much about the relationships as possible, and solving for values which are mutually consistent are steps in the process of applying analysis to the solution of economic problems.

Time Series Charts

One special use of two-dimensional charts is to portray changes in a variable over time. Time series graphs are encountered very fre-

---

[12] As you may already know, this may be solved by means of simultaneous equations, as follows:

$$y = 2x + 4 \qquad 13 - x = 2x + 4 \qquad y = 2x + 4$$
$$y = 13 - x \qquad\qquad 9 = 3x \qquad\qquad y = 6 + 4$$
$$\qquad\qquad\qquad\qquad 3 = x \qquad\qquad y = 10$$

quently in economics, and the student should be familiar with their construction and use.

When charting a time series, it is customary to measure time along the horizontal axis and the related variable along the vertical axis (see Fig. 1-5). It is most important that the scale on the vertical axis begin with zero at the origin. If this is not done, an erroneous impression of the extent of change may be created, as in Fig. 1-6.

FIG. 1-5 Plotting a Time Series

Billion dollars

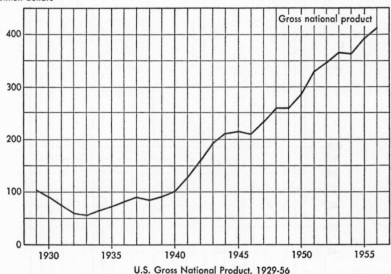

U.S. Gross National Product, 1929-56

FIG. 1-6 Misleading Plotting of a Time Series

Billion dollars

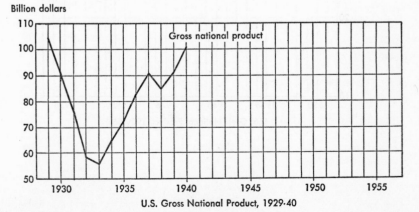

U.S. Gross National Product, 1929-40

FIG. 1-7   Plotting a Time Series: Semilogarithmic Scale

Billion dollars

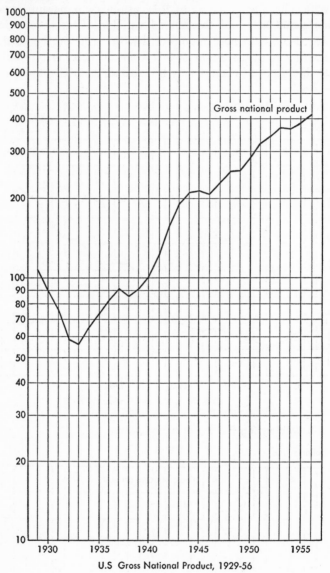

U.S Gross National Product, 1929-56

Even when the chart is properly constructed, it is sometimes difficult to compare relative rates of change on conventional graph paper. For example, in Fig. 1-5 it is not immediately apparent that United States Gross National Product was increasing at a much faster rate from 1933 to 1937 than from 1949 to 1953. In order to overcome this difficulty and enable the reader to perceive relative rates of change quickly and easily, economists frequently use semilogarithmic charts [13] rather than the conventional type discussed above. On this type of chart, changes in time along the horizontal axis are measured as usual. On the vertical scale, however, the distances between units are proportional to the *logarithms* of the units rather than to the units themselves.[14] For example, since the logarithm of 4 is to the logarithm of 2 as the log of 2 is to the log of 1, the distance between 4 and 2 is the same as the distance between 2 and 1. In other words, on a regular scale, equal distances represent equal *absolute* amounts of change; on the logarithmic scale, equal distances represent equal ratios or proportions or *relative* amounts of change (see Fig. 1-7).

The great advantage of the logarithmic scale is that one can compare relative rates of change merely by looking at the slope of the curve or curves. A variable which is changing at a constant percentage rate over time, for example, will result in a straight line on such a chart.

One important difference between a logarithmic and conventional scale is that the former can never show a value of zero. It is designed to show relative or percentage rates of change, and change from zero to a positive value would represent an infinitely great percentage increase and hence cannot be shown.

CASE 1-13   Use of charts

1. From the curve in Fig. 1-3 find the values of x when y has the following values:

y	x
1	
5	
10	

2. Plot five points based on the following equation, and then draw the curve which represents the equation:

$$y = \frac{4}{x}$$

---

[13] These are sometimes referred to as "ratio" or "ratio scale" charts.

[14] Hence the name *semi*logarithmic chart. There is also a *double* logarithmic chart where the scales on both the vertical and horizontal axes are based on logarithms.

3. a. Draw a curve from the following figures:

x	y
0	0
2	2
5	12.5
8	32

b. From this curve attempt to find the values of y corresponding to the following values of x:

x	y
3	
4	

4. Redraw the curve which represents the equation in Question 2, using the same horizontal scale but doubling the scale on the vertical axis. Does this curve represent the same relation as that in Question 2? Why do the curves look different on your graph paper?

CASE 1-14   Regular vs. special checking account

Sid Farmer and his wife Harriet are debating the merits of a special checking account vs. a regular checking account. Harriet is in favor of a regular account, pointing out that the bank charges 50 cents per month plus 10 cents per check on the special account (which requires no minimum balance). Sid reminds Harriet that in order to have a regular account they must maintain a minimum balance of $500 at all times, which money could otherwise be deposited in a savings bank and earn interest at the rate of 3 per cent per year.

Questions

1. Set up the *cost per check* of each type of account as a *general* functional equation, using symbols to represent the variables.
2. *Define* the functional relationship as best you can, still using symbols.
3. Substitute the actual figures given, solve the problem, and advise the Farmers as to what they should do.
4. Plot the functional relationship between *total cost of checks* and number of checks for each type of account and solve the problem graphically.

CASE 1-15   Comparing rates of change

FIG. 1-8   Personal Consumption Expenditures and Gross Private Domestic Investment, 1948–1955

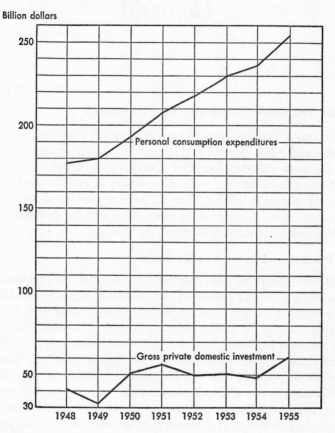

Billion dollars

Questions

1. What criticisms may be made of the above graphical presentation?
2. Present the same information in a new chart which will facilitate comparisons of the rates of change of the two variables.

CHAPTER TWO

Demand

USE OF THE TERM "DEMAND" IN ECONOMICS

The term "demand" is used by economists in a number of different contexts, and it is important to distinguish carefully among the various uses. Students will, therefore, find it necessary to apply the term with caution and to be precise as to its meaning in each context. Several particular meanings will be taken up in later sections of this chapter. In this section we consider the general nature of the demand concept and look briefly at some of its chief applications.

The Demand Concept in Economics

Demand frequently has a different connotation for economists and for noneconomists. To the economist, demand (regardless of the context in which it is used) implies that there is someone who is willing and able [1] to pay for a commodity or service. The term "demand" is not a synonym for "need," "desire," or "want," although it is often incorrectly used as such by noneconomists. Unless "need" or "desire" or "want" is accompanied by a willingness and ability to pay, demand is not present in any economic sense of the term. As we will see later, willingness and ability to pay are not the *only* necessary elements in the complete definition of demand; but they are, nevertheless, essential elements in the concept.

It is also important to distinguish between demand and actual expenditure. While demand reflects a willingness and ability to spend, it does not imply that actual expenditures have taken place. In order for expenditures to take place, commodities or services must be available, and transactions between buyers and sellers must be consummated. Expenditure therefore depends upon demand, but is not synonymous with it.

---

[1] "Able" simply implies having the money to pay for the commodity or service. It does not imply that commodities or services are necessarily available for purchase.

Applications of the Demand Concept

In developing the demand concept, we must first of all distinguish among different types of demand. We first make a broad distinction between (a) the demand for *particular* commodities or services and (b) *aggregate* demand, which may be defined as the total demand for all commodities or services produced during a specific period of time. The types of demand situations that can be identified within these broad classifications are considered below.

Demand for particular commodities or services.   With respect to the demand for particular commodities or services, there is an important distinction between *consumer demand* and *business (or producer) demand.* The first term applies the demand concept to consumer commodities or services, i.e., commodities or services which are expected to give direct satisfaction to the user (for example, shoes, toothbrushes, haircuts, and laundry services). Consumer commodities may be subdivided into durable commodities (such as automobiles and television sets) and nondurable commodities (such as food and clothing). When we study consumer demand we may be interested in studying the demand of a particular individual for a particular commodity or service; but we may also be interested in the demand of *all* consumers for that commodity or service. The latter is referred to as *market demand,* and will be dealt with in detail later in this chapter.

Business firms and others engaged in production also have a demand for commodities and services. These include commodities used up or converted in production (such as iron ore in steel production, soybeans in the plastics industry, electric power in all sorts of industries); labor services of many different kinds; the services of productive property either in the form of land or of productive plant and equipment; and capital funds which can be used to purchase productive property. Business demand is sometimes referred to as *derived demand.* A businessman never wants a producer commodity or service for the direct satisfaction it yields, as is true of consumer demand; he wants it only because it will help him to produce. If there is no demand (either existing or potential) for his output, the businessman would have no demand for producer commodities or services, or for labor, land, or capital funds. Thus, the demand for these things is said to be *derived* from the demand for the final product.

The distinction between producer commodities and consumer commodities is not always clear-cut. Some commodities may be classified as one or the other depending upon their use. An automobile bought for family pleasure trips, for example, is a consumer commodity, whereas one bought by a traveling salesman for business purposes is a producer commodity. The demand for automobiles, therefore, contains elements of business demand as well as consumer demand.

Aggregate demand. When we add up the total demand for all particular goods and services during a given time, we arrive at what economists call *aggregate demand.* But this total is not reached simply by adding total consumer demand to total business demand. Government also buys goods and services, and there is usually a demand for the goods and services of one nation on the part of other nations outside its borders. Moreover, we find that the pattern of business demand for new plant and equipment—what is called aggregate investment demand—behaves somewhat differently from other types of demand. For these reasons the concept of aggregate demand is better reserved for separate treatment in Chapter 9.

In this chapter we are primarily concerned with consumer demand, and mainly with the consumer demand for particular commodities and services. Business demand is considered briefly at the end of the chapter.

CASE 2-1   Use of the demand concept

1. "The demand for housing is great, but people do not have the money to pay for it."
2. "The demand for long underwear isn't what it used to be."
3. "We, the members of the Greenback party, demand cheap money."
4. "The prosperity of the postwar period has been an important factor in the strong demand for automobiles."
5. "When the government raised the price of butter, the demand for margarine increased."

Questions

1. In which of these statements is "demand" being used in an economic sense?
2. How should the remaining statements be reworded to bring out their specific meaning?

CASE 2-2   Types of commodities and services

1. Telephones
2. Water
3. Apples
4. Diesel oil
5. Fertilizer
6. Tricycles
7. Clothing
8. Grain elevators
9. Newspapers
10. Coal
11. Bulldozers
12. Blast furnaces
13. Medical care
14. Railroad transportation
15. Opera
16. Typing
17. Baseball games
18. Restaurant meals

Questions

1. Identify the commodities and services listed on page 30 as (a) primarily consumer, (b) primarily producer, or (c) both.

2. Why might economists find it useful to distinguish between consumer demand and other kinds of demand?

CASE 2-3   The need and demand for physicians

"In the field of medical care, a shortage in personnel or in facilities is conceived of as the difference between the numbers available to render service and the numbers needed. The use of need as the standard of adequacy is common to all discussions of medical care, both technical and popular, and is adhered to with remarkable consistency.

Why is need the accepted standard in medical care when it is, at best, a subordinate concept in other areas of economic activity? I believe that need rather than consumer behavior in the market is the prevailing standard in medical care because by tradition we aim to make medical care of good (or adequate) quality available to all people, regardless of economic status and willingness to pay for it. . . .

Usually the need for physicians is estimated on the basis of ratio of physicians to population that currently prevails at a selected point in an array of states or health service regions.

The National Health Assembly employed as one of its standards the weighted ratio of physicians to population in the twelve states with the highest individual ratios and arrived at an estimated need for 254,900 physicians in 1960 and projected a shortage of 42,000.

In 1949, Mountin, Pennell, and Berger, of the U.S. Public Health Service, estimated need on the basis of three alternative standards, representing ratios of physicians to population at the 12th, 16th, and 37th health service regions, respectively, in an array of 126 regions.

Gross needs, inclusive of retired physicians, are estimated for 1960, as follows: Standard A, 272,000; Standard B, 261,000; Standard C, 244,-500. Estimating a maximum availability of 227,000 physicians in 1960, the anticipated shortages are 45,000, 34,000, and 17,500, respectively. It should be noted that the estimates assume that all regions below the standard ratio will be raised to it, but that regions which are above the standard will retain their present ratios. . . .

Let us examine the policy decision that need is our standard of adequacy for medical care. If medical care were subjected to the test of the market place, like most other goods and services, what could be said about the demand for physicians relative to the present number?

Professor Dickinson and others take the position that there can be no serious shortage of physicians because consumers receive what they pay for (and the indigent continue to receive whatever services they require). Indeed, they argue, consumers are currently receiving extra benefits. As is well known, consumers spend approximately 4 per cent of their total expenditures for medical care. They spend larger shares of the total on other items, such as liquor, recreation, personal services, etc. Moreover, between 1940 and 1949, the prices charged by physicians rose less than most other prices, only 38 per cent against a rise of 69 per cent in the cost of living. Relative to other items of expenditure, physicians' services have become a better buy. If consumers want more medical services supplied by more physicians, they should devote more money to this purpose. . . .

Comparison of consumers' expenditures for medical care with those for other items can be misleading, as many persons have noted. Expenditures for tobacco, liquor, or recreation may be considered by some as morally reprehensible, but they are certain, regular, low-priced per unit of purchase and, usually, pleasurable. Until the advent of health insurance, expenditures for medical care were uncertain, irregular, low-priced to some and very costly to those with serious illnesses, and scarcely pleasurable. . . .

It has been suggested that by the very nature of the service, consumers' expenditures on medical care are bound to be too low. As in education, free consumer choice tends to result in too low an expenditure because the return is uncertain and social benefits exceed private benefits by a large margin. It is, therefore, advocated that consumers' choice either be abandoned or guided in order to increase expenditures for medical care. . . .

As for the conclusion that increased consumers' expenditures for medical care would bring about an increase in the volume of services, it is subject to qualification. . . . A high degree of product differentiation makes the sliding scale possible, and it acts to raise the average level of charges for medical care. Incomes of physicians can rise without a corresponding expansion in services rendered.

Some students of medical care, especially economists, point to the incomes of physicians as indicative of a shortage in the field. Friedman and Kuznets concluded that as much as one-half of the difference in average income between physicians and dentists is accounted for by the greater difficulty of entry into medicine. . . .

This pressure for admission to medical school by a large number of qualified applicants is sufficient proof of a shortage in the medical profession, independent of any income differentials, if one accepts the test of the market for the allocation of manpower. In practice, this test is not applied in the medical field lest an increase in the number of physicians produce certain undesirable consequences.

Dean Rappleye has given two major arguments against a substantial increase in the output of physicians: the quality of medical training would suffer; and the ethical standards of the medical profession might be impaired. Dr. Rappleye has stated: 'Economic competition [in medicine] would [not] result in the maintenance of high standards of medical care because laymen cannot be expected to have a basis for judgment of professional competence.' Nor, in his opinion, can effective control be exercised by other means. . . .

If need is accepted as the basis for determining requirements for medical care for individuals, the market cannot perform the test of adequacy of care. However, it is not possible to rely on 'medical' criteria alone to establish a standard of need; economic costs, in the sense of alternatives foregone, must be taken into account. . . ." [2]

Questions

1. Can you distinguish "demand" from "need" in this situation? How?
2. Do you agree that need rather than consumer behavior in the market should be the standard in medical care? Why?
3. In your opinion, should the "need" for physicians be met without regard to economic considerations?

CASE 2-4   The desire and demand for education

"Corporate aid to higher education reached a record level in 1956, but much more support must be forthcoming if the nation's colleges and universities are to meet current and future needs.

Business and industry—from General Motors, the world's largest corporate enterprise, to Joe's Dry Cleaning and Laundry in the small town of Oberlin, Ohio—gave an estimated total of $100,000,000 to higher education, according to the Council on Financial Aid to Education.

This estimate—which some educators, businessmen, and research workers feel may even be a little on the conservative side—represents an increase of $25,000,000 over 1954 and a gain of $60,000,000 since 1950.

Only last week, Dr. Frank H. Sparks, chairman of the commission on colleges and industry of the Association of American Colleges, described the increase in corporation support of higher education as being of 'revolutionary proportions.'

Total voluntary private contributions to higher education from all

---

[2] Herbert E. Klarman, "Requirements for Physicians," *American Economic Review*, Vol. 41, May 1951, pp. 633–44. © 1951 by the American Economic Association.

sources exceeded $500,000,000. But this sum, too, is inadequate when measured against the need.

According to Dr. Wilson Compton, the council's president, the nation's colleges and universities will need an average of more than $500,000,000 additional each year for the next ten years 'if they are to meet rock-bottom requirements of maintenance and growth.'

Two-thirds of the additional funds that the council estimates are needed will be required by the private colleges and universities, and the remainder by the tax-supported institutions. Two-thirds of the total funds required by both groups of institutions will be needed for plant improvement and expansion, and one-third for operating expenses. A major share of the operating expense needs would be used to improve faculty salaries.

From where are these needed funds to come?

'Some of this support,' Dr. Compton said, 'may come from increased tuitions in private and tax-supported institutions alike—aided by student loans and scholarship funds. But much of it will have to come from alumni, business concerns, the professions, foundations, related church bodies, labor unions—the general public.

Ironically, a major reason why colleges are in financial difficulty is that there has been a tremendous demand for their products: college-educated men and women. Last fall's enrollment of 3,000,000 students was a record. However, by 1970, it is estimated that twice that number will be enrolled in colleges and universities.

The increasing enrollment has forced the colleges to expand their facilities and increase their faculties. All this happened, moreover, during the period of rising costs and proportionately decreasing income. Tuition fees have been raised 100 to 150 per cent in many institutions since World War II, but even so tuition income now covers only about half the per capita cost of education in many colleges. The rest of the cost has to be provided by the college—very often at the expense of faculty salaries.

AD CAMPAIGN PLANNED

With the cooperation of the Advertising Council, the Council for Financial Aid to Education is planning to start shortly a public service advertising campaign on the plight of the colleges. It will call attention to the need for increased support. This campaign will be similar to one that in recent years was responsible for increased interest in 'better schools.'

Business and industry will not be asked to carry the burden of providing the additional funds—not even the educators want this—but they will be asked to step up their support.

According to the latest statistics from the Internal Revenue Service, corporations gave 1.24 per cent of their net taxable income to philanthropy—and about one-fifth of this amount went to higher education purposes. Without officially urging this—it does not want to tell business how much to give—the Council on Financial Aid to Education has recently suggested that 1 per cent of net taxable income might be a fair amount. Based on last year's estimated taxable income of $40,000,000,000, this percentage would have meant $400,000,000.

Although corporation aid to education has increased rapidly in recent years and more is now heard about it than ever before, it is not a new development. Westinghouse started an aid-to-education program about forty years ago, and other companies also were making grants. But the scope was limited and the total of funds given was not sizable.

It was not until after World War II that business corporations really began to get interested in aiding education. Three leading corporation executives were largely responsible for that development, although it came about under fairly unusual circumstances.

ABRAMS RECALLS SPEECH

In 1947, Frank W. Abrams, then chairman of the Standard Oil Company (New Jersey), made a speech on 'The Stake of Business in American Education.'

'When I got through,' Mr. Abrams recently recalled, 'I don't know whether I persuaded anybody else, but I sure persuaded myself.

'Something like the same thing,' he continued, 'happened to Irving S. Olds, then chairman of United States Steel, at just about the same time, and to Alfred P. Sloan, then chairman of General Motors. Mr. Olds made a speech at Yale and Mr. Sloan wrote an article for *Collier's*—and they both bought their own medicine.

'I found out later all three of us also got the same kind of reaction not only from educators, but from other businessmen. We began to get a lot of letters of commendation and invitations to appear and say it again.

'We had apparently said some things that had been germinating in the minds of a great many people. In other words, we had hit the market at the right time.'

EXECUTIVES FOLLOW SUIT

The three were soon joined by other executives, who felt that the future of the nation and the fate of their companies depended in large measure on the American system of education. Corporation aid to education was recognized as a good business investment. One businessman commented:

'Corporations and their shareholders have a stake in higher education. Higher education is important to them in the matter of markets—an educated public and a high standard of living go hand in hand. It is important in the development of products and processes. And it can no longer depend on the charity of private individuals struggling under current tax loads.'

But before corporation contribution could assume major proportions, a rather formidable hurdle had to be cleared.

For despite their sympathy to the plight of higher education and their personal willingness to do something about it, many corporation directors were not at all sure whether they had a legal right to make unrestricted corporate gifts to colleges and universities. In the absence of legal precedents, the directors ran the risk that they might have to repay the corporation personally for any grants they made.

In 1953 several stockholders of the A. P. Smith Company in East Orange, N.J., sued to stop a $1500 gift of unrestricted funds to Princeton University. The company's profits, they contended in effect, should be used to further the company's business or be distributed to the stockholders. The New Jersey Supreme Court held that the gift was legal and the precedent was set.

BASE OF GIVING WIDENED

With the impetus furnished by the Smith decision and sparked by those who saw the needs and knew the answers, corporation giving began to take giant strides. Not only did the dollar volume increase, but, just as important, the base of giving was broadened.

Whereas most of the early aid-to-education programs were designed to benefit the donor directly, the new programs often provided money with no strings attached—the funds could be used at the discretion of the institution. All sorts of programs and plans were developed—involving direct grants, indirect grants, scholarships, fellowships, supplemental aid, matching grants, and other types of aid. . . .

UNIONS VOICE FEARS

The rise in corporation contributions and the importance being attached to this source of support by educators, have caused concern in some circles, particularly among labor unions. This concern is motivated by the fear that increased dependence on corporate grants might bring the nation's colleges and universities under the influence of the corporations. Educators are quick to deny these charges.

Dr. Compton, a former college president, declared:

'While the college campus and business have become more interdependent, the former has had to sacrifice none of its independence. In all my experience with college administrators—and I was one of them for many years—I have heard no complaint and seen no evidence that industry, through its financial aid or in any other way, is attempting to dictate educational policy or to meddle in academic affairs.

'Business is not throwing its weight around the college campus. Rather it is helping the colleges to help themselves. The ties that unite the long-range interests of higher education and business are not ties that bind.' " [3]

Questions

1. Is the demand for a college education increasing? If so, why is the need for subsidies also increasing?
2. Since business is willing to contribute to the cost of education, can it be said that there is a demand by business for education?
3. Should students be required to pay the full cost of their education? Give reasons for your answer.

CASE 2-5   Consumer demand for services

"City package tours that include theatre tickets were given the blessing of legality yesterday by the Court of Special Sessions.

In a unanimous decision, Justices Louis B. Heller, George M. Carney, and Vincent R. Impellitteri granted a defense motion to dismiss charges against the Paul Tausig & Son Travel Agency of 29 West 46th Street [New York City].

The agency, in business more than fifty years and offering package tours for the last seven years, was charged in a criminal information with reselling theatre tickets without a city license.

Following the presentation of the prosecution's case by assistant corporation counsel Paul Farkas, Solomon A. Klein, the defendant's attorney, moved for dismissal of the charges.

Mr. Klein likened the travel agency to an errand boy in one case and to a dentist in another. He said that just as an employer might send a clerk to a theatre to buy a ticket for him, so the travel agency acted as an agent for its customers.

In the analogy to a dentist, Mr. Klein explained that when a dentist put a gold filling in a tooth, he wasn't selling gold but was performing a service, just as the Tausig Agency was doing.

The decision is expected to affect many other agencies offering tours that include a stay at a New York hotel, a sightseeing trip, entertainment at a night club, and tickets to a hit show.

Mr. Klein pointed out that the statute under which the agency was

---

[3] Leonard Buder, "Industry Steps Up Gifts to Colleges," New York *Times,* January 13, 1957. © 1957 by The New York Times Company.

being prosecuted was enacted 'to safeguard the public against fraud, extortion, and exorbitant rates.'

'We are innocent; we are moral; we have not violated the statute in any way,' he said, adding: 'We have never sold a theatre ticket at any profit.

'The interpretation of the statute that has been given by the License Department is absurd. It helps only one group of people—the ticket scalpers and the black market ticket speculators who would like to drive us out of business because they cannot compete with us.'

Mr. Klein asserted in his motion that 'the economic welfare of the city' was at stake in the case. He observed that tourism brought a billion dollars a year into the city, and that one agency alone brought in as much as 30,000 visitors and $8,000,000 in business.

Samuel Mandell, assistant corporation counsel who opposed the motion, maintained that his office was charged with enforcing the statutes 'no matter who gets hurt.'

He accused the Tausig Agency of setting up a 'scheme in order to facilitate the sale of theatre tickets' and charged the agency with 'circumventing the law.'

Presiding Justice Impellitteri said that the 'evidence is conclusive that the main part of the bill of the tour is for hotels and other entertainment and the theatre end is incidental' in the package." [4]

Questions

1. Is the demand for theatre tickets in this case consumer demand or producer demand?
2. What is the travel agency selling?
3. Can ticket scalping be classified as a service? In what way does it differ from the business of the tourist agency?

CASE 2-6   The demand for real estate brokers

"Many a lively discussion has been started on the question of whether a prospective home purchaser or seller should work through a real estate broker or attempt to go it alone. As long as there are active real estate boards, and until the last house has been sold without benefit of brokerage, the argument can be expected to rage on.

People on both sides of the debate offer reasons to support their views, and, strangely enough, the complexity of a realty transaction is the crux of both their contentions. Brokers say that laymen are generally not trained to handle such deals. Individual sellers or buyers argue that brokers, striving for a large turnover, cannot be relied upon to consider details.

---

[4] Jack Roth, "City Package Trip Upheld by Court," New York *Times,* December 19, 1956. © 1956 by The New York Times Company.

Speaking for the Westchester County Realty Board, John J. Donohue, its president, gives some of the reasons why brokers are indispensable to a successful transaction in a typically residential area.

Tracing the process from its beginning, Mr. Donohue explains that a broker, better than almost anyone else, can steer the potential seller to the most advantageous asking price. In many cases, he says, owners succumb to an understandable pride in their properties or to overoptimism in seeking unrealistic yields from their houses. A broker, discussing the matter when the home is listed for sale, can point out to the owner that asking too much is a waste of time.

POOL OF POTENTIAL BUYERS

Once the home is placed on the market with one or more brokers, Mr. Donohue continues, the seller has at his immediate disposal a pool of potential buyers who have at one time or another asked the agents to be on the lookout for a property of approximately that description. These buyers can be contacted and brought to the house within a reasonably short time.

But this is not done in random fashion, the realty spokesman explains. On the contrary, the broker acts as a buffer to prevent unwarranted intrusions on the seller's privacy. If, for example, a home-seeker has flexible requirements, but insists on a two-car garage, a broker is unlikely to disturb a seller whose house may meet the needs but has only a one-car garage.

At the same time, brokers can serve everybody concerned by screening potential purchasers in matters of finance. Mr. Donohue says that an astute agent knows not only the value of a dwelling, but also its financing potential. Such a broker is not likely to take a purchaser who needs a thirty-year mortgage to a property that, because of age, commands no more than a ten-year term.

With varying degrees of subtlety, brokers also try to elicit from home-seekers their financial status as it applies to their ability to meet the carrying charges entailed in the price bracket in which they are looking.

Mr. Donohue himself tries to obtain this information without asking the question directly. But, in many cases, novices in search of a house put their cards on the table, asking his advice on what price range and type of financing they should consider in view of their incomes. This, of course, clears the air when specific houses are under consideration.

The realty men's contention is that a broker's skill in matching income and savings with price and financing protects a seller against an inconclusive sale. Too often, they contend, an inexperienced home-seller considers the deal closed when someone selects his property and agrees on the price. He makes arrangements to move elsewhere, only to find out at the eleventh hour that the purchaser is unable to obtain the necessary mortgage. This, Mr. Donohue maintains, is less likely to happen when a broker handles the sale.

Those who prefer to sell their properties without benefit of brokerage seem to agree with few if any of the points made by the realty spokesman. Their views, expressed in telephonic conversations based on their efforts to sell their homes through direct advertising, are as follows:

Most commonly, such sellers object primarily to the customary 5 per cent commission paid to brokers in home sales. Paid by the seller, the commission reduces the net yield of the sale if the price represents the actual value of the dwelling, they say. If, on the other hand, the seller wants to preserve the full measure of the net yield, he must then raise the price by 5 per cent to compensate for the commission.

The usual objection of sellers to paying the commission is that it seems to them unnecessary to cut a broker in on the yield of a home sale. Raising the price to make up for the commission meets with the argument that the resulting price level becomes too high to attract purchasers. In fact, sellers with this point of view ask, why should either party to the transaction pay a premium for consummating it?

The realty men's answer to this is that the commission does not distort the market value of a property. Moreover, they say, their participation in the deal may bring the price closer to the true market. They believe that an inexperienced purchaser may well pay a sum far too high for the house because no expert was there to advise him on its true worth.

ANOTHER POINT OF VIEW

By the same token a seller who may have become impatient might settle for something well below what he could have netted. In either case, say the brokers, it would have been worth either party's while to absorb what the brokers prefer to call a professional fee of 5 per cent.

Another viewpoint expressed by the home-owners who plan to forego the aid of brokers is that there is a distinct difference between the ideals and the actual practices of the realty profession. They discount the buffer theory, saying that brokers have brought to their homes many lookers who should have been eliminated as potential buyers.

Sellers in this category also feel that they are capable of protecting themselves against deals that cannot be financed. Before they commit themselves to vacate their houses for a buyer, they make certain that the latter is financially able to go through with the deal. If they are not equipped to ascertain it themselves, they say, they rely on their attorneys for this task.

One of the facets of this debate that may account for some of the divergence of opinions is the question of loyalty. Under the law, brokers are the agents of the sellers because the sellers pay the commissions (even if they are absorbed by the purchasers in the price). Sellers, therefore, expect brokers to represent their interests to the utmost.

Mr. Donohue points out, however, that even though a broker is the seller's agent of record, a conscientious realty man will keep the interests of purchasers in mind also as a matter of ethical practice.

It does little good, he says, for a broker to treat buyers otherwise, because callousness to their needs will eventually deplete the list of potential buyers who look to brokers in their search for homes. This, in the long run, would hurt the sellers." [5]

Questions

1. What is the service that a real estate broker renders? Is it a consumer service or a producer service? Why?
2. Who is the demander of this service: the buyer or the seller?
3. In practice, who pays for the service? In your opinion, who should pay for it?

SPECIFIC MEANINGS OF THE TERM "DEMAND"

It was indicated in the previous section that the term "demand" has different meanings depending upon the context in which it is used. Two important but sometimes confusing uses of the term are those relating to the concepts of the *quantity demanded* and the *demand schedule*.

Quantity Demanded

Demand is sometimes used to indicate the "quantity demanded" by the consumer. Thus, if one speaks of the demand of consumers for oranges, he may be referring specifically to the quantity of oranges consumers are willing and able to buy.

We may now ask what determines the quantity of a commodity or service which will be demanded by a consumer.[6] The factors which influence the quantity demanded will be referred to as the *determinants of quantity demanded.*[7]

---

[5] Walter H. Stern, "Is a Broker Worth 5%?" New York *Times*, November 11, 1956. © 1956 by The New York Times Company.

[6] Quantity demanded is always expressed as a quantity per unit of time, e.g., so much demanded per week or per month. The same demand may be expressed in more than one way, just as a car may be said to have a velocity of a mile per minute or 60 miles per hour. Also, as in the case of the speeding auto, the demand for a product need not remain constant over time but may change.

[7] Some writers refer to these factors simply as the *determinants of demand.*

If we consider a specific individual, Bob Smith, and his demand for a specific commodity, beer, we can observe some of the things which determine the quantity of beer he is willing and able to buy during any specific period of time. We may list the following: his income, the price of beer, the prices of other goods he may wish to buy, his liking for beer, the weather, the amount of entertaining he expects to do, the amount of advertising by beer manufacturers, and so on. The last four items, and many others of a similar nature, are usually lumped together into a general category called *taste*. This is a catchall category which includes all the factors other than income or prices which influence the quantity demanded.

What is true of Bob Smith with respect to beer is true of any consumer with respect to any commodity or service. The variables which determine the quantity of a commodity which will be demanded (per unit of time) may be summarized as (a) the price of the commodity, (b) the prices of other commodities, (c) income, and (d) taste. Occasionally, we may also have to consider the consumer's expectations about income and prices. For example, if Bob Smith expected the price of beer to rise, he might temporarily buy more; similarly, if he expected his income to fall, he might cut back his beer purchases somewhat in an effort to economize.

Through the use of symbols, we can express the determinants of quantity demanded in a simple equation, $Q_d = f(p, Y, op, t)$, which says that the quantity demanded (Q_d) is functionally related to the price (p), income (Y), other prices (op), and taste (t).

Demand Schedules and Demand Curves

The demand schedule. We are now ready to consider another specific meaning of the term "demand" which has acquired particular importance in economic analysis. We have seen that the quantity demanded of a commodity or service is a function of several variables. One of these variables, the price of the commodity or service in question, is often singled out for special attention. The relationship between price and the quantity demanded is described by a demand schedule.

The concept of the demand schedule is based on the assumption that the determinants of quantity demanded other than price, namely, income, other prices, and taste, remain unchanged (i.e., are held constant). Therefore, under conditions of *ceteris paribus*, the quantity demanded can be thought of as a function of price alone, $Q_d = f(p)$, since the other variables are fixed.

Economists believe that the variables Q_d and p are related in a particular way, namely, that as one increases the other decreases and vice versa. When two variables have this type of relationship, one is known as a decreasing function of the other. In the case of demand, the relationship may be stated as follows: other things being constant, the higher the price the smaller the quantity demanded, and the lower the price the greater the quantity demanded. Alfred Marshall, the great British economist (1842–1924), referred to this as the "one general law of demand." In a later chapter we will examine the theories which economists have developed showing why and under what conditions this law must be true. For the present, we may note that it is confirmed by everyday experience. The best test of a theory is the predictions that it yields, and this one yields good predictions.

You should be careful not to infer from the law of demand more than it implies. The law does not say anything about the absolute or relative amounts of decrease or increase in prices and quantities; it says only that the relationship is inverse. The demand schedules presented below are hypothetical schedules for consumers A, B, and C, all conforming to the general law of demand.

DEMAND SCHEDULE A		DEMAND SCHEDULE B		DEMAND SCHEDULE C	
Price (dollars per unit)	Quantity (units per month)	Price (dollars per unit)	Quantity (units per month)	Price (dollars per unit)	Quantity (units per month)
5	5	5	75	5	240
4	6	4	84	4	300
3	7	3	91	3	400
2	8	2	96	2	600
1	9	1	99	1	1,200

In the remainder of this book, unless otherwise indicated, the term "demand" will be used to denote a demand schedule. Thus, demand, used in this way, refers not to a single price and quantity, but to a whole schedule of prices and related quantities.

Market demand schedule. Up to this point we have been concerned primarily with the demand schedule of an individual consumer. Of much greater practical importance is the demand schedule of all potential consumers in a particular market for a commodity or service, sometimes referred to as *market demand.* This schedule is simply the sum of all the individual demand schedules. Thus, if A, B, and C above represent three consumers in the same market, their total or market demand is obtained from their individual demand schedules by adding together the quantities demanded at each price by each of the consumers, and constructing a new schedule showing the results.

MARKET DEMAND SCHEDULE OF A, B, AND C

Price (dollars per unit)	Quantity (units per month)
5	320
4	390
3	498
2	704
1	1,308

The demand curve. The transition from a demand schedule to a demand curve is a fairly simple one. Drawing on our discussion of two-variable charts in Chapter 1, we can set up a chart with quantity demanded per unit of time (Q) measured along the horizontal axis, and the price per unit (P) measured along the vertical axis.[8] Each pair of related variables (Q and P) from our schedule can now be plotted as a single point on the chart. (In Fig. 2-1 we have plotted the points indicated in the market demand schedule shown above.) When all these points are plotted, we may connect them with a smooth line. The result will be the demand curve which corresponds to the schedule. (It is conventional to use the letter D to label such a curve.)

FIG. 2-1
A Demand Curve

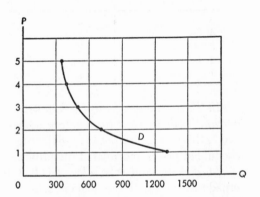

The demand curve differs from the demand schedule in one notable respect. In drawing the curve, we have taken the discontinuous variables of the schedule and given them the appearance of continuity. The result is that we can now read off a price-quantity relationship for any conceivable price or quantity within the range shown. This is a

[8] It is conventional in drawing a demand curve to show Q on the horizontal axis and P on the vertical axis.

considerable convenience; however, we must bear in mind that all the price-quantity relationships that we read from the curve (except those that are taken directly from the schedule) are approximations. It obviously follows that the more complete the schedule, the better will be the approximations we can obtain from the corresponding demand curve.

According to the general law of demand, all demand curves must slope downward to the right as we look at the chart. This is referred to as a negative slope, and tells us at a glance that as the value of the horizontal variable increases, the value of the vertical variable decreases. If the situation were to be reversed, i.e., if the value of the vertical variable were to increase with an increase in the value of the horizontal variable, the curve would slope upward to the right. A demand curve that behaved in this manner would be an exception to the general law of demand. Although such exceptional cases may exist, they require a special interpretation.

What the demand curve tells us.   We must always remember that neither the demand schedule nor the demand curve gives us the actual price of the commodity or the actual quantity bought. The schedule (and the curve drawn from the schedule) is only a statement of possibilities. It answers the question: "What will be the quantity demanded *if* the price is such and such?" or, alternatively: "What must be the price *if* the quantity demanded is to be such and such?" In this respect the demand schedule is like another, more familiar type of schedule, the football schedule. The hypothetical schedule below does not tell us that today *is* October 15 and that the opponent is Yale, but only that *if* the date is October 15, the opponent will be Yale, and vice versa.

COLUMBIA FOOTBALL SCHEDULE 1960	
October 1	Army
October 8	Michigan
October 15	Yale
October 22	Notre Dame
October 29	U.C.L.A.

Changes in the quantity demanded.   You will notice that demand schedule B (p. 43) tells us that if the price is $4, the quantity demanded will be 84. It also tells us that if the price should drop to $3, the quantity demanded would be 91. This change is referred to as an increase in the *quantity demanded*. If the price should rise to $5, the quantity demanded would be 75. This would be called a decrease in the *quantity demanded.* In graphical terms, a change in the quantity demanded means a change from one point on the curve to another on the same curve.

Notice that we do not say there has been an increase or decrease in *demand.* Changes in the price of the commodity do not of themselves produce changes in demand. Again the analogy with the football schedule is instructive. If on October 15 Columbia plays Yale, and then on October 22 plays Notre Dame, no one would refer to this as a change in the schedule. A change in opponent, yes; but this is exactly what the schedule told us to expect. Similarly, changes in price result in changes in the quantity demanded, according to the schedule, but do not produce changes in the demand schedule itself.[9] In the next section we will look into situations in which the demand schedule itself changes, and the demand curve therefore occupies a different position when plotted on a chart.

CASE 2-7 Consumer demand for food

The following excerpts suggest some of the factors influencing the quantity of food demanded by consumers:

1. "The 33 million babies born during the past 9 years [1945–1953] will affect more than a few specialized markets. They will constitute a kind of bulge in the U.S. population during their entire life cycle; their impact on both the size and age composition of the nation will not be transitory. Neither will their impact on the market.

As a case in point consider the food market. . . . Though their requirements are special . . . babies are not spectacular food consumers. A child of one needs less than 1,000 calories a day, a child of six less than 2,000. Since an extraordinary proportion of our population has been in the six-and-under group in recent years—it is now around 17 per cent—total U.S. calorie requirements have not kept pace with the rise in population. But the postwar babies will soon be growing into ravenous teenagers. A seventeen-year-old boy ordinarily consumes *more* calories than a grown man." [10]

2. "H. J. Heinz Co. has been working for five years on types of food for the aged designed to keep them alive longer. They claim that food for

---

[9] Except possibly in some unusual cases where taste is affected by the price, e.g., perfume, or where expectations about future price changes are affected.
[10] "Sixty-Six Million More Americans," *Fortune,* January 1954, pp. 94–95. © 1954 by Time, Inc.

the old should have more proteins, vitamins, and minerals and less carbohydrates than for others. It should also have less salt because of the tendency toward high blood pressure on the part of the aged.

This preoccupation with a new type of food is due to the fact that the age composition of America is changing. The population of persons 60 years and older was 18.3 million in 1950, and is expected to be 23 million by 1960." [11]

3. "As compared with 1910, the average American now eats only half as many potatoes, only three-fourths as much bread and other cereal products, but a third more eggs, and a fourth more fruits and vegetables." [12]

Questions

1. What determinants of quantity demanded are illustrated in the above case?
2. How would the quantity demanded of commodities other than food be affected by the changes that are described?
3. What other factors can you think of that affect the demand for food?

CASE 2-8   A consumer's demand for automobiles

Jones has a large family and lives in the suburbs. He is accustomed to driving his car into the city every day when he goes to work. He now faces the problem of either abandoning this practice or purchasing a second car for the use of his family while he is away. Jones has a modest income, and would prefer not to buy a second car. His wife, however, insists on having a car for shopping and for driving the children to school. She also points to the neighbors, most of whom have two cars. When Jones says that he cannot afford two cars, his wife replies that he must be more ambitious and look forward to earning more in the future. She reminds her husband that bus and taxi fares have risen considerably, and that it has become more expensive to use public transportation to get around. She also tells him that prices of automobiles are likely to rise, and that buying a second car now is a good investment. If worst comes to worst, she assures him, they could always give up their summer trip to Maine and find a cheaper vacation.

Questions

1. Identify the determinants of quantity demanded in the above situation.
2. Who is demanding a second car, Jones or his wife? Explain your answer.

[11] Wall Street Journal, June 2, 1955. © 1955 by Dow Jones and Company, Inc.
[12] American Assembly (Columbia University), United States Agriculture: Perspectives and Prospects, N.Y., 1955, p. 15.

CASE 2-9   Variables affecting consumer demand

1. "From the reflections and investigations that have been reviewed in the previous sections, we arrive at the hypothesis that the following factors may have been capable of exerting a significant impact . . . on the course of aggregate shoe buying in the United States in the interwar period: consumer disposable income, recent changes in income, expectations about future income, changes in income distribution, the price of shoes relative to that of other things consumers buy, perhaps stocks of usable shoes that people hold, and, finally, a group of factors that for the period reviewed tended to change in one direction over time and that may consequently be impounded in a time trend—factors such as aspects of some of the variables already mentioned, development of goods that competed with shoes for the income dollar and, opposing it, growing interest in style in clothing, changes in what the shoe industry offered its customers, changes in age and family composition of the population, as well as in its size, and shifts from rural to urban living." [13]

2. "The subject of primary interest concerning consumer demand has become the consumer himself—that is, his actual behavior and the kind and degree of regularity that characterize it. How, in what directions, and in what degree is the current spending of individual families influenced by the size of the family, the age of its members, their occupation, their place of residence, their income, any recent shift in their income, their highest past income, the amount of their liquid assets, their stock of durables and semidurables, recent changes in their buying, their highest past spending, their expectations concerning future incomes and prices, the amount and kind of their neighbors' buying, and by still other factors? How, in what directions, and in what degree is the consumer spending of a nation influenced, among other things, by the distribution of individual incomes, by the amount of capital gains or losses, by changes in the general level of prices, by the dispersion of individual price movements, by the terms on which consumer credit is extended, by the introduction of new commodities, by advertising expenditures, by the rate of formation of new families, by the geographic mobility of the population? These are some of the questions now being put by economists; and while none have as yet been answered with precision and some have hardly been answered at all, the rough foundations of an empirical science of consumption are slowly beginning to take shape." [14]

---

[13] Ruth P. Mack, *Factors Influencing Consumption: An Experimental Analysis of Shoe Buying,* Technical Paper 10, National Bureau of Economic Research, N.Y., 1954, p. 45. © 1954 by the National Bureau of Economic Research, Inc.

[14] Arthur F. Burns, *The Instability of Consumer Spending,* 32nd Annual Report,

Questions

1. Do the above discussions relate to consumer demand for particular commodities, aggregate consumer demand, or both?
2. Identify the variables discussed according to whether they involve primarily (a) price, (b) income, or (c) taste.

CASE 2-10   Drawing a demand curve

1. Given the following demand schedule, plot and draw the demand curve.

P	Q
(dollars per dozen)	(dozen per week)
$10	40
8	60
6	100
4	200
2	250
1	300

2. What will be the quantity demanded if:

$$P = 7?\ P = 5?$$

3. What is the highest price at which you can sell 50 dozen per week? 240 dozen per week?

CASE 2-11   Swimming pool attendance

Mrs. Leonard and Mrs. Martin were discussing the new swimming pool which was to open soon in their neighborhood. The admission price had not yet been announced and the women were guessing as to what it might be.

"If they are smart, and set admissions at fifty cents," said Mrs. Leonard, "my family will probably be steady customers, several times a week. If it is a dollar, we might go about once a week, and if it is higher, only on the very hottest days." "Not our family," said Mrs. Martin, "we will probably go more often if it is one dollar than if it is fifty cents."

Questions

1. Does the Leonard family's demand conform to the general law of demand? How would you show it graphically?
2. Does the Martin family's demand conform to the general law of demand? Can you show it graphically?

National Bureau of Economic Research, N.Y., May 1952, p. 13. © 1952 by the National Bureau of Economic Research, Inc.

CASE 2-12   Tropicade Soda, I

The XYZ Bottling Company was preparing to introduce a new carbonated beverage made with the juice of an exotic tropical fruit and to be sold under the name "Tropicade." They planned to introduce the drink in the New York market first, and the president of the company asked the sales manager, Bill Johnson, to prepare some estimates of their potential sales volume at various prices. Johnson submitted the following figures as part of his report:

PRICE PER 8 OZ. BOTTLE	ESTIMATED ANNUAL SALES (*millions of bottles*)
15 cents	1
2 for 25	2
10	5
2 for 15	8
5	11

Questions

1. Does the demand for Tropicade conform to the general law of demand?
2. If we are to treat these estimates as a demand schedule, what assumptions must be made?
3. On the basis of this information, would it be possible for the company to determine the best selling price for the product?

CASE 2-13   Adding demand curves

FIG. 2-2   Adding Demand Curves

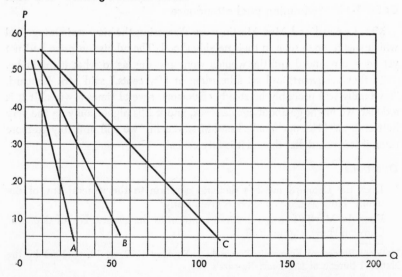

Questions

1. Draw the market demand curve which is the sum of demand curves A, B, and C.
2. What is the market demand at $P = 30$? At $P = 20$?
3. Is it possible to draw two or more demand curves (each of which conforms with the general law of demand) so that their total or market demand curve does not conform?

CASE 2-14   The discount house

"Bergen County shoppers will be buying cut-price goods from a well-known discount house for at least six months before two huge department store shopping centers, to be opened near Paramus, N.J., woo them for customers.

Masters, Inc., will open a store on Route 4 on Sept. 10. It will be just about midway between the R. H. Macy Paramus Center and Bergen Mall, a big multistore project of Allied Stores, the country's largest department store chain, less than a mile to the east. Both department store centers are now under construction and are scheduled to open next spring.

L. Bamberger & Co., a Macy subsidiary, will have a branch in the Paramus Center, and so will Alexander's. Stern Brothers, an Allied Stores affiliate, will dominate Bergen Mall, and another big-name department store also will be there.

All will find that at least part of their potential clientele have been accustomed to buying at Masters. Department store antipathy toward discount houses is well known.

The Paramus coup represents the latest outmaneuvering of big, conservative, conventional storekeepers by 43-year-old Stephen Masters, president of the discount house. Nineteen years ago, he and his brother Philip set out with borrowed capital of $500 to start a new kind of retailing.

LOW PRICES WAS KEY

The key was low prices. Discounts ranging up to 60 per cent were given to customers reached by mail. A tiny room at 48 West Forty-eighth Street was Masters when it opened. Against the establishment in a city just emerging from the depression were the combined might of nine well-established department stores and hundreds of appliance stores.

Today, Masters sells, at cut prices, $20,000,000 worth of merchandise a year. Its headquarters remain on Forty-eighth Street, but the number has been changed to 66. Branch stores are operated at Miami and Washington. Now the suburbs are being invaded. In addition to the Paramus venture, Masters will open a discount house on Oct. 1, near Elmsford,

N.Y., a five-minute automobile drive from Westchester's huge and bustling Cross County Center. . . .

The low prices were offered for two reasons. The first was low overhead. No floorwalker with a flower in the buttonhole of his jacket ever paced in a Masters' store. There never were any highly paid merchandise managers supervising battalions of buyers.

Mr. Masters is one of four central buyers who obtains the varied merchandise to stock the chain. This now takes in 8,000 different items, including furniture, all kinds of appliances, radio and television, drugs, giftware, clothing, luggage, records, sporting goods, tools, and almost everything else a customer might want. The tiny room in 1937 sold radios only.

Masters' customers are bargain hunters of the informed kind. They know exactly what they want and the so-called 'list' price prevailing in conventional stores. This is the price sometimes suggested by the manufacturer, sometimes fixed rigidly by him (under the Fair Trade Act), or generally observed by stores when they are not running sales. The shoppers demand a lower price and usually get it. They are encouraged to carry small articles away. This cuts delivery expense. Masters maintains its delivery of larger items, and servicing is as good as that of any retail establishment in the country.

No discounts are given in the New York store on 'fair traded' merchandise when a court injunction prevents Masters from selling at prices under manufacturer-set minimums. However, customers often are told to write to the Washington store since there is no fair trade law in the District of Columbia.

Mr. Masters sums up the retail operation that he pioneered as follows: 'Reputable discount houses are operated for the most part by men who get up earlier than their competitors and work later, who use their creative brains to procure and move wanted merchandise at lower costs, and [who] pass on the resultant economies to an enthusiastic public.'

This involves lightning decisions that bring in a quantity of goods at low prices from manufacturers and distributors. Mr. Masters and his three buyers make these decisions, and no salesman with a 'good deal' is kept waiting very long. All goods are sold at what the chief thinks is a fair profit. There are no loss leaders (items sold below cost to attract customers into a store to be steered to higher-priced goods) at Masters." [15]

---

[15] Alfred R. Zipser, "Discount House Gets Thar Fust," New York *Times*, July 15, 1956. © 1956 by The New York Times Company.

Questions

1. In analyzing demand for a product sold at different prices in regular department stores and in Masters, Inc., would you need a single demand schedule for each product, or separate schedules? Why?
2. Describe the effect of "fair trade" (resale price maintenance) practices on demand.
3. To what extent does the emergence of the discount house affect the demand schedule for "fair-traded" items?

CASE 2-15   Demand for shoes

"Shoe production this year is heading for a new high of 600,000,000 pairs, according to Irving Edison, executive vice-president of Edison Brothers Stores, Inc.

Speaking yesterday at the breakfast meeting of the Popular Price Shoe Show of America at the New Yorker Hotel, Mr. Edison said that an increase in population and the fulfillment of many hard-line needs had enlarged the opportunity for shoe sales. Consumers are spending, he said, with no fear of depression.

'We are catering to a consumer market with tastes, psychology, finances, and knowledge that are far more advanced than ever before,' Mr. Edison said.

The easy accessibility and ample free parking facilities are not the only attractions of the new shopping centers, which are having a sharp impact on the shoe industry, he said. Shoppers like the environment, the roomier stores, and the cheerier atmosphere, he said. . . ." [16]

Questions

1. What determinants of demand are illustrated in the above case?
2. In the light of the factors that are stressed in this case and in the previous case, do you think that discount houses would be successful in selling shoes? Explain your answer.

CHANGES IN DEMAND

In the previous section we saw that a demand schedule relates price changes to changes in the quantity demanded, but not to changes in demand. This distinction now calls for further clarification.

What do we mean by a change in demand, as opposed to a change in the quantity demanded? We mean a change in the *demand schedule itself*. For example, in the Tropicade Soda case (Case 2-12) if the

---

[16] "Shoe Output Seen Heading for High, with Ample Sales," New York *Times*, May 7, 1957. © 1957 by The New York Times Company.

quantity demanded at 15 cents should shift from one million to two million bottles, at 12½ cents from two million to four million, at 10 cents from five million to six million, and so on, we would say that there has been an increase in demand. This would mean that we have a new schedule in which the quantity demanded at each price is greater than in the old schedule. (Another way to describe the change is to say that each of the old quantities is now demanded at a higher price.) Similarly, a decrease in demand would signify a change in the demand schedule, such that at each price the quantity demanded is less than before.

Since a change in price brings about a change in quantity demanded and not a change in demand, we may deduce that the latter is brought about by changes in other variables. So long as the other determinants of demand—income, other prices, and taste—remain unchanged, the schedule is fixed and there can be no change in demand. If changes do occur in one or more of these other determinants, however, the schedule itself will change. Suppose, in the Tropicade case, that consumers experience an increase in income; there would then very likely be an increase in demand. Or suppose the prices of other drinks were reduced; this would in all probability result in some decline in the demand for Tropicade. Finally, suppose the consumers' taste should change. The result would then be either an increase or a decrease in demand, depending on the direction of the change in taste.

In general, we may summarize the effects of changes in determinants as follows. An increase in income is likely to produce an increase in demand, but may have the opposite effect for certain goods. A change in taste will result in either an increase or decrease depending upon the nature of the change. An increase or decrease in the price of some *other* good may result in either an increase or a decrease in demand, depending upon whether the other good is a substitute or complement for the one in question. Tea and coffee, for example, are substitutes for one another, and a rise in the price of tea is likely to result in an increase in the demand for coffee. Sugar, on the other hand, has a complementary relationship with coffee and tea, and increases in the price of sugar will tend to decrease the demand for both coffee and tea.

The point to remember is that a change in quantity demanded means a change from one point on a schedule to another point on the same schedule, while a change in demand signifies a shift in the demand schedule itself. The former results from a change in price, while the latter is brought about by a change in one or more of the other determinants of quantity demanded. In graphical terms, a change in demand means a movement from one curve to another. If the new curve is above and to the right of the old curve, there has been an increase in demand. If the new curve is below and to the left of the old one, there has been a decrease in demand. If there is no change in an existing schedule and curve, we may assume that the determinants of quantity demanded other than price have remained constant, or that such changes as may have taken place have exactly canceled one another. Fig. 2-3 shows the original demand curve (D), the new curve following an increase in demand (D_1), and the curve resulting from a decrease in demand (D_2).

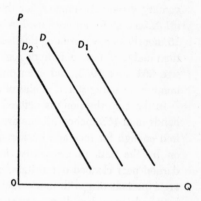

FIG. 2-3
Changes in Demand

CASE 2-16   Consumer demand for coffee

High coffee prices have caused Americans to drink less of the beverage, according to a survey reported to the annual convention of the National Coffee Association in October 1955.

Lawrence E. Benson told the coffee group that a survey by his firm, Benson & Benson, Princeton, New Jersey, disclosed that 23 per cent of all households—or an estimated 11 million—were using less coffee than two years before, while 16 per cent were using more; that 20 per cent were making coffee last longer by weaker brewing or by using left-overs in order to reduce waste.

According to the survey, 96 per cent of American homes use coffee. One per cent had stopped using coffee entirely, and 6 per cent had cut out the use of coffee for certain meals or occasions due to high prices.[17]

Questions

1. Does the above situation reflect a change in the quantity demanded or a change in demand?

[17] Adapted from a story in the *Wall Street Journal*, October 13, 1955.

2. How would you account for the 16 per cent of households using more coffee in spite of the higher prices?

CASE 2-17   Ponies and portraits

1. "For more than a half century the horse has been steadily disappearing from the American scene. But during the last five years the pony has galloped into a new place in the life of U.S. youngsters, who have rediscovered the old-fashioned fun of owning an animal big enough to ride and gentle enough to serve as a backyard pet. Traditionally the luxury of the rich, the pony has now become a familiar plaything. Montgomery Ward this summer, for the first time, lists ponies in its catalogue ($179.95 cash for an untrained, purebred Shetland colt, or $18 down and 15 months to pay). Among Shetlands, the most popular pony in the U.S., the number of new purebreds registered this year has jumped an impressive 30% over 1955, and even bigger gains have come in the countless numbers of unregistered ponies of all breeds.

In the U.S. the pony is defined as a type of horse no more than 14.2 hands high (58 inches). Some are small enough for toddlers, others spirited enough for teen-age buckaroos. To meet the new demand, brought on by the nation's prosperity, importers have raided Europe. 'We've darned near cleaned out Britain,' says one. Some American pony raisers are experimenting with fancy new types, and in Oregon a motel operator has made pony breeding a promising sideline. In Maryland a riding instructor has doubled her business since 1952, and still had to turn away pupils this year. Ponies, which were once seldom seen even at horse shows, now have whole shows of their own. And in the two years since it was organized, the U.S. Pony Club has sprouted more than 40 member clubs." [18]

2. "Portraiture as a fine art, most critics agree, is all but dead. But portrait painting as a business is currently enjoying its biggest boom in 40 years. All across the U.S., portrait specialists are turning out—with the rapidity and often the similarity of an assembly line—a profusion of likenesses of business heads, college presidents, government officials, society leaders, children, pets, homes, and, as one painter put it, 'just plain pleasant people.'

The portrait boom has gone hand in hand with the country's prosperity. 'Most people,' remarks a museum director, 'like themselves enough to want to be painted. Now they have the money to get it done.' As a result Portraits, Inc., a New York clearing house for portrait commissions, has in-

[18] "A Galloping Popularity for the Pony: A Luxury of the Rich Becomes a Familiar Child's Pet," *Life*, August 13, 1956, pp. 84–85. © 1956 by Time, Inc.

creased its business tenfold since 1946, and popular portraitists like Lloyd Embry make well over $50,000 a year." [19]

Questions

1. What determinants appear to have been most influential in the shifts in demand described above?
2. How would the shifts in demand described above be affected by a substantial decrease in the prices of portraits and ponies?

CASE 2-18   Hurricanes and candles

"An ill wind, often of hurricane force at this time of the year, is blowing financial good to candle makers.

Whenever the electricity fails, candles that ordinarily adorn mantels, tables, and buffets assume a new role in providing light until the emergency is over.

Since a few years ago when the heavily populated Northeast began to be plagued with hurricanes in late summer and early fall, the candle industry has had a large increase in output. Production has gone up 12 per cent since 1953, a whopping rise for a small industry. . . ." [20]

Questions

1. How do hurricanes produce a shift in the demand for candles?
2. What is the effect of the hurricanes on the demand for electricity?

CASE 2-19   Tobacco consumption in the U.S.

"From 1880 to 1954 annual total tobacco consumption per person over 14 years of age increased from 5.41 to 12.20 lbs. During the same period cigarette consumption increased from 0.047 to 9.84 lbs. per person. Except for snuff, consumption of other tobacco products declined. Chewing tobacco was the leading tobacco product in 1880; in 1954 its consumption outranked only that of snuff.

During the years 1880–84 only 1% of total tobacco consumption was in the form of cigarettes; from 1950–54, 80%. Since World War I the annual consumption of cigarettes per person over 14 has increased by more than 8 lbs., approximately a sixfold increase. About 41% of this increase may be

[19] "A Peak for Portraits: Prosperity Turns Art into a Big Business," *Life*, August 13, 1956, p. 77. © 1956 by Time, Inc.
[20] Alexander R. Hammer, "Hurricanes Promoting Candle Sales," *New York Times*, August 26, 1956. © 1956 by The New York Times Company.

regarded as additional tobacco consumption, the remaining 59% as a shift from other tobacco products to cigarettes." [21]

Consumption of Each Tobacco Product Expressed as a Percentage of Total Consumption of Tobacco

Year average	Cigarettes %	Cigars %	Smoking tobacco %	Chewing tobacco %	Snuff %
1880–84	1	26	14	56	2
1885–89	2	25	15	56	3
1890–94	3	24	16	53	3
1895–99	3	24	18	52	4
1900–04	2	27	21	45	4
1905–09	3	27	25	41	5
1910–14	7	26	25	37	5
1915–19	16	25	22	31	5
1920–24	26	25	18	25	5
1925–29	38	21	16	20	5
1930–34	44	17	20	14	5
1935–39	53	15	17	10	4
1940–44	65	13	11	7	4
1945–49	76	11	5	5	3
1950–54	80	10	4	4	3

Questions

1. Do the figures above represent demand schedules? Why or why not?
2. On the basis of the above figures, what inferences might you draw about changes in the demand for various forms of tobacco? Why are these merely surmises?
3. To what do you attribute the substantial increase in tobacco consumption as a whole?

CASE 2-20 The demand for cigarettes

"The year 1953 was a year tobacco-makers aren't likely to forget. It was the year that ended a 21 year upclimb in domestic sales. It was the year when regular size cigarettes encountered the worst publicity they have ever had. The long-percolating talk of a possible link between lung cancer and smoking finally boiled over. Even though the industry insists the evidence is lacking, there are some signs that the talk is making a difference in smoking habits. . . .

---

[21] Benno K. Milmore and Arthur G. Conover, "Tobacco Consumption in the U.S., 1880 to 1954," *Agricultural Economics Research*, Vol. 3, No. 1, January 1956, pp. 9–13. The table comes from the same source.

TOTAL DOMESTIC CIGARETTE SALES

1940	180.5 billion cigarettes
1945	267.2
1950	360.8
1951	378.7
1952	394.9
1953	387.0

CIGARETTE SALES BY TYPE

	1952	1953
Regular size	314.8 billion cigarettes	273.0 billion cigarettes
King size	73.3	100.5
Filter tip	5.3	12.3
All other	1.5	1.2

P.S. Sales of Vanguard Press' book, *How to Stop Smoking*, are running nearly 3,000 per month—against 1,000 a few months ago." [22]

Questions

1. Does this case alter the conclusions you reached in the preceding case?
2. What would happen if the industry lowered cigarette prices in an effort to counteract the effect of the talk about cigarette smoking and cancer?
3. Assuming that cigarette sales continue to decline, would you expect to see an increased demand for other forms of tobacco consumption?
4. Cigarette sales in 1954 were $369,000,000; in 1955, $382,000,000; in 1956, $392,000,000. How would you explain this resurgence of sales?

CASE 2-21 The demand for vodka

"A tasteless, odorless, and colorless product has become popular among America's imbibers of alcoholic beverages.

It is vodka, made from grain mash at 190 proof, watered down to either 100 or 80 proof, and bottled and sold without flavoring or aging. While some people drink it straight or 'on the rocks,' most prefer it in a martini or in such concoctions as 'screwdrivers' (with orange juice) or 'bloody Mary's' (with tomato juice). Still others like it mixed with ginger beer, or soda, or a soft drink. . . .

The rate of growth is the most startling aspect of the vodka picture. One source of liquor statistics, Clark Gavin Associates, estimates that last

[22] "Cigarettes: Is This a Turning Point?" *Business Week*, January 2, 1954, pp. 74–76. Copyright, 1954 by McGraw-Hill Publishing Company, Inc. Reprinted by permission.

year vodka consumption reached 6,234,662 gallons, 90 per cent above the 1954 level. In a study made for *True* magazine, Gavin estimated that first quarter consumption this year was more than 190 per cent above that in the similar period of last year. . . .

The leader in vodka sales is not a big distiller but G. F. Heublein & Bro., Inc., Hartford, Conn., a company long known for its sauces and as the distributor for Bell's Scotch whisky. Its Smirnoff brand, industry sources estimate, accounts for half of the sales of vodka in this country.

Heublein started the trend toward vodka drinking in this country. It purchased the Smirnoff name in 1939 but didn't begin to exploit it until 1948, when Californians began drinking a concoction of vodka and ginger beer. Thereafter, Smirnoff became the subject of heavy advertising campaigns, first on the West Coast and then in the East. . . .

There are said to be more than 100 brands of vodka on the market, and many retail liquor dealers devote extensive displays and promotion to their sale. Five years ago many such establishments carried only a token number of brands. Now all bars carry at least a couple of brands, and most bartenders have been schooled in making the new vodka drinks." [23]

Questions

1. What, in your opinion, accounts for the popularity of vodka in the U.S.?
2. On which of the demand-determining factors does advertising have its chief effect?
3. Using graphs showing before-and-after demand curves for vodka, demand for other alcoholic beverages, and total demand for all alcoholic beverages, show what takes place if: (a) the increase in the demand for vodka reflects an increase in the demand for all liquor; (b) the increase in the demand for vodka has taken place at the expense of the demand for other types of alcoholic beverages.
4. What would happen to the demand for vodka if there were to be a substantial rise in the price of orange juice, tomato juice, and other vodka mixers?

CASE 2-22   Cashmere sales decline—why?

"Producers of cashmere fabrics suffered a substantial set-back in sales this year. Estimates in some quarters put volume as much as 30 per cent behind a year ago. The severity of the decline is causing many to re-evaluate the place of cashmere coatings in next year's plans.

A check of the leading producers turns up some of the points that are said to have contributed to the poor showing:

[23] James J. Nagle, "Vodka Is Growing Fast in Favor with America's Beverage Users," New York *Times,* August 12, 1956. © 1956 by The New York Times Company.

1. Spiraling raw materials costs followed by sharp increases in fabric prices. Fabric quotations went as high as $4.50 a yard over a year ago, moving garment prices up as much as $30 at the retail level.

2. Styling of cashmere coats has undergone no major change in recent years. Most makers continued to offer the 'classic' model with only minor variations.

3. The adoption of cashmere by a number of manufacturers whose capital did not allow them to tie up finances for very long. The movement of coats slowed up, and, under pressure to meet obligations, many cutters were forced to liquidate piece goods and/or coats at prices that tended to depress the market.

4. Stores have overplayed the term 'cashmere' as an off-price drawing card. The availability of these sales leaders in great quantity—many offering legitimate big savings—has caused the consumer to hesitate before buying a regular price coat." [24]

Questions

1. Are we dealing, in the above situation, with a change in demand or a change in quantity demanded?
2. Can the decline in sales correctly be ascribed to both a rise and a fall in price as suggested above? Explain.

CASE 2-23 The demand for color TV

"A five week color television set promotion in . . . [the Milwaukee] area was reported . . . to have 'demonstrated conclusively that the public is ready to buy' color television 'in large volume.'

Martin P. Bennett, merchandising vice-president for the Radio Corporation of America, said that sales of color sets in Milwaukee County during the campaign, which has just ended, averaged 106 a week. This, according to Mr. Bennett, was 783 per cent above the average of 12 a week before the campaign. He estimated that the program had put between 500 and 600 new R.C.A. color sets in homes.

Walter J. Damm, president of station WTMJ–TV, the Milwaukee Journal's television station, said there had been about 3,300 color sets of all makes within range of his station before the campaign.

Mr. Bennett declared that the promotional techniques that proved successful in the Milwaukee 'test' would be used in other drives to sell color sets in every major market in the country. These techniques included newspaper, radio, and television advertising, telephone and door-to-door solicitations, and home demonstrations.

[24] Story by Sanford J. Parker, *Women's Wear Daily*, November 27, 1956, p. 24. Copyright, 1956 by Fairchild Publications, Inc.

Local television stations averaged seven and a half hours of color broadcasts a week during May. R.C.A. said this was more than had ever been presented anywhere for a comparable period.

'The success of the Milwaukee campaign,' Mr. Bennett declared, 'clearly demonstrates four points: first, that public interest in color television is higher than ever; second, that color TV is priced right for large-volume sales; third, that the public will buy color when it is properly exposed, promoted, and demonstrated; and fourth, that dealers—far from being apathetic about color as is sometimes said—are actually enthusiastic in their support of it.'

As for prices, Mr. Bennett went on, the Milwaukee campaign showed that the sets are not priced beyond reach. 'Seven out of ten people who bought color sets passed up the $495 model in favor of higher-priced sets ranging up to $850,' he said.

James A. Taylor, president of the Taylor Electric Company, R.C.A. Milwaukee area distributor, said, however, that dealers had given some discounts off factory-suggested list prices. But he emphasized that prices received during the campaign were far higher than those before it began. . . .

Money spent on the Milwaukee campaign and others like it that will follow is above the normal R.C.A. advertising and promotional budget, according to [an R.C.A. representative]. Pointing out that R.C.A. already had spent $100,000,000 on all phases of color television, he declared:

'We're going to get color off the ground, whatever the effort.' " [25]

Questions

1. Does the fact that R.C.A. was able to sell more sets at prices "far higher than . . . before" indicate an exception to the general law of demand?

2. Do you agree with Mr. Bennett that the campaign clearly demonstrates "that public interest in color television is higher than ever"?

THE RELATIONSHIP BETWEEN INCOME AND DEMAND

Thus far we have been discussing a particular type of demand schedule, namely, that relating changes in price and quantity demanded. But economists are also interested in other types of demand schedules or curves. The *income demand schedule*, for example, is based on the relationship between the quantity demanded and income. It is obtained by holding constant the other determinants of quantity

[25] Alfred R. Zipser, "Drive Lifts Sales of Color TV Sets," New York *Times*, June 6, 1957. © 1957 by The New York Times Company.

demanded, including the price of the commodity or service in question, and treating the quantity demanded as a function of income: $Q_d = f(Y)$. The curve which may be drawn from an income demand schedule is often referred to as an Engel curve in honor of the nineteenth-century German economist who conducted some famous investigations using this concept. Income demand curves are drawn with income (Y) measured on the horizontal axis and quantity demanded (Q_d) measured on the vertical axis.

We have defined the income demand schedule in terms of the relationship between quantity demanded and income. It does no violence to the concept, however, to speak of the dollar value of the amount demanded ("dollar demand") as a function of income. Since price is assumed to remain unchanged, the amount demanded in dollars is equivalent to the quantity demanded multiplied by the given price. As may be seen in Figs. 2-4 and 2-5, the two curves are identical. Similarly, a table or chart showing the percentage of income spent on a good as a function of total income (Fig. 2-6) may be regarded as merely another version of the same basic concept. Through the use of simple arithmetic, this percentage of income curve can be used to derive either of the curves in Fig. 2-4 and Fig. 2-5.

FIG. 2-4 Quantity of Commodity X Demanded at Price $5.00

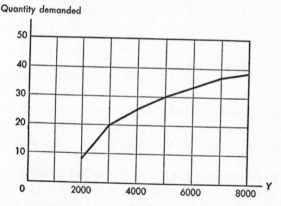

Unlike the general law of demand which underlies the price demand schedule, the relationship between the variables Y and Q_d is usually positive, i.e., the quantity demanded usually rises as income rises and falls as income falls. There are exceptions, however. In the case of some commodities, such as margarine, or some services, such as shoe repair, consumers may buy less as income rises. The additional

FIG. 2-5   Dollar Demand for Commodity X at Price $5.00

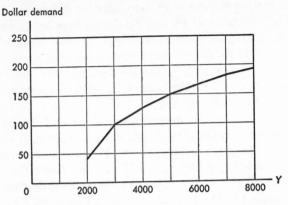

FIG. 2-6   Per Cent of Income Spent on Commodity X at Price $5.00

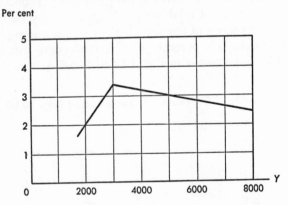

income may make it less desirable or necessary to substitute margarine for butter, or shoe repair for the purchase of new shoes. Commodities and services which fall in this category are referred to as "inferior goods."

The Engel curve refers to the demand of a particular consumer. Of much greater practical importance is a schedule or curve which relates quantity demanded of a commodity to changes in income for the country as a whole. If such a schedule can be estimated,[26] a businessman would then have valuable information as to how the demand for his product will change with changes in aggregate income.

---

[26] There are many theoretical and practical difficulties. One problem concerns the distribution of income. Changes in the distribution of income could change the quantity demanded, even if aggregate income remains the same. To illustrate,

One aspect of consumer demand which has received a great deal of attention in recent years is the total spending by all consumers for all goods. According to a system of analysis developed by John Maynard Keynes (1883–1946) and his followers, such spending is considered to be primarily a function of income. The relationship between income and spending for consumer goods is called the *consumption function* or the propensity to consume. This concept plays a very important part in the Keynesian analysis of changes in national income and employment. The relationship is usually expressed symbolically as $C = f(Y)$, meaning that consumption (C) is a function of income (Y). When shown on a graph, it is customary to measure income along the horizontal axis, and spending for consumption in the vertical direction. We will return to this concept in Chapter 9.

CASE 2-24   Consumer purchases of fur

Analysis of Consumer Purchases of Fur in Selected Cities, 1935–36 [27]

INCOME CLASS	AVERAGE EXPENDITURE PER FAMILY		
	New York and Chicago	New England and East Central Cities	Southeastern
500– 999	$ 1.08	$ .28	$ —
1,000–1,499	1.39	2.34	.10
1,500–1,999	1.11	3.49	.62
2,000–2,999	3.13	4.48	1.57
3,000–3,999	7.96	3.90	4.14
4,000–4,999	10.58	11.55	12.38
5,000–7,499	28.93	$5,000 and over 13.72	19.23
7,500 and over	84.23		

consider the possible influence of a change in income distribution on total expenditures for automobiles. The following table shows what might happen if aggregate income remains unchanged, but distribution among families changes.

I. ANNUAL INCOME	ANNUAL EXPENDITURE FOR AUTOMOBILES	II. ANNUAL INCOME	ANNUAL EXPENDITURE FOR AUTOMOBILES
Family 1 $ 3,000	$ 0	$ 20,000	$1,500
Family 2 10,000	1,000	30,000	2,000
Family 3 87,000	3,000	50,000	2,500
Total $100,000	$4,000	$100,000	$6,000

[27] *Study of Consumer Purchases, Family Expenditures in Selected Cities,* 1935–36, Vol. 3, *Clothing and Personal Care,* Bureau of Labor Statistics Bulletin No. 648, Washington, D.C.

Questions

1. Do expenditures on fur rise as income rises? Show this situation graphically for "New York and Chicago."
2. Does the curve you have drawn for the previous question represent the sum of the income demand schedules of individual families? Why or why not?
3. Describe what would be signified by (a) movement along the curve and (b) a shift in the curve with respect to (1) the curve you have drawn, and (2) the income demand curve for an individual family.
4. Between 1946 and 1955 retail fur sales in the U.S. fell about 40 per cent, while personal income in the U.S. increased about 70 per cent. How would you explain this decline in sales in the light of the figures shown above?

CASE 2-25   Tropicade Soda, II

The XYZ Bottling Company (see Case 2-12) decided to go ahead with its new product, Tropicade. A price was set, distribution arranged, and the company began to accumulate inventories of fruit and sugar based upon their anticipated sales.

At just about that time, a national conference of businessmen and economists warned that a recession in business seemed likely in the near future. The president again asked his sales manager, Bill Johnson, to prepare some figures for him. This time he wanted estimates of how sales might be affected by changes in income. The manager presented the following schedule:

(REAL) DISPOSABLE PERSONAL INCOME	ESTIMATED SALES (millions of bottles)
$300 billion	5.00
290	4.97
280	4.90
270	4.75
260	4.50

Questions

1. How should Johnson have interpreted this schedule for the president of his concern?
2. If you had been in Johnson's place, what kinds of information would you have found useful in preparing this schedule?
3. Suppose that the decline in income in the above case was primarily a decline in corporate dividends. Would this have the same effect as an equivalent decline in wages?

CASE 2-26   Changes in personal consumption expenditures

Between 1929 and 1955 disposable personal income increased from $83.1 billion to $270.6 billion. Total personal consumption expenditure increased from $79.0 billion to $254.0. The table below shows expenditures for each of the twelve major categories of expenditure, and also for certain selected items. You will note that the increases for some items were much greater than the average, while some were much smaller.

Changes in Personal Consumption Expenditures, 1929–1955 [28]

	1929	1955	Per cent increase
MAJOR GROUPS			
Food and tobacco	$21.2 billion	$81.4 billion	284
Clothing, accessories, and jewelry	11.2	25.6	129
Personal care	1.1	3.2	190
Housing	11.4	30.6	168
Household operation	10.7	33.8	216
Medical care and death expenses	3.5	12.5	257
Personal business	5.1	12.8	151
Transportation	7.6	32.4	326
Recreation	4.3	13.0	202
Private education and research	.7	2.9	314
Religious and welfare activities	1.2	3.4	183
Foreign travel and remittances net	.8	2.3	187
SELECTED ITEMS			
Shoe cleaning and repair	$ 164 million	$ 214 million	30
Laundering in establishments	475	976	105
Domestic service	1,716	3,353	95
Physicians	959	3,070	220
Dentists	482	1,017	111
User operated transportation	6.0 billion	29.1 billion	385
Purchased local transportation	1.1	2.1	91
Books and maps	309 million	542 million	75
Pari-mutuel net receipts	8	426	5,225
Interest on personal debt	584	3,416	485

Questions

1. Pick out several items of each type and indicate why, in your opinion, they departed significantly from the average increase.
2. Does this table tend to support or refute the statement that the quantity demanded is a function of income?

---

[28] U.S. Department of Commerce.

CASE 2-27   The demand for housing

"Residential construction outlays (including expenditures for additions and alterations but not repairs and maintenance), measured as a proportion of either gross national product or gross capital formation, have experienced a marked decline since about 1890 in addition to the more familiar major swings. Even the current housing boom has not attained the relative strength of the 1920's, and falls considerably short of the relative levels achieved during the 1890's. Since residential capital formation is closely geared to increases in population and households, the declining rate of population growth in itself would provide a sufficient explanation for its diminishing relative importance without further examination of the role of the consumer.

But the burden of this paper is that the decline of non-farm housing construction in total output, rendered inevitable by demographic trends, has been powerfully reinforced by changes in consumer behavior. For not only has housebuilding declined in relation to total production, but the per capita real value of the standing stock of housing has failed to show any marked trend during the first fifty years of this century, and the average real value per dwelling unit standing has declined perceptibly. . . . These phenomena suggest, at least, that there has been a downward shift in consumer preferences for housing.

Value Per Capita and Per Dwelling Unit of Residential Capital, 1890–1950 (1929 dollars)

YEAR	PER CAPITA VALUE	PER DWELLING UNIT VALUE
1890	$658	$2,651
1900	793	3,355
1910	792	3,320
1920	747	3,119
1930	870	3,135
1940	770	2,662
1950	740	2,381

The findings on average real values per capita and per dwelling unit are astonishing in view of the rise in per capita real income over the past fifty years. . . .

Why has the per capita use of housing capital failed to show any marked increase over a half-century? Complete understanding of why the flow of resources into the residential real estate sector has been so insensitive to gains in real income may never be attained. But a few observations are offered.

First, consumers have chosen to spend part of their increments in income not directly on shelter but on many kinds of consumer capital related to the house and considered a vital part of household operation. Statistical measures of residential capital formation are dependent upon an arbitrary definition of items to be included or excluded in measuring outlays on construction, a definition which falls increasingly short of the full outlay for a dwelling unit as seen from the consumer's point of view. Thus, while certain consumer durables, such as oil burners and bathtubs, are captured by the construction data, others, like mechanical refrigerators, washing machines, garden equipment, venetian blinds, etc., are not. An expansion of the definition of residential capital formation to embrace items of this kind might possibly lead to a different conclusion; namely, that per capita use of housing resources has increased.

Thus, while the proliferation of consumer durables has offered serious competition to all other goods in the consumer basket, the outlays for these durables—so many of which have become complementary to the dwelling unit—appear to have been substituted for construction expenditures as currently defined in greater measure than for other forms of consumer outlays.

Second, the size of the capital outlay a family is willing to make for a house is not independent of the annual level of carrying costs. To the extent that the latter increases the former may shrink. If annual costs may be measured by the aggregate rent bill (imputed rents for home-owners plus contract rents for the tenants), the evidence points to a more rapid rise in rents than in capital values. Rent charges seem to have kept pace with income; that is, in spite of variations from decade to decade, there does not appear to have been any substantial long-run change in the ratio of rent to income; in the meantime the ratio of residential capital to income has been declining. The relatively greater increase in rents is attributed to the proliferation of services other than pure shelter, such as heat, light, janitorial and municipal services, and to the relatively greater amount of depreciation stemming from electric wiring, central heating, and kitchen equipment—all shorter-lived than the shell of a house. A larger and larger proportion of the annual rental bill is occasioned by services other than pure shelter, the costs of which are imputed or actually paid in the form of rent.

Third, the apparent refusal of consumers to allow their rising income to be reflected in larger increases in space per person is also understandable in view of the housekeeping problems created by the large house calling for expensive domestic and maintenance services. At the same time the need for more housing space was becoming less urgent as many activities, recreational and domestic, were shifted from the household as a result of the automobile and the trend towards increased purchase of commodities and services traditionally produced in the home. . . .

It is clear that some future revision of consumer preferences in favor of housing would serve as a powerful lever in raising the level of residential construction. Such an alteration in consumer standards could, demographic trends aside, arrest or even conceivably reverse past trends in the share of output absorbed by residential capital formation. Among the factors involved in any radical shift in tastes would be a willingness on the part of home-owners and tenants to change old for new dwelling units at a more rapid and continuous pace. An accelerated exchange of old for new products would involve a more rapid decline in prices for old dwellings relative to those for new dwellings, with the ultimate prospect of displacing the least desirable part of the housing stock altogether because it would become worthless, or of making it available to groups which otherwise could not afford separate dwelling units.

A change in consumers' attitudes towards housing could conceivably be induced or strengthened by product innovation. Larger numbers of households might trade old for new units if the latter were vastly superior in design, style, location, or quality, and if the process of innovation could be kept alive so as to be sufficiently persuasive. In such an event, builders would develop a 'replacement market' akin to that for other durable goods, in addition to the market hitherto served. . . .

Plotting the future course of consumer behavior with respect to residential construction is no less hazardous than the projection of aggregate consumer spending. But the probability of an autonomous change in favor of housing on the part of the consumer within the next generation must be questioned. It can hardly be anticipated that there will be no further development of new goods and services which will compete for a place in the family budget. Moreover, the position of housing in the budgets of large numbers of consumers may have suffered from rent control during and after the war. Tenants living in controlled apartments have become accustomed to paying a much smaller proportion of income for rent than was customary before the war and have adjusted their expenditures to this pattern. For these households, a spectacular change in consumers' preferences would be required to induce a demand for new housing that could only be satisfied at rents or carrying charges much greater than the controlled rents they have been paying for many years. . . .

In the absence of public action the one factor now visible that portends a possible reversal of past experience is the suburbanization movement. It is conceivable that an intense repugnance towards city residence may lead to absolute declines in central city population. The resulting increase in vacancies and fall in rents and prices might fail to check new construction in the suburbs because the competitive relation between city and suburban housing markets will weaken. Also, suburban living tends to become centered on family and home and may bring about larger and more expensive houses. But the modern suburbanization movement is at least thirty-five years old and, thus far, no such changes have come to pass.

Finally, the profound and increasing interest of government in housing must be taken into consideration. In a broad sense the concern of government with housing and its financing, while it originated in depression emergencies and was intensified by war and postwar dislocations, must be viewed as a lasting and probably increasing influence on residential construction. This concern, by no means limited to housing conditions of the poor and indigent, expresses deep-seated social forces which cause housing to be clothed with substantial and probably growing public interest, although the scope and means of government action may differ in varying political and economic climates. Continued and probably intensified use of federal aids for residential construction is likely not only because they are tools in a broad program to improve housing conditions, but also because they fit in with full employment policies." [29]

Questions

1. What are the determinants of the demand for housing?
2. In your opinion, do individual families tend to buy more housing as their incomes rise?
3. In the light of the tremendous rise in income between 1890 and 1950, how would you explain the apparent fact that per capita purchases of housing have not increased in real terms?

BUSINESS DEMAND

As in the case of consumer demand, we may also use a demand schedule and curve to show the relationship between price and quantity demanded with respect to a businessman's demand for particular inputs (e.g., the productive services he uses in production). Such a schedule is based on the assumption that the prices of other inputs, technology, and the demand schedule for the businessman's output are all constant. Under these conditions, the quantity demanded of an input is an inverse function of its price. Economists cite two reasons

[29] Louis Winnick, "Housing: Has There Been a Downward Shift in Consumers' Preferences?" *The Quarterly Journal of Economics,* Vol. 69, Harvard U. Press, Cambridge, Mass., February 1955. Copyright, 1955 by the President and Fellows of Harvard College. Reprinted by permission of the publishers.

for this. First, if the price of an input falls, the businessman will find that it pays to use more of it as a substitute for others. If the price of machinery should fall, for example, some businessmen would find that it pays to substitute machinery for labor. Second, a fall in the price of an input means a decrease in the cost of production, and in all probability a decrease in the price of the final product. In accordance with the general law of demand, a fall in the selling price will lead to an increase in the quantity demanded of the final product, which in turn will result in an increase in the quantity demanded of all inputs. (We will have more to say on this matter in Chapters 3 and 7.)

Just as the sum of the demand of all consumers for all goods is known as aggregate consumer demand, so is the sum of all business demand for new plant, equipment, and inventories known as aggregate investment demand. Unlike aggregate consumer demand, however, aggregate investment demand is not considered to be primarily a function of income. Instead, in the Keynesian analysis it is held to depend primarily upon profit expectations and the rate of interest. More detailed discussion of aggregate demand and other Keynesian concepts is reserved for Chapter 9.

CASE 2-28   The demand for air freight

In hearings before the Civil Aeronautics Board some years ago one airline submitted estimates of the annual air traffic volume which could be expected at various rates. The figures were as follows: [30]

RATE PER TON-MILE (cents)	TON-MILES (millions)
35	30
30	60
25	100
20	200
15	800
12	3,550
10	5,000
8	7,400

Questions

1. Does this case reflect consumer demand or business demand? Explain.
2. How would you explain the fact that the curve has a negative slope?

[30] Exhibit SA-4B Slick Airways, Inc. (C.A.B. Docket No. 1705, *et. al.*), p. 13. Quoted in R. M. Alt & W. C. Bradford, *Business Economics*, Richard D. Irwin, Homewood, Ill., 1951, p. 186.

CASE 2-29 New uses for nylon

"Nylon—long regarded by many solely as a covering for dainty limbs—is doing more and more heavy duty on the industrial front.

About 5,000,000 yards of coated nylon fabrics were used last year. The market has been growing by some 400 per cent a year.

Early merchandising efforts in the field were aimed mainly at selling truck tarpaulins. But now a seemingly endless number of uses has been developed. Some textile officials believe that nylon will soon replace cotton canvas tarps just as nylons have replaced silk hose.

Nylon has carved out a growing market in the marine industry, as hatch and boat coverings, sails, and awnings. Along the agricultural front it is being used for grain storage tents, trench silos, haystack covers, and implement shelters.

Considerable work is now going into the adoption of the fabric for irrigation ditch linings and tubings. Oil drilling rig shelters of nylon have won wide acceptance. In the backyard, coated nylon is moving into the wading pool and swimming pool cover markets. And now the armed forces are using large quantities for geodesic domes, as portable shelters.

The success of coated nylon is predicated on its light weight, high tear strength, waterproof quality, flexibility, resistance to rot, mildew, and chemicals such as oil and gasoline, and its relative ease of repair.

LIGHTER, HENCE CHEAPER

How these features result in economies is illustrated by a study conducted by E. I. du Pont de Nemours & Co. in the trucking industry. The company says that the initial cost of a coated nylon cover is greater than that of a conventional tarp.

However, because of nylon's lighter weight, up to 40 per cent can be saved on the cost of transporting the cover over the road. (The American Trucking Association says a trucker can save $1 a year for every pound of dead weight removed from the truck.)

Then, too, a nylon cover usually has double the life of a regular tarp. And the infrequent repairs that are needed can be made by anyone with a simple kit. An intangible saving is ease of handling—one man can handle a nylon cover as opposed to the two or three usually required. All of these factors combine to give truckers a total saving of 50 per cent over conventional tarps, according to du Pont.

A typical nylon cover is made of a base fabric of nylon plus a coating of neoprene or vinyl. Neoprene is a synthetic rubber that has excellent weathering properties. Vinyl is a synthetic resin noted for high resistance to abrasion and chemicals.

Reports indicate that neoprene will out-perform vinyl where considerable flexing of the fabric is required. In all other respects the vinyl-coated materials will perform equally well, du Pont officials say.

Tests have also shown that black and silver are the only suitable colors for use with neoprene. Colors have no effect on the performance of vinyl coatings, and a wide range is being used.

Last week the Brandywine Music Box, a music-circus tent theatre, set up business about ten miles north of Wilmington, Del. Its vinyl-coated nylon tent is made of 26,000 square feet of fabric in a fashionable shade of robin's-egg blue.

Neoprene-coated tarps are nothing new to Dodger fans. Brooklyn has been using this type of covering at Ebbets Field for about six years.

At the first sign of rain the ground crew races out and covers the infield with two tarps each measuring 85 by 165 feet. The Dodgers claim their ground crew holds the major-league record for covering a field in the fastest time—one minute and fifteen seconds.

When the Dodgers decided to play some of their games this year in Jersey City's Roosevelt Stadium, they bought two new coverings. The old ones were sent to Jersey, the new ones to Ebbets Field.

The club says it now uses half the manpower previously required to roll out the old tarps. Many other ball clubs are using nylon now.

Another use was discovered in New Mexico last year, when Khapra beetles began an alarming invasion. Three huge warehouses in which the beetles had been found were wrapped tightly with nylon tarps and sealed. The buildings were fumigated and kept under wraps for six months, until the beetles were killed.

Thus far nylon has hogged the coated-fabric market because its strength by weight exceeds that of other synthetic fibers. However, Dacron, Orlon, and rayon have certain properties that conceivably could make them suitable for coated fabrics." [31]

Questions

1. To what extent would you attribute the increased use of nylon described above to changes in price? To other factors?
2. As described above, is nylon a consumer good or a producer good? Explain.
3. With the information given above as a starting point, how would you go about preparing a demand schedule for nylon?

CASE 2-30 The demand for labor in the steel industry

"Wage increases won by national unions in basic industries have often been called a primary cause of the postwar inflation. The following state-

---

[31] Carl Spielvogel, "New Uses for Nylon," New York *Times*, July 15, 1956. © 1956 by The New York Times Company.

ment by Admiral Ben Morell, president of the Jones and Laughlin Steel Corporation, typifies this view:

> 'Raises in one strategic industry have been followed by similar raises in another, and then by equivalent raises "across the board." Our price level has been on an upward spiral dictated in large measure by labor leaders.'

At this writing, a renewed inflation seems well under way, and inquiry into the role of large-scale collective bargaining as a possible cause of inflation again assumes great practical importance. If collective bargaining is indeed a basic cause of inflation, it should be regulated in the public interest. If it is not a cause of inflation, or is only a minor contributing cause, then other means of controlling inflation must be found, and regulation of collective bargaining must be justified, if at all, on other grounds.

The first questions to be answered in such an inquiry are: Has large-scale collective bargaining during the postwar period raised wages above the levels which would have prevailed in its absence? If so, to what extent?

I have sought to answer these questions for the basic steel industry for the period 1945–48. . . .

TABLE 1   Money and Real Earnings in the Basic Steel Industry, 1939–40 and 1945–48

Year	AVERAGE HOURLY EARNINGS			AVERAGE WEEKLY EARNINGS	
	Current dollars		1935–39 dollars	Current dollars	1935–39 dollars
	amount	index (1939=100)			
1939	.845	100.0	.850	29.88	30.06
1940	.851	100.7	.849	31.49	31.43
1945	1.188	140.6	.925	52.44	40.84
1946	1.291	152.8	.927	48.25	34.64
1947	1.439	170.3	.904	55.95	35.14
1948	1.579	186.9	.922	62.40	36.45

The effects of the first three rounds of wage increases on money and real earnings in the basic steel industry are shown in Table 1. . . .

The increase in the industry's demand for labor is shown in part by employment data. The estimated employment of production and related workers rose from 458,000 in 1945 to 525,000 in 1948, despite the increases in wages indicated by Table 1. The sharp increase in the demand for steel also indicates a probable increase in the demand for steel labor. The rise in the demand for steel is shown in part by the following price and output data: In 1945 finished steel output was approximately 57,000,-000 tons at an average base price of 2.4 cents a pound; in 1948 output had increased to almost 66,000,000 tons, despite an increase in the average base price to 3.4 cents a pound. . . .

There is considerable evidence that the industry experienced a shortage of labor at current wage rates during the postwar period. Such a shortage would cause the bidding up of wages in the absence of collective bargaining, and an increased willingness on the part of employers to grant wage increases under collective bargaining. It is particularly significant that shortages existed soon after wage increases were negotiated, indicating that negotiated rates at these times were probably below those which would have prevailed in the absence of bargaining. . . .

Factors other than collective bargaining seem adequate to account for the wage increases which took place. The principal factors which would have operated in the absence of bargaining were the tremendous increase in the demand for steel, the consequent increase in the demand for labor by the steel industry, and the shortage of labor relative to the quantity demanded at existing wage rates. The sharp increase in the cost of living and the substantial increase in output per man-hour might have been less important contributing factors. . . ." [32]

Questions

1. Explain the increase in demand for steel from 1945 to 1948.
2. How did the increase in the demand for steel affect the demand for steel labor?
3. Can you explain the effect of the rise in wages for steel workers on the demand for steel labor?

CASE 2-31   Union efforts to raise wages

"A union can also affect prices and wage rates through influencing demand by policies intended to shift the whole schedule or by activities which counteract decreases in demand that would otherwise take place. Such programs may be undertaken in cooperation with the firms in the industry or on the sole initiative of the union. A survey of union activities intended to increase demand for the industry as a whole (with corre-

[32] Albert Rees, "Postwar Wage Determination in the Basic Steel Industry," *American Economic Review*, Vol. 41, June 1951, pp. 389 ff. © 1951 by the American Economic Association.

sponding effects on the wage bill) reveals several typical patterns. (a) The union may instigate and secure the cooperation of all parties interested in the industry in a program of mass advertising and promotion. If the product is typically purchased by the general public, a wide sales campaign may prove effective. Unions in the producers' goods area would ordinarily have to resort to other methods. (b) Political pressure may be used to exclude or restrict the introduction of competitive products, as is exemplified in the support of tariffs on foreign goods. . . .

The International Ladies' Garment Workers' Union sponsored an extensive promotional program for the New York Dress Industry in negotiations for a renewal of an agreement in early 1941. . . .

The United Hatters, Cap, and Millinery Workers have also initiated and supported campaigns to increase the demand for the products of their industry in order to increase the wage bill. . . .

The Glass Bottle Blowers strongly supported a higher tariff on French perfume bottles. The union sent representatives to France to compare costs of manufacturing; others appeared before the Congressional committees to explain the position of the union. The same union has striven to maintain sales in the industry by vigorous opposition to paper substitutes. An attempt was made to impose a 1-cent tax or premium on milk sold in paper containers. The support of the teamsters and other unions was solicited. The photoengravers resorted to more usual business tactics in making 'substantial regular monthly contributions . . . to provide greater distribution of *More Business* being published by the American Photo-Engravers Association for the purpose of further interesting the buyer of engravings of the full possibilities of the process, and thus encourage an increasing demand for our product.' The same union complained of the increasing share of advertising business going to radio stations, and made favorable mention of European systems of radio control. The market for engravings was being affected by radio competition. The typographical union also has been much interested in radio competition with printed material; it has fought against higher postal rates for second-class mail. The hosiery workers are concerned with the fashion of slacks among women. The brewery workers were opposed to prohibition. The teamsters protested the purchase of gasoline and oil in tank-car lots by large consumers. The carpenters have opposed legislation against billboards. The United Mine Workers' political opposition to the St. Lawrence project is a protest, in part, against a possible decrease in the demand for coal. Virtually every trade union, with the possible exception of those constituting exceedingly narrow bargaining units, comes to be interested in factors affecting product demand of the industry. Furthermore, trade-union leaders are usually remarkably well-informed as to conditions of the trade. But the extent and methods of shifting market demand vary enormously from union to union." [33]

Questions

1. How would an increase in demand for the product affect the demand for labor?
2. Would a decrease in the price of the product have the same effect? Explain.

---

[33] John T. Dunlop, *Wage Determination Under Trade Unions*, Augustus M. Kelley, Inc., N.Y., 1950, pp. 97 ff. © 1950 by John T. Dunlop.

CHAPTER THREE

Supply and Costs

SUPPLY SCHEDULES AND CURVES

We have seen that demand implies a willingness and ability to pay for some commodity or service. In a similar manner, supply implies a willingness and ability to produce, offer, or make available some commodity or service in return for payment. The term "supply" is used with reference to many different things: the supply of raw materials, of manufactured goods, of services, of labor, of land, or of money. As in the case of demand, we can speak of supply meaning either quantity supplied or a supply schedule. In this chapter the term "supply" will be used to mean a supply schedule, unless otherwise stated.

You will recall that the demand schedule shows the relationship between quantity demanded and price. Similarly, the supply schedule shows the relationship between the quantity that will be supplied (produced or offered) and price. The demand schedule answers the question, "What will be the quantity demanded if the price is such and such (other things being equal)?" The supply schedule answers the question, "What will be the quantity supplied if the price is such and such (other things being equal)?"

The concept of a supply schedule must be applied with caution. In order for the schedule to be meaningful in the sense in which we have defined it, a prospective supplier must be faced with a price over which he does not exercise control.[1] This is most likely to be true if the supplier is in a highly competitive situation, i.e., if (a) the supplier is one of a great many suppliers in a market, (b) the total amount that he could possibly supply is very small relative to the total market, (c) the several suppliers do not engage in collusion, and (d) there are

---

[1] This is also true of the demand schedule; i.e., the assumption must be made that the prospective demander has no control over price. Such an assumption was made throughout Chapter 2. We may now note that the assumption is almost always justified for consumer demand, but may not always be true for business demand.

no important differences among the products of the various suppliers; i.e., the product is fairly standardized. It will also be true if the price is set by government decree, as under price control. In other situations, however, where the supplier himself has some control over his price, the concept of a supply schedule must be redefined to take this factor into account. For this reason, much of our discussion of the basis of the supply schedule must be reserved for the later chapter on marginal analysis. For the time being, we may note that where we refer to a supply schedule, we may use it in much the same way as the demand schedule.

As in the case of demand, we may write an equation $Q_s = f(p)$ which says that the quantity supplied (Q_s) is related to the price (p). We may represent this by a curve plotted on a chart with quantity measured along the horizontal axis and price measured in the vertical direction. Individual supply curves (e.g., the curves of individual firms) may be combined to obtain the industry supply curve. Finally, we may discuss movements along the curve (called changes in the quantity supplied) and we may study shifts in the supply schedule itself (referred to as changes in supply). (See Fig. 3-1.)

We must note, however, some major differences between supply curves and demand curves. First, unlike demand, supply curves usually slope upward to the right, indicating a positive relationship between price and quantity supplied.[2] Second, while the principal determinants of quantity demanded are price, income, other prices, and taste, the major determinants of quantity supplied are price and costs. Whereas shifts in a demand curve are the result of changes in income, other prices, or taste, shifts in the supply curve are the result of a change in *costs*.

When we think about the supply schedule for a firm or an industry, it is not difficult to grasp the notion that supply will be related to costs of production. When we consider the supply of a type of labor service (such as that of schoolteachers or firemen), the significance and meaning of cost as the determinant of the supply schedule may not be as readily apparent. On reflection, however, we can see that the cost factor in such instances is represented by the costs of preparation for the occupation and by the loss of alternative opportunities, including the opportunity for leisure. Part of the costs of any type of work are the foregone rewards, both financial and psychic, which could be enjoyed by the person if he were not spending his time in that work.

Since an understanding of cost is essential to an understanding of

---

[2] However, there is no general law of supply corresponding to the general law of demand.

FIG. 3-1   Supply Curves

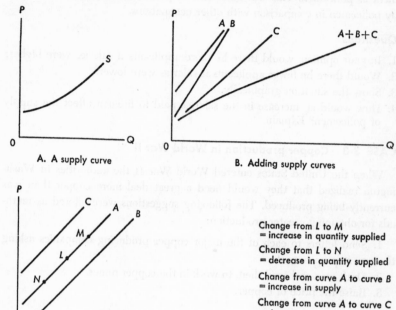

A. A supply curve

B. Adding supply curves

C. Changes in quantity supplied and changes in supply

Change from L to M
= increase in quantity supplied

Change from L to N
= decrease in quantity supplied

Change from curve A to curve B
= increase in supply

Change from curve A to curve C
= decrease in supply

supply, we will devote the next section to a discussion of this concept and some of its applications in economics.

CASE 3-1   Drawing supply curves

Assume a supply schedule which satisfies the equation,

$$Q_s = \frac{P}{2} - 5$$

1. Plot and draw the supply curve.

2. How would you indicate graphically a change in quantity supplied? A change in supply?

3. How would you alter the equation to indicate such changes algebraically?

CASE 3-2   New York policemen

New York City Police Commissioner Stephen Kennedy recently reported difficulty in obtaining a sufficient number of qualified applicants for appointment as policemen. This was attributed in part to the low salaries received by policemen in comparison with other occupations.

Questions

1. In your opinion, would there be more applicants if salaries were higher?
2. Would there be fewer applicants if salaries were lower?
3. Show the situation graphically.
4. How would an increase in the salaries paid to firemen affect the supply of policemen? Explain.

CASE 3-3   Copper production in World War II

When the United States entered World War II the authorities in Washington realized that they would need a great deal more copper than was currently being produced. The following suggestions were offered as methods for obtaining greater production:

1. Send letters to each of the major copper producing companies asking them to step up output.
2. Draft men and send them to work in the copper mines.
3. Raise the price of copper.

Questions

1. Which of these methods would have resulted in movement along a supply schedule?
2. Show this graphically.
3. In your opinion, which of the three proposals had the most merit? Why?

USE OF THE TERM "COST" IN ECONOMICS

In applying the cost concept we encounter two important distinctions frequently made by economists. These are (1) the difference between the economist's approach to cost as opportunity foregone and the businessman's approach to cost as money paid out, and (2) the difference between fixed cost and variable cost. These distinctions are discussed below.

Alternative or Opportunity Cost

The economist uses this term to emphasize the fact that the cost of anything is best measured by the alternative opportunity which is given up or foregone. This is recognized in everyday speech, as evidenced by such comments as "I managed to pass the course, but at great cost to my social life," or "My fooling around last semester cost me a passing grade." The concept has important practical applications as well as usefulness in analyzing basic economic problems of society.

This use of the term "cost" differs from the customary usage of the term in business or business accounting, where the stress is usually placed on *historical* cost, i.e., what was paid for something when it was acquired, regardless of when or how it is to be used. Thus a piece of machinery is valued by the accountant according to how much was paid for it at the time of its acquisition, with suitable allowance for depreciation. The economist, on the other hand, tends to regard historical cost with less interest. He is more concerned with the present opportunity cost, i.e., the alternative uses to which something can be put at the present time.[3] From the point of view of the economist, the present value of a resource as determined by its alternative uses is a more meaningful measure of cost than the historical cost, and provides a better guide to economic policy. Thus the piece of machinery which was valued by the accountant in terms of its historical cost might be dealt with by the economist in terms of the price it would bring in the current market.

A related distinction in the use of cost concepts may be observed in the stress placed by businessmen and business accountants on money paid out. In accounting terms, cost reflects an actual expenditure in dollars and cents, or the incurring of debt. Economists emphasize, however, that even if no money is paid out, the use of resources represents a cost in terms of what those resources could have earned in alternative uses. Accountants, for example, frequently do not treat the services of a self-employed person as a cost of the business; the economist, on the other hand, would regard the potential earnings of such services in other uses as the present cost of those services in their present use. Similarly, an owner who uses his own property does not have to pay rent, and accordingly need not incur a cost in an accounting sense. In economics, however, the "cost" of using the property would be the rent it would earn if the owner chose to lease the property instead of using it himself.

Fixed and Variable Costs

Another distinction which economists have found very useful is the difference between fixed and variable costs. The former refers to costs which do not change in total amount as the rate of output is

---

[3] What is opportunity cost in a given situation will depend upon whose point of view is being considered. Thus there is the opportunity cost of using a machine for one purpose rather than another within the same firm; the opportunity cost of using it outside the firm but in the same industry; and the opportunity cost of using it in some other industry. In the first instance we would be considering the opportunity cost to the firm; in the second, the opportunity cost to the industry; and in the third, the opportunity cost to society as a whole.

changed.[4] Variable costs are those costs which do change in total amount as the rate of output is changed. For example, the rent of a factory building is usually a fixed cost for a firm. Whether the firm operates at full capacity, or at half, or does not produce at all, the rent is a fixed cost for the duration of the lease. Similarly, if the firm owns its own building, real estate taxes are usually a fixed cost. Raw materials, on the other hand, are normally a variable cost—if the rate of output increases, the amount spent for raw material rises; if it falls, the business will incur less expense for that item.

The fixed and variable costs referred to above are the *total* fixed costs and *total* variable costs of the firm. It is also useful to know the fixed cost per unit of output, and the variable cost per unit of output. These quantities, which are also known as *average* fixed cost and *average* variable cost, are obtained by dividing total fixed cost and total variable cost, respectively, by the number of units produced. The relationship between total and average costs is shown in Table 3-1 below.

TABLE 3-1   Total and Average Costs

RATE OF OUTPUT (*units per week*)	TOTAL FIXED COST	TOTAL VARIABLE COST	TOTAL COST	AVERAGE FIXED COST	AVERAGE VARIABLE COST	AVERAGE COST
0	$300	$ 0	$300	$ ∞	$ 0	$ ∞
1	300	80	380	300	80	380
2	300	150	450	150	75	225
3	300	210	510	100	70	170
4	300	280	580	75	70	145
5	300	375	675	60	75	135
6	300	540	840	50	90	140

CASE 3-4   Souvenirs of Cape Cod, I

Jared Hunter, a retired sea captain living on Cape Cod, found that the postwar inflation made it extremely difficult for him and his wife to live on his small pension. He decided to supplement his income by manufacturing ceramic souvenirs and selling them to the tourists who invade the Cape each summer.

He withdrew most of his savings, about $5,000, from the bank and bought machinery and an initial supply of raw material. He and his wife fitted a

---

[4] These costs resemble those referred to as overhead costs by businessmen, although the correspondence is not always exact.

downstairs room of the house as a workshop, and they spent the winter and spring making brooches and ashtrays which bore the inscription "Souvenir of Cape Cod."

When summer came they set up signs and displays on the front porch, and Captain Hunter and his wife alternated between waiting on customers and making additional units as their stock ran low.

In the fall, the Captain decided to draw up a rough statement of income and costs to see whether the venture had been a profitable one. The figures were as follows:

	INCOME		
Sold:	606 Ashtrays @ $1.50	$ 909	
	1,197 Brooches @ 1.00	1,197	
	Total		$2,106
	COSTS		
	Ceramic clay	$ 615	
	Other materials and supplies	230	
	Depreciation on machinery ($4,500 over 10 years)	450	
	Signs, advertising, etc.	150	
	Electricity	94	
	Total costs		$1,539
	Profit		$ 567

"Well," said Captain Hunter to his wife, "that's a nice profit for a small business. Looks as if we ought to plan to go ahead again next year."

"Not if I can help it," she replied. "You haven't figured your costs correctly. According to my calculations the business showed a loss."

Questions

1. Why did Mrs. Hunter say the costs were not figured correctly?
2. In your opinion, how should costs be calculated in this case?
3. Can Captain Hunter's conclusion be justified?

CASE 3-5   The cost of World War II

There are two entirely different ways of measuring the cost of World War II.

1. The financial cost:
   a. Taxes paid to support the war
   b. Money borrowed by the U.S. government to finance the war
   c. Taxes paid since the war for
      (1) interest on war debt

(2) obligations to veterans

(3) other expenses arising out of the war

2. Commodities and services which could have been produced with:

a. Materials used in war

b. Labor used to produce war materials

c. Capital equipment used to produce war materials

d. Labor of men in armed forces during the war

e. Labor of men killed or disabled during the war

Questions

1. In the light of the above, discuss the statement, "The cost of World War II will be borne by our children and our children's children."

CASE 3-6   The cost of driving an automobile, I

An advertisement of the Ethyl Corporation gave the following figures for yearly driving costs, quoting the American Automobile Association as the source: [5]

FOR 5,000 MILES		FOR 15,000 MILES
$481.33	Depreciation	$481.33
104.39	Insurance	104.39
16.86	License fees	16.86
116.00	Gasoline and oil	348.00
37.00	Maintenance	111.00
25.50	Tires	76.50
$781.08	*Total*	$1,138.08

Questions

1. According to the AAA, which items represent fixed costs for the automobile owner? Which are treated as variable? Do you agree with the AAA?

2. What would correspond to the rate of output in this case?

3. What cost has been completely neglected?

CASE 3-7   Souvenirs of Cape Cod, II

Questions (Refer to Case 3-4):

1. Which of Captain Hunter's costs are fixed? Which are variable?

2. Assuming that:

a. one ashtray requires twice as much clay as one brooch, and

b. one ashtray requires the same amount of labor, electricity, and other materials as one brooch,

---

[5] *Life,* September 21, 1956. By permission of the Ethyl Corporation and the American Automobile Association.

can you calculate the average fixed and average variable costs for ashtrays and for brooches?

CASE 3-8   Cost curves and break-even charts

Just as we can plot a demand or supply curve from a demand or supply schedule, we can plot cost curves if we have a table of costs. One practical application of cost curves is their use in break-even charts. A simple break-even chart may be constructed as follows (see Fig. 3-2 and Table 3-2). We set up our chart with rate of output (and sales) per month measured on the horizontal axis and total cost (and revenue) in dollars measured on the vertical axis. Let us suppose that the firm has fixed costs of $6,000 per month. The fixed cost curve (TFC) will then appear as a horizontal straight line at a height of $6,000. Let us further suppose that total variable cost increases at a constant rate of $4 per unit. This assumption gives us curve TVC. When we add total fixed cost and total variable cost, we arrive at total cost (curve TC). Total revenue (TR) is obtained by multiplying the rate of sales by the selling price, which in this case is assumed to be $7.50.

We may now observe that at low rates of output the total cost curve lies above the total revenue curve, and the difference between the two represents the loss to the firm. At point A, where the two curves cross, total cost and total revenue are exactly equal; this is the break-even point. At rates of output beyond the break-even point, total revenue exceeds total cost and the firm operates at a profit.

FIG. 3-2   A Break-Even Chart

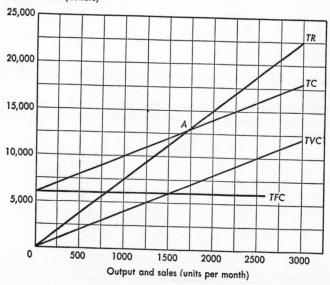

Cost and revenue (dollars)

Output and sales (units per month)

TABLE 3-2

RATE OF OUTPUT (SALES) (units per month)	TFC	AVC	TVC	TC	AR	TR	PROFIT OR LOSS
0	$6,000	$4	$ 0	$ 6,000	$7.50	$ 0	$−6,000
1,000	6,000	4	4,000	10,000	7.50	7,500	−2,500
1,500	6,000	4	6,000	12,000	7.50	11,250	− 750
2,000	6,000	4	8,000	14,000	7.50	15,000	1,000
3,000	6,000	4	12,000	18,000	7.50	22,500	4,500

Questions

1. Assuming that fixed costs are $7,000 per month, find the break-even rate of output.
2. Find the break-even point when fixed cost is $6,000 per month, but variable cost is (a) $5 per unit; (b) $3 per unit.
3. Find the break-even point when fixed cost is $6,000 per month, variable cost is $4 per unit, but selling price is (a) $9 per unit; (b) $5 per unit.
4. Find the break-even point when fixed cost is $6,000 per month, selling price is $7.50 per unit, but variable cost behaves as follows:

RATE OF OUTPUT	TOTAL VARIABLE COST
500	$ 2,500
1,000	4,500
1,500	6,000
2,000	9,000
2,500	12,500

Can you think of any reasons why variable cost might behave in this manner?

5. Find the break-even point when fixed cost is $6,000, variable cost is $4 per unit at all rates of output, but the demand curve facing the firm is as follows:

PRICE	QUANTITY (units per month)
$14	500
12	1,000
10	1,500
8	2,000
6	2,500
4	3,000

CASE 3-9   Department store economics

Mr. Hanson runs a moderate-sized department store in Southern California. For purposes of merchandising and financial control, the store is divided into three departments: A, clothing; B, household goods; C, miscellaneous. A buyer is in charge of each department with full responsibility. Each buyer is paid a small salary plus a bonus at the end of the year which is based upon the performance of his department. In 1956 the figures for each department were as follows:

	Dept. A	Dept. B	Dept. C
Net sales	$360,000	$300,000	$240,000
Cost of goods sold	240,000	190,000	140,000
Direct costs within dept.	62,000	60,000	58,000
Dept.'s share of fixed costs of store ($90,000)	36,000	30,000	24,000
Net profit	22,000	20,000	18,000

In 1957, Sam Jones, the household goods buyer, launched a more aggressive merchandising program which included smaller markups, bigger commissions to the salesmen, and faster turnover of merchandise. As a result, he was able to double the volume of the department as compared with the previous year, while the other departments in the store turned in exactly the same figures as in 1956. Jones looked forward eagerly to his bonus, but after the profit figures were calculated, he received a smaller bonus than he had the year before. He asked Mr. Hanson for an explanation, and was shown the following:

	Dept. A	Dept. B	Dept. C
Net sales	$360,000	$600,000	$240,000
Cost of goods sold	240,000	410,000	140,000
Direct costs within dept.	62,000	130,000	58,000
Dept.'s share of fixed costs of store ($90,000)	27,000	45,000	18,000
Net profit	31,000	15,000	24,000

"Mr. Hanson," said Jones, "your method of calculating is all wet. I should get a bigger bonus this year."

"Mr. Jones," said Mr. Hanson, "we are interested in profit, not volume. You're fired!"

Questions

1. Who was right, Jones or Hanson? Explain.

MARKET, SHORT–RUN, AND LONG–RUN SUPPLY

In speaking about supply, economists have found it useful to distinguish among three different situations: (1) immediate or market supply, (2) short-run supply, and (3) long-run supply. The distinction rests upon the length of time we have in mind when we ask the question, "What will be the quantity supplied if the price is such and such?" The answer to this question may well be different depending upon how long we are assuming that "such and such" a price has prevailed.

The *immediate* or *market* supply schedule refers to the quantity currently available, and is independent of price. An example would be the supply of paintings of an artist who is now dead, or the current supply of a highly perishable commodity. One important use of this concept is when we speak of the supply of money, meaning the amount of coin and currency in circulation plus the amount of demand deposits in commercial banks. The immediate or market supply is represented graphically by a vertical line (see Fig. 3-3).

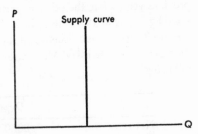

FIG. 3-3
Market Supply

The *short-run* supply schedule is based on the assumption that there is time for the producer to change his rate of output in response to changes in price, but not sufficient time to change the size of his plant. In other words, a producer can vary the quantity supplied by varying certain of his inputs. There are other inputs, however, which in the short run are fixed. In the short run a manufacturer, for example, can usually change the amount of raw material and direct labor that he uses, but cannot change the number of machines or the size of his factory.

The *long-run* supply schedule presumes that businessmen have had an opportunity to change the size of their firms and plants, and that firms have had an opportunity to enter or leave the industry in response to price changes.

The question of time is one of the most difficult aspects of economics, and although concepts such as short run and long run are useful, we might also remember that time "is itself absolutely continuous; Nature knows no absolute partition of time into long periods and short, but the two shade into one another by imperceptible gradations, and what is a short period for one problem, is a long period for another." [6]

Increasing, Decreasing, and Constant Costs

One question of considerable interest in economics concerns the shape of the long-run cost curve, i.e., the behavior of average costs as the size of the plant or firm is changed. Do average costs decrease as size increases? If so, we refer to this as decreasing costs. If average costs increase, we then speak of increasing costs. If average costs do not vary with changes in size, the situation is referred to as one of constant costs (see Fig. 3-4). The pattern is clearly different in different industries (e.g., in dress manufacturing costs begin to increase at a relatively small size, in aluminum refining at a relatively large size), and has a great influence on the number and relative size of firms in an industry. This is a subject of great practical importance to businessmen, and is also a major consideration in the enforcement and interpretation of antitrust laws and other aspects of public policy relating to the control of business.

FIG. 3-4   Costs in the Long Run

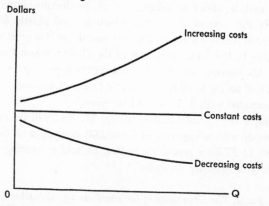

<hr>

[6] Alfred Marshall, *Principles of Economics*, preface to 1st ed., reprinted in 8th ed., p. vii. Copyright, 1920 by The Macmillan Company, N.Y. Reprinted by permission.

CASE 3-10   The supply of silver fox [7]

YEAR	AVERAGE PRICE PER SKIN	QUANTITY OF SKINS PRODUCED ON U.S. FARMS
1944	$50.35	233,720
1945	38.18	235,762
1946	35.45	238,484
1947	17.37	243,543
1948	12.96	140,297
1949	10.96	61,530
1950	11.64	36,734
1951	14.76	29,916
after 1951	below 15.00	below 10,000

Questions

1. Do the figures shown above represent a market, short-run, or long-run supply schedule, or none of these? Explain.
2. What sort of relationship seems to exist between the price of silver fox and the number of skins produced?
3. When prices fell 50% from 1946 to 1947, why do you suppose there was no decrease in production?
4. If the price of silver fox should again rise to $50, what do you think would be the effect on the quantity supplied?

CASE 3-11   Descending zirconium

"The atomic-age metal zirconium is following the traditional price curve of metals under development; as production soars, the price plunges. In the case of zirconium, which is used mostly for structural applications in nuclear reactors, the downward curve is particularly steep. Gen. Clinton F. Robinson, president of the Carborundum Company, said yesterday his concern was turning out 325,000 pounds of zirconium a year now, and selling it all to the Atomic Energy Commission at $12.50 a pound, compared with $15 a pound last year.

However, a new plant at Parkersburg, W. Va., will be in production by September with a capacity of 1,200,000 pounds, and the price will be reduced to $7.50 a pound thereafter, he told a meeting of the New York Society of Security Analysts." [8]

---

[7] Victor R. Fuchs, *The Economics of the Fur Industry*, Columbia U. Press, N.Y., 1957, p. 122. © 1957 by Columbia University Press.
[8] New York *Times*, May 15, 1957. © 1957 by The New York Times Company.

Questions

1. What does the above suggest about the long-run cost curve for zirconium?
2. If the government can pay $12.50 a pound for zirconium, why should the Carborundum Company cut its price to $7.50?

CASE 3-12   Burlington's switch

"Synthetic textiles came into the news last week with the announcement that Burlington Industries, the largest producer, had sold four of its converting divisions, which cater to the women's wear trades. It appears that Burlington is reverting to the theory that mills should stick to turning out the basic cloth, and that distributors, or converters, should be charged with finishing this cloth to the specifications of cutters and retailers.

Burlington will continue, however, to sell finished goods in the men's wear field, where much larger quantities of a given pattern are used, and where style changes are not so frequent and so violent.

For Burlington, this marks almost a complete cycle. Until World War II, the company stuck mainly to selling unfinished or gray goods. In the period of fabric shortages, the company, along with other textile manufacturers, embarked on a wide program of selling finished goods, attracted no doubt by the larger profits involved. When textiles were in short supply, anything that was produced could be easily sold.

When the textile industry returned to its traditional heavy competition, it appeared that the large companies were at somewhat of a disadvantage in filling demands for small runs of varied patterns. Textron, Inc., was the first large producer to limit its finished goods business in the women's wear trades. It has retained for the most part only those synthetic goods plants that supply gray goods.

The 'dream' of the textile industry about two decades ago was vertical integration, where one company could manufacture the product from yarn to garment. It was argued that only in this way could the textile producer guarantee quality to the ultimate consumer, because he could keep track of every step along the way. But proponents of vertical integration did not take into account the fickleness of Dame Fashion, and the fact that physical distribution of marketing was a function that could be operated more efficiently by numerous smaller entrepreneurs than by one large producer, at least in the textile and apparel trades.

And so the dream of vertical integration is about dead." [9]

---

[9] Herbert Koshetz, "The Merchant's Point of View," New York *Times*, November 18, 1956. © 1956 by The New York Times Company.

Questions

1. What does the above imply regarding the long-run cost curve?
2. In the light of the widely held opinion that the efficiency of American production is attributable to a considerable degree to large-scale operations, how do you account for the developments described above?
3. What other industries, in your opinion, might exhibit similar characteristics?

CHANGES IN SUPPLY

When we speak of a change in supply, we mean a shift to a new supply schedule. This will usually depend upon a change in costs, which in turn are controlled by two factors, one technological and the other economic.

On the technological side, every output (e.g., automobiles) comes into existence as a result of the use of productive resources, called inputs (e.g., machinery, labor, steel). The output at any given time is, in a physical sense, a function of the inputs of the productive services. This relationship is called the "production function." Production functions change over time. New inventions and discoveries tend to increase the output that can be achieved from a given amount of inputs, or to decrease the amount of inputs needed to obtain a given amount of output. This means lowered costs. If costs are lowered, then businessmen will find that at each possible price for the article it pays to produce *more* than before. In graphical terms, the supply curve will have shifted to the right.

The other determinant of cost is the price of inputs. When the prices of inputs rise, other things remaining constant, costs rise. A rise in costs usually means that at each possible price the quantity that people are willing and able to supply is smaller than before; i.e., there is a decrease in supply. In graphical terms this will mean a curve which is to the left of the old one. When input prices fall, on the other hand, costs fall, and this will usually stimulate an increase in supply.

CASE 3-13   Chemistry and farm costs

One of the major contributions of modern chemistry has been to decrease the cost (raise the yields) of agricultural products. The following are a few examples of the changes which have taken place:

1. "It now costs one-half as much as formerly to control rangeland and cropland pests; the control efficiency has risen from 60 per cent to 98 per cent.

2. The control of greenbugs with the new insecticides has increased wheat yields in Oklahoma by as much as 400 per cent; alfalfa seed production in Utah has risen 150 per cent; hybrid corn production increases due to better insect control are estimated at 30 per cent; Maine potato production can be increased 100 per cent.

3. Requirements for producing a bale of cotton are sinking toward ten man-hours from a prechemical high of 155." [10]

Questions

1. Show graphically the effect of these changes on the supply of agricultural products.
2. Do you see any connection between the above and the "farm problem"?

CASE 3-14   Hi-fi diamond needles

"The diamond needle before long will be standard equipment on ready-assembled hi-fi record players in the medium-price range, in the view of Robert Walcutt, president of Walco Products, Inc., East Orange, N.J.

Mr. Walcutt based his prediction on his concern's achievement, after two years of research and the expenditure of some $500,000 in pilot products, in perfecting a process for automatic manufacture of diamond phonograph styli.

The immediate effect of the advance, he said, would be a cut in the list price of the diamond needle from $25 to $14.95.

In the next twelve months, Mr. Walcutt said, Walco will produce 3,000,000 diamond needles, more than the total sales for the industry last year.

The new automatic process, introduced by Walco, in effect moves diamond grinding and polishing out of the arts into the category of electronic science. Production will be 2,000 per cent faster, with rejects almost completely eliminated. Also, smaller and less costly diamonds are usable with automatic precision engineering.

The key to the process is a revolutionary technique of bonding the diamond tip to a steel shank. Walco combined its own research and development efforts with those of the research laboratory of the Sylvania Electric Products Corporation." [11]

Questions

1. Does the above imply a movement along a supply curve or a shift in supply?

---

[10] "Farming's Chemical Age," *Fortune*, November 1953, p. 202. © 1953 by Time, Inc.

[11] William M. Freeman, "Hi-Fi Diamond Set for Mass Output," *New York Times*, July 20, 1957. © 1957 by The New York Times Company.

2. Does the above imply a movement along a demand curve or a shift in demand?

CASE 3-15   Synthetic gasoline too costly

"The world's first plant for the manufacture of gasoline from natural gas will be shut down as uneconomical, it was announced today by the Amoco Chemicals Corporation.

The plant, at Brownsville, Texas, will be closed within the next few months, with a reduction of the work force to begin Oct. 1.

J. H. Forrester, president of Amoco, a subsidiary of the Standard Oil Company (Indiana), said: 'We have determined that the Brownsville plant cannot make gasoline and chemicals from natural gas at present market prices as cheaply as they can be made by other processes.' . . .

Mr. Forrester said that production at the Brownsville plant had been 'at a very low level.' He declared: 'We have proved the technical soundness of the process. However, results indicate that the units are more costly to operate and maintain than we had anticipated.' " [12]

Questions

1. Under what circumstances might synthetic gasoline be considered part of the supply of gasoline?
2. Since the manufacturers have "proved the technical soundness of the process," isn't it wasteful to close down the plant (a) from the point of view of the firm; (b) from the point of view of society?

[12] New York *Times*, September 14, 1957. © 1957 by The New York Times Company.

CHAPTER FOUR

Equilibrium

THE CONCEPT OF EQUILIBRIUM

Meaning of the Concept

The concept of equilibrium plays a central role in many branches of science, both natural and social. The most general definition of the term suggests a *balance*. In physics, for example, an object is said to be in equilibrium when the various forces acting upon it are in such perfect balance that the object does not change its position if at rest, or does not change its direction and speed if in motion. This equilibrium will continue to exist as long as no disturbance occurs to upset the balance. Perhaps the most familiar example of equilibrium is that of a pendulum when it is at rest.

Application of the Equilibrium Concept to Economics

As applied to economics, equilibrium is a conceptual tool for analyzing situations in which certain types of adjustments are assumed to have taken place. Equilibrium exists in an economic situation when the relationship between the relevant economic variables is such that in the absence of a disturbing force there is no disposition for any variable to change. Should a disturbing force occur, the relationship between the variables would change until a new equilibrium position was reached. All parts of the economic system, in the view of most economists, always tend to move toward equilibrium following the impact of a disturbing force.

If we can identify the economic forces which are at work in a given situation, the concept of equilibrium provides us with a tool for analyzing the results of the interplay of these forces. For example, in this chapter we will examine in some detail the process by which the forces of demand on the one hand and supply on the other determine the equilibrium price (and quantity) for a commodity or service in a particular market. To find equilibrium in this situation, we will look for that price where supply and demand are in such balance that there is no tendency for the price either to rise or fall. We may also expect to find that the price, if not already at the equilibrium point, will tend to move in that direction.

Equilibrium Rarely a Description of Reality

In the real economic world, a complete state of equilibrium is rarely achieved. In most situations it is likely that we can observe only a tendency toward equilibrium rather than the complete working out of the forces which bring us to that point. This working out takes time; and with the passage of time the forces may change, and new forces may appear. For this reason, the concept of equilibrium is more useful as a theoretical tool of analysis than as a description of any existing situation. It is, nevertheless, a very useful device. If we know the equilibrium position in a given situation, we can study the forces which tend to move things into or out of balance, and thus find a basis for predicting the probable direction of movement.

Types of Equilibrium Situations

We use the concept of equilibrium in many types of situations, ranging from the very simple to the very complex. The range of complexity depends upon how many conditions of equilibrium are involved. By conditions of equilibrium we mean the relationships which must be fulfilled for equilibrium to exist. For a simple case of two economic variables, such as price and quantity in a particular market, a single condition of equilibrium exists, namely that the quantity supplied must equal the quantity demanded. When we deal with more complicated relationships involving many variables, additional conditions become necessary for the definition of the equilibrium position. Other equilibrium situations in economics, many of which will be discussed in later chapters, may be described briefly as follows:

1. Equilibrium of the consumer—with respect to the allocation of income to the purchase of different goods.
2. Equilibrium of the firm—with respect to the rate of output and rate of use of various productive resources.
3. Equilibrium of the industry—with respect to the entry and exit of firms, size of firms, and rates of output.
4. Equilibrium of the entire economic system—encompassing equilibrium for consumers, firms, industries, and owners of productive resources.
5. In a somewhat different vein, John Maynard Keynes and his

followers have used the concept of equilibrium to describe a situation where the aggregate level of activity in the economy, especially as measured by the national income, is stable. Such an equilibrium is said to be achieved when the rate of total purchases of commodities and services at current prices is equal to the rate of total production.

The terms *partial* and *general* equilibrium are sometimes used to describe the range of equilibrium situations as they progress from the simple to the complex. By partial equilibrium we mean the equilibrium of a particular part of the economic system; by general equilibrium we mean the equilibrium of the entire system. Actually, the difference between partial and general equilibrium is only one of degree. As compared with the equilibrium of a single firm, which is clearly partial, equilibrium of an entire industry is certainly more general; nevertheless, the latter situation is referred to as partial equilibrium in order to distinguish it from equilibrium throughout the entire system. If general equilibrium is achieved, then each firm and industry within the system must be in equilibrium.[1] The fact that an individual firm or industry is in equilibrium, however, does not mean that the entire system must be in equilibrium. We must also note that the Keynesian concept of aggregate equilibrium is not the same as that of general equilibrium; aggregate equilibrium does not imply equilibrium for every firm and industry, but only that, on the average, total production and total purchases over a given time period are in balance.

Most of this chapter is concerned with partial equilibrium; it concludes with a brief discussion of general equilibrium. Aggregate equilibrium is treated in Chapter 9.

CASE 4-1   Equilibrium in economics

". . . We know from experience what kind of relations subsist between prices and quantities, by virtue of which they influence each other. This we express by saying that prices and quantities of all goods and services are *interdependent* and form a *system*. The quantities are really rates per element of time, but for some purposes it is more convenient to eliminate the time factor and to speak of absolute quantities. . . .

The first and foremost task of economic analysis is to explore the properties of that system. The method of doing this is analogous to the method known in mechanics as the method of virtual displacements. What we

---

[1] The above refers to a "closed" system, i.e., international trade is not taken into account. Actually, it is possible to make the concept of equilibrium even more general in application by specifying that all aspects of economic relations among different countries be in balance as well.

want to learn before anything else is whether or not the relations known to subsist between the elements of the system are, together with the data, sufficient to determine these elements, prices and quantities, uniquely. For our system is logically self-contained only if this is the case: we can be sure that we understand the nature of economic phenomena only if it is possible to deduce prices and quantities from the data by means of those relations, and to prove that no other set of prices and physical quantities is compatible with both the data and the relations. The proof that this is so is the magna charta of economic theory as an autonomous science, assuring us that its subject matter is a cosmos and not a chaos. It is the rationale of the idea of variables that do not vary, the justification of the scheme of a stationary economic process. The values of prices and quantities which are the only ones, the data being what they are in each case, to satisfy those relations, we call *equilibrium values*. The state of the system which obtains if all prices and quantities take their equilibrium values we call the *state of equilibrium*." [2]

Questions

1. What is meant by "variables that do not vary"? Is this likely to be the case in the real world?
2. How should we interpret the writer's distinction between the elements of the system and the data?
3. Why is it important to have a logically self-contained system?
4. Does the writer seem to be discussing partial or general equilibrium? Explain.

EQUILIBRIUM IN A PARTICULAR MARKET

How to Find the Equilibrium Position

The most useful application of the equilibrium concept is in determining the equilibrium price and quantity for a particular commodity or service in a particular market. Let us suppose that the demand and supply schedules for commodity X are as follows:

P	Q (demanded)	P	Q (supplied)
$5	5	$5	13
4	6	4	10
3	7	3	7
2	8	2	4
1	9	1	1

[2] Joseph A. Schumpeter, *Business Cycles*, Vol. 1, pp. 41–42. Copyright, 1939 by McGraw-Hill Book Co., Inc., N.Y. Reprinted by permission.

What is the equilibrium price and quantity? The point of equilibrium will be at a price of $3 and a quantity of 7 because at that point, and only at that point, are the forces of demand and supply in balance, i.e., there is no tendency for the price to either rise or fall. If we choose a price higher than $3, the quantity supplied would exceed the quantity demanded, suppliers would tend to lower the price in order to increase sales, and the price would tend to fall. At all prices below $3, the quantity demanded would exceed the quantity supplied; buyers would tend to bid the price up, and the price would tend to rise.

If we use curves to represent our demand and supply schedules, as in Fig. 4-1, we can see the meaning of equilibrium in graphical terms. The equilibrium point is where the two curves cross; it is the only point on the chart where demand and supply are in balance. The equilibrium price and quantity can be determined by referring to the respective axes as shown by the dotted lines.[3]

FIG. 4-1   Equilibrium of Supply and Demand

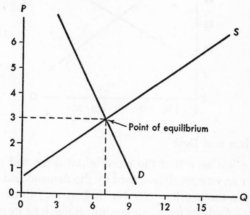

Such an equilibrium position is said to be *stable*, meaning that if the price is temporarily above or below the equilibrium position, it will tend to return to equilibrium. There is also a type of equilibrium which is said to be unstable, but which is of less interest to economists. Its

---

[3] The problem could also be solved algebraically as follows:

1. The first schedule is represented by the equation $Q_d = 10 - P$
2. The second schedule is represented by the equation $Q_s = 3P - 2$
3. The condition of equilibrium is that $Q_d = Q_s$
4. It follows that $3P - 2 = 10 - P$
$$4P = 12$$
$$P = 3$$

existence, however, does point up the importance of assuming that we are dealing with equilibrium positions that are stable. Let us suppose, for example, that the demand curve sloped upward to the right and the supply curve downward to the right (as in Fig. 4-2). A slight decrease in price below the equilibrium level would now lead to further decreases in price; similarly, a slight increase in price above the equilibrium level would lead to further increases in price. Under these conditions, no forces would exist to restore the equilibrium position. Since prices in the real world seldom fall to zero or rise to infinity, we need not concern ourselves further with the question of instability at this time.

FIG. 4-2   Unstable Equilibrium

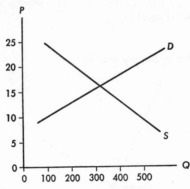

Equilibrium and Time

We have just seen that the equilibrium price and quantity for a commodity or service are determined by the demand and supply schedules. We saw in the previous chapter that we may think of several different supply schedules for a commodity: immediate or market supply, short-run supply, and long-run supply. You may therefore suspect that there may be more than one equilibrium price for a commodity, depending upon which supply schedule is used; this is in fact the case. We may speak of:

1. Immediate or market equilibrium—meaning that the supply schedule represents only the quantity currently available, and is therefore represented by a vertical straight line.

2. Short-run equilibrium—meaning that the supply schedule reflects the responses of businessmen to changes in price with respect to their rates of output, but not with respect to size or number of firms.

3. Long-run equilibrium—meaning that businessmen may change

the size of plants and firms, and that firms may enter or leave the industry.

Furthermore, long-run *demand* schedules may also differ from short-run demand schedules, reflecting the time needed to find out about price changes and the time needed by consumers to use up goods which they already own and to make adjustments in their patterns of living and spending.

Fig. 4-3 suggests how the equilibrium position may differ depending upon the time period being analyzed.

FIG. 4-3   Market, Short-Run, and Long-Run Equilibrium

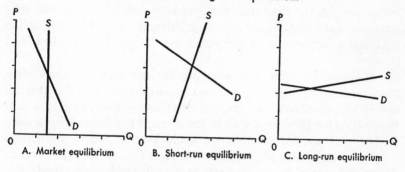

A. Market equilibrium   B. Short-run equilibrium   C. Long-run equilibrium

Changes in Equilibrium

If the underlying data (forces) of a situation change, there will be a new equilibrium position. In the case of the equilibrium price and quantity of a commodity, the underlying data are the demand and supply schedules. If there is a change in either or both, there will be a new equilibrium position. If we are using charts in our analysis, this will be represented by new curves on the chart (see Fig. 4-4). (Note: You may find it helpful at this point to review those sections of Chapters 2 and 3 which discuss shifts in the demand and supply schedules.)

FIG. 4-4   Changes in Equilibrium

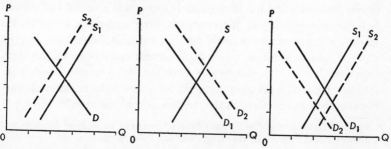

The question of shifts in schedules should not be confused with the discussion of short- and long-run schedules. A shift in schedules occurs when there is a change in the underlying data. In the case of demand, this means a change in income, other prices, or tastes; in the case of supply, it means a change in costs resulting from changes in the prices of inputs, in technology, or opportunity costs. No such changes are implied by the distinction between short and long run. A short-run schedule may shift, in which case there is a new short-run schedule. The same is true of long-run schedules. But the move from short-run analysis to long-run analysis does not involve a shift in either schedule. The long-run schedule is a different schedule, and usually has a different shape than the short-run schedule; both schedules, however, exist simultaneously, and merely represent different ways of looking at the relationship between quantity demanded, or quantity supplied, and price.

It should be noted that when we are analyzing the equilibrium price for a commodity or service we usually assume that the demand and supply schedules are independent of one another, that is, a shift in one does not produce a shift in the other. If the demand for a commodity increases, for example, we would look for a new equilibrium point where the new demand curve crosses the old supply curve. In the special case of the interest rate as the price of loanable funds, this assumption may not be warranted. If we think of the supply of such funds as being determined by savings, and the demand for such funds as being dependent upon businessmen's intentions to spend for investment goods, we must realize that shifts in the latter may have important repercussions on the over-all level of income in the country, and thus cause shifts in the savings (supply of funds) curve as well.

CASE 4-2   Demand and supply

"As in any other kind of market, demand sometimes exceeds supply in the credit market, and supply sometimes exceeds demand. As a result, interest rates rise and fall in response to changes in demand and supply. It is the responsibility of the reserve banking authorities to watch the market, to help correct disorderly market conditions should they develop, and generally to foster an orderly flow of credit and money. Of the measures described in later chapters as available to the reserve banking authorities, those with the most pervasive influence on the credit market are the ones that operate through the medium of bank reserves." [4]

---

[4] Board of Governors of the Federal Reserve System, *The Federal Reserve System, Purposes and Functions,* Washington, D.C., 1954, p. 13.

Questions

1. Do the terms "demand" and "supply" have the same meaning in the first and second sentences of the above passage?
2. How would you rewrite the first two sentences to eliminate any ambiguity in the use of these terms?
3. Use a graph and the concept of equilibrium to help explain the above quotation.

CASE 4-3   Changes in equilibrium

Assume that you begin with the demand and supply curves shown in Fig. 4-5. What would happen to the equilibrium price and quantity if, *ceteris paribus*, there were:

1. An increase in demand
2. An increase in supply
3. An increase in supply and demand
4. A decrease in supply
5. A decrease in demand
6. A decrease in supply and demand
7. A decrease in demand and an increase in supply
8. An increase in demand and a decrease in supply

FIG. 4-5

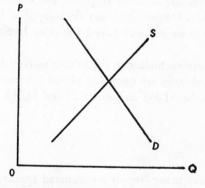

CASE 4-4   Demand for wool balances supply

"The world's supply and demand of wool appear to be in close balance. Despite the heavy supplies dumped on the market upon the termination of the Australian dock strike ten days ago, prices have remained relatively steady.

Since last fall prices have moved in comparatively narrow ranges. The trade showed some trepidation when the Department of Agriculture announced that surplus supplies of wool would be sold. But demand for the limited amounts released each month by the department has been excellent, and these supplies did not upset the price structure.

Consumption by clothing makers in the United States has been good. While synthetics are here to stay, their novelty appeal seems to have worn off and wool is holding its own or gaining in appeal. In Europe the recent cold weather has increased the demand for wool clothing.

The Australian dock strike started on January 23 [1956] and lasted twenty-three days. On the final trading day before the strike, wool top futures for March delivery were quoted at $1.588 a pound on the New York Cotton Exchange. Speculators entered the market, and the trade bought to cover needs as soon as it became apparent the strike might last several days.

On the last day of the strike, February 14, March futures were at $1.625. Speculators dumped their holdings and took profits when the strike was terminated, causing prices to fall 4 cents a pound to $1.585 by February 17.

Supplies of wool piled up at the piers in Australia during the strike. The auctions were postponed for two weeks because the supplies could not leave the country. Many observers expected these large supplies to discourage buying and weaken the market.

However, when the auctions reopened the demand was good and prices were steady. Despite the heavy dock supplies, buyers bid aggressively at the auctions and maintained the price levels of the pre-strike offerings.

Despite the nervous trading in the futures market during the last two weeks, March deliveries are quoted at almost the exact level of the day preceding the strike, $1.588 on January 20 and $1.585 cents a pound last Friday." [5]

Questions

1. What does it mean to say "supply and demand appear to be in close balance"? Aren't they always in balance?
2. Why did the price rise in early February? Why did it fall later in the month?
3. "Many observers expected these large supplies to discourage buying and weaken the market." Can you suggest a reason why this did not occur?

---

[5] George Auerbach, "End of Australia Dock Strike Brought No Price Upsets in Futures Market," New York *Times*, February 26, 1956. © 1956 by The New York Times Company.

CASE 4-5   The price of pigs

"When meat and livestock prices were high—as they were a few years ago—the consumers were unhappy. When prices of livestock and meat declined, as they have recently, the livestock producers became deeply concerned.

Getting people to understand what makes meat prices is a difficult problem. Basically, price is determined by the supply of meat on one side of the counter and the amount of money that consumers have, and are willing to spend for meat, on the other side of the counter.

When a homemaker buys a quantity of meat, the effect of her decision is felt in a long line of competitive sales and purchases—from retailer back to livestock producer.

In this process, the meat packer encounters some unique problems. To start with, he has no control over the supply of his raw materials. He doesn't know from one day to the next how many meat animals will come to market, or what competition will force him to pay for them. Nor does he know what meat prices will be in the future because of inevitable variations—not only in livestock marketings, but also in general trade and business conditions, the weather, and the many other factors.

Unlike most manufacturers, the meat packer cannot hold much of his product for future sale. Meat is highly perishable. A relatively small amount is canned or frozen. Some of it is cured and smoked. Some is made into sausage. About three out of five pounds of meat produced is sold fresh—without further processing. Because of its perishability, every pound of fresh meat has to be sold at a price that will move it promptly into consuming channels. Therefore, the price must balance supply and demand. Sometimes this means a profit; sometimes a loss.

In the last few months the spotlight has been focused on lower prices of cattle and hogs. The seriousness of this price drop is shown by the fact that hog prices in December of 1955 were 37 per cent lower than in December 1954. During the same time the price of choice grade cattle dropped 24 per cent.

What brought on this sharp price decline? The simple answer is that livestock marketings far outstripped that level of consumer demand for meat which would have sustained favorable livestock prices.

There has been a rapid and continuing build-up of cattle numbers, beginning in 1948. When such a build-up levels off, there is always a large increase in marketings. The first flood of cattle came to market in 1953—with about a 30 per cent increase over the previous year. In 1954, and again in 1955, beef production reached all-time peaks.

Pork production in the last two months of 1955 increased 17 per cent over the same period in the previous year. These unusually heavy supplies of both cattle and hogs, coming to market at the same time, resulted in the severe price drop.

One may ask, why did this overabundance occur? The simple reason is that it was profitable to increase livestock production in the war and post-war period. Profits provided farmers and ranchers the incentive and the capital for the purchase of new equipment, new labor-saving facilities and other improvements, all resulting in greater efficiency in livestock raising and feeding. One of the results has been the substitution of mechanical horsepower for horses. Ten million horses and mules have been elimi-nated since 1940. This has made more pasture land available for live-stock. In addition, feed grain supplies during the build-up period were plentiful.

It should be borne in mind that livestock production is not subject to quick and easy adjustment. It takes up to two years, for example, to raise and fatten a steer." [6]

Questions

1. What has been happening to the price of meat? Can we speak of an equilibrium price in this case?
2. What reason does the writer give for the movement of price?
3. Do you agree with his analysis? Can you think of any major factors which have been neglected?

CASE 4-6   Mill curtailment balances cloth supply

"Basic print cloth prices fell 6 cents a pound in the past year but cur-tailment 'is gradually correcting the present dislocation of supply and de-mand in the market,' W. Ray Bell, president, The Association of Cotton Textile Merchants of New York, told the group's annual meeting yester-day.

While print cloth quotations were off 6 cents, raw cotton costs de-clined only 1.75 cents a pound, he stated. He thought cotton goods at current levels represent attractive buys and that 'fabrics have been squeezed to the point of unprofitable sale.' Curtailment of 3 per cent in the third quarter of 1956, of 6 per cent in the fourth period, and still more so far in 1957, is gradually correcting the present oversupply situation, Mr. Bell reported.

. . . 'Further liquidation of spindles had taken place with a loss of 666,000 in the year and a new low number now operating,' Mr. Bell said. 'Textile equipment has been eliminated to the extent that the average spindle in each of the past two years has had to run in excess of 6,000 hours to provide only enough cotton textiles to keep up with the increase

---

[6] "Meat Processors and the Farm Problem," address by John Holmes, Chairman of the Board, Swift and Company, January 29, 1956, pp. 3–5.

of population. Average hours operated cannot increase much from this point and a period of expansion in the industry lies in the foreseeable future.'

For the shorter term, Mr. Bell estimated normal national requirements for 1956 of 10.9 billion square yards of cotton goods and stated that the actual amount produced was closely in line with this. However, inventory liquidation in trade channels, and a quarter billion yards of low priced imports from Japan, added to this, had affected the markets strongly and contributed to a depressed price structure.

The threat of heavy Japanese imports, he said, has been abated by Japan's five year quota system announced in January." [7]

Questions

1. Why had print cloth prices been falling? Show this graphically.
2. If prices fell below the cost of production, would quantity supplied be likely to be greater in the short run or in the long run? Explain.

CASE 4-7   The demand for wheat in 1699

"The first 'empirical' demand schedule was published in 1699 by Charles Davenant in *An Essay Upon the Probable Methods of Making a People Gainers in the Balance of Trade*. It was presented with admirable brevity:

'We take it, that a defect [shortage] in the harvest may raise the price of corn in the following proportions:

Defect				*Above the Common Rate*
1 tenth	raises the price			3 tenths
2 tenths	"	"	"	8 tenths
3 tenths	"	"	"	16 tenths
4 tenths	"	"	"	28 tenths
5 tenths	"	"	"	45 tenths' " [8]

(Note: In England wheat is often referred to as corn.)

Questions

1. Can you use your knowledge of equilibrium and of supply and demand curves to show how the above information describes a portion of the demand curve for wheat?

(Note: It is assumed that the supply curve of wheat for any one year is a vertical line.)

---

[7] "Bell Says Mill Curtailment Will Balance Cloth Supply," *Women's Wear Daily*, February 15, 1957, p. 24. Copyright, 1957 by Fairchild Publications, Inc.

[8] George J. Stigler, "The Early History of Empirical Studies of Consumer Behavior," *Journal of Political Economy*, Vol. 42, No. 2, April 1954. © 1954 by the University of Chicago.

CASE 4-8   A rise in beef prices

"Two principal reasons were given today by meat dealers and packers and marketing experts for the current rise in the price of top quality beef.

But opinions on the implications of the rise ranged from one man's 'it's seasonal and doesn't mean anything important' to another's prediction that it foreshadows a general increase in living costs.

Virtually everyone questioned by the *Post* expressed the opinion that the chief cause of the price boost was the shortage of top quality grain-fed steers.

'The livestock men are not putting the feed into steers to mature them to prime capacity,' a market analyst said. 'They are marketing them earlier, figuring they'll do as well by selling now as by waiting until the steers are "well-finished."'

'If there were a chance of a shortage in poultry or pork this fall, it would be different,' he said. 'Then it would be worth their while to hold on because they could count on a big demand for beef.

'But with the highest turkey run on record expected, and the potential of a great amount of pork, they figure there will be a slump in the demand for beef, so they can't see any sense in keeping the steers on feed for the longer period.'

Thus, there is plenty of average, but a shortage of top quality beef.

'There is a proportionally large cattle population,' a Department of Agriculture spokesman said, 'even a little higher than last year. But the farmers just aren't sending as much prime cattle to market.'

The second major reason advanced for the rise was the imminence of the Jewish holidays with the concomitant increased demand for top quality forequarters of beef, the only beef used for the Kosher market.

'When this market absorbs more than its usual amount of the available quality beef,' one packer pointed out, 'a shortage naturally develops and that, in turn, leads to increased prices.'

A spokesman for a large chain of food stores saw the shortage as general rather than a matter of top quality beef only.

'Beef prices were away down,' he said, 'and the government asked everyone to promote beef sales. As a result, an unusually large amount of beef has been consumed and now there is a shortage.'

To support this argument, he cited a recent report by John A. Logan, president of the National Association of Food Chains, which said the food chain industry spent an estimated $50,000,000 on meat promotion in the 12 months ending June 30.

'As a result,' said the Logan report, 'consumers piled more meat on their dinner tables than in any period since 1908.'

In opposition to those who believe the rise is only the beginning of a general increase of living costs, several packers predicted that the price would settle down again in a few weeks with the end of the holidays and the traditionally greater demand in cool weather for pork and poultry." [9]

Questions

1. Is there an equilibrium price for top quality beef? How is it determined?
2. Which determinants of supply and demand are referred to in this case? To which of these would you attach the greatest importance? Why?
3. What factors would determine whether or not the price rise of top quality beef is more than a temporary phenomenon?
4. Why should "the highest turkey run on record" be expected to result in a "slump in the demand for beef"?

CASE 4-9   Sugar prices get sweeter

"The law of supply and demand, working within the structure of the sugar quota system, raised prices for the raw commodity yesterday.

About 30,000 tons of raw sugar were purchased yesterday for delivery here at 6.12 cents a pound, duty paid, the highest since 1954. Most of the sugar, due in port late this month or early in August, will come from the Philippines, some will come from Cuba and Puerto Rico. Additional shipments will arrive in New Orleans and in Savannah.

The previous high for the year was 6.1 cents a pound, established late last week. The year's low was 5.83 cents, on January 3. Prices last year ranged between 5.75 cents (on April 14) and 6.08 cents (on July 22).

Trade sources attribute the price rise to a change in the quota system and to a seasonable increase in demand during the hot months.

Recently the Sugar Act was amended to permit domestic beet and cane areas to sell more sugar than in past years and to reduce the amount to be imported.

Beet sugar producers now are selling most of their supplies in the West. This has forced Eastern refiners to purchase cane sugar from domestic or foreign growers. A result is a temporary heavy demand for cane sugar to supply Midwestern and Eastern areas.

Trade interests believe the present marketing quotas are in close relation to the expected consumption of sugar in this country. Few expect the quotas to be increased soon.

During the summer months, the demand for sugar increases. Sizable quantities are used by ice cream producers and soft drink manufacturers.

---

[9] Nancy Seely, "Rise in Beef Prices Laid Chiefly to Lack of Top Quality Steers," New York *Post*, August 30, 1956, p. 6. Copyright, 1956 by New York Post Corporation. Reprinted by permission.

Importers expect prices to remain at the present level or inch higher unless import quotas are raised. The price will ease later in the year, they say, when domestic beet sugar producers ship supplies farther east." [10]

Questions

1. Which way has the supply schedule moved? Which way has the demand schedule shifted? Illustrate this graphically.
2. Why does the demand for sugar increase in the hot months?
3. Would you expect the price of ice cream also to rise in the summer? Why or why not?
4. What are some of the reasons, other than those given in this case, why the demand for sugar might change?
5. In the absence of other changes, what factors would determine the limits of a price increase caused by the usual seasonal increase in demand?

CASE 4-10   Price of lumber

" 'Tell me whether it is going to rain,' a lumber dealer in Portland, Oregon, is reported to have said, 'and I'll tell you where the lumber market is going.'

The lumber industry prospers on catastrophes, bad weather, rail car shortages, or strikes. An example of this was the long spell of bad weather in Oregon in the spring of 1955. Over double the normal rainfall was recorded in Portland, Oregon, for April, making it the third wettest April in 84 years. These late rains meant unusable logging roads and snow in the higher elevations, thus creating unfavorable conditions for sawing down wood. When sunny skies finally broke through the overcast, prices for lumber dropped $2 to $3 per thousand board feet on good grade, undried 2 x 4's in random length—an important item in home building. Prior to the price break, there had been seven successive weeks of price increase, bringing the price for this type of lumber to $78 or $79 per thousand board feet. This price was 20% above the price two months earlier, and 23% above the price a year ago." [11]

Questions

1. To what do you attribute the rise in price? What assumptions must be made about demand?
2. Show how the analysis of the price of lumber would be affected if bad weather persisted for a much longer period of time.

[10] "With Imports Curbed, Sugar Prices Set High," New York *Times*, July 18, 1956, p. 35. © 1956 by The New York Times Company.
[11] *Wall Street Journal*, May 9, 1955. © 1955 by Dow Jones and Company, Inc.

CASE 4-11 Japanese blouses

1. Assume that the demand for blouses in the United States can be described by the following equation:

$$Q_d = 20,000,000 - 2,000,000P$$

where Q_d = quantity demanded per year and P = price per blouse in dollars.

Assume further that U.S. blouse manufacturers cannot afford to produce any blouses at prices below $8, but can produce unlimited quantities at that price. Draw the supply and demand curves and find the equilibrium position for this industry.

2. Now assume that Japanese manufacturers can produce and ship *identical* blouses to the U.S. in unlimited quantities at $4 per blouse, but not for less. If there are no restrictions on imports, what will happen in the U.S. blouse market? Show the results graphically.

3. Now assume that a quota is imposed so that only 1 million Japanese blouses per year can enter the United States. What will be the result? Show this result graphically.

4. In what respects are the above assumptions unrealistic? How would more realistic assumptions affect the analysis?

CASE 4-12 Equilibrium price for rubber

The following are paraphrased reports from the columns of the *Wall Street Journal*:

1. *October 19, 1954*

Natural rubber prices rose to 27¢ per pound, an increase of 5¢ per pound since mid-August. The rise is ascribed to (a) increased purchases of crude rubber by U.S. tire manufacturers who boosted output as the new car models came into production; (b) entry of Russia into the market for large quantities of Indonesian rubber; and (c) the closing of British rubber inventories from foreign markets by the London dock strike. Dealers, however, express doubts that the price rise will continue. They note a growing switch to synthetic rubber, which is almost 4¢ per pound cheaper than natural.

2. *October 22, 1954*

Synthetic rubber sales decreased 21% from 1953. The total sales expected for 1954 is 448,000 tons. Production for 1955 is expected to be 550,000 to 600,000 tons. This estimate is based chiefly on the fact that synthetics sell for 23¢ per pound versus a natural rubber price of 27¢.

3. *December 7, 1954*

Natural rubber prices slipped one cent per pound since the two-year high mark of 29¢ per pound set early in November 1954. Synthetic rubber is now in greater demand. Some expect a 20% jump in sales of synthetic rubber in 1955.

Questions

1. What demand or supply factors were responsible for the rise in the price of natural crude rubber? Show this graphically.
2. Can you suggest the direction in which the equilibrium position *for natural rubber* is likely to move in the future?

CASE 4-13   Effects of export restrictions

On October 21, 1954, it was reported in the *Wall Street Journal* that U.S. steel producers would request the government to stiffen export restrictions on iron and steel scrap. Removal of tight export controls by the government on April 1, 1954 had opened the gates to large exports of scrap for the first time since before Pearl Harbor. As a result, scrap exports jumped during the first eight months of 1954 to 671,000 tons in comparison to the 271,000 tons exported during the whole of 1953. Domestic scrap prices rose from $25 per ton to $34 per ton in October. It was feared by the steel producers that large exports would further increase the price for scrap.

In support of their position, the steel producers contended that iron and steel scrap is a scarce natural resource which should be conserved for domestic use in case of another military emergency. The scrap dealers, on the other hand, opposed the restoration of government export controls on the ground that there is no prospect of any future shortage of scrap so long as U.S. steel mills continue to operate far below capacity. Steel production for October 1954 was reported to be 73.6% of theoretical capacity.

Questions

1. Show graphically why the lifting of export restrictions on steel scrap resulted in a rise in price.
2. Would the argument for stiffening export restrictions be stronger if the U.S. steel mills were producing at, or near, capacity? Why or why not?

CASE 4-14   Interest rates hit new high

"Several news developments last week were of significance to any businessman interested in borrowing money. Michigan's Consumers Power Co. raised $40 million in the bond market at an average interest cost of 3.986%, the highest rate paid by any top-flight utility since the early 1930's. Long-term Treasury bond prices dropped to new 1956 lows. And the interest rates on bankers' acceptances rose one-eighth of a percentage point, reaching the highest levels in more than two decades.

Back of these developments is the simple fact that the demand for money is growing faster than the available supply. The inevitable result is higher interest rates. As was noted in this space last week, the supply is being limited both by the slow rate of increase in savings and by actions of the Federal Reserve System to restrict the funds the commercial banks have available for lending." [12]

Questions

1. What is bringing about the rise in interest rates? Show this graphically.
2. What was the connection between the rise in interest rates and the drop in prices of long-term Treasury bonds?
3. Suppose business suddenly decided to sharply curtail expenditures for plant and equipment. Explain, with the aid of charts, how this might affect interest rates.

EQUILIBRIUM OF ADMINISTERED PRICES

The determination of the equilibrium price through the interaction of demand and supply is most easily seen for homogeneous products traded on organized exchanges. If we consider wheat, for example, it is clear that (excluding government action) no one person or firm "sets" the price of wheat, but rather that it is entirely the result of impersonal market forces. Likewise, there is only *one* price for any grade of wheat at any one time in a single market. There are many commodities, however, for which this is not the case. Prices of these commodities, superficially at least, appear to be set by the producer, and economists refer to them as "administered prices." The cases dealing with such prices, however, reveal that even administered prices are subject to the forces of demand and supply, although the achievement of the equilibrium position may not come as quickly or as automatically as in the case of wheat. During the period when the price is not at the equilibrium level, the quantity demanded at that price will not be equal to the quantity supplied. If Q_d is greater than Q_s, the situation is sometimes referred to as a "sellers' market." If Q_s is greater than Q_d, it is called a "buyers' market."

CASE 4-15 Administered prices

"In terms of their behavior as well as the nature of the markets in which they are set, several differences may be noted between market prices and administered prices. Market prices fluctuate more frequently under the impact of changing economic pressures. On the great commodity exchanges, these changes may take place every few minutes. In contrast, when administered prices are set, they may remain unchanged for sub-

[12] *Wall Street Journal*, August 20, 1956, p. 1. © 1956 by Dow Jones and Company, Inc.

stantial periods of time. When changes are made in administered prices, they usually take the form of step-like arrangements rather than the erratic movements found for market prices. The record of price changes for such products as rayon, bricks, potash salts, refrigerators, steel, automobiles, and many retail prices illustrates this tendency. Usually an accumulation of pressures is necessary before the administered price is changed." [13]

Questions

1. According to the above, would administered prices always be at their equilibrium level? Why or why not?
2. In your opinion, what is meant by "an accumulation of pressures"?

CASE 4-16   Accent on price

"A month or so from now, when the budget-conscious housewife buys a new automatic washer or clothes drier made by Borg-Warner Corporation's Norge division, she will pay from $10 to $90 less than today's customer.

Judson S. Sayre, Norge president, gave no reason for lower prices when he introduced the new line to distributors the other day. Another Norge spokesman, however, said the lower tags represent 'a realistic appraisal of the home laundry industry.'

In plain English, the statement means people are buying fewer washers and driers—possibly because they think prices are too high. So far other laundry appliance makers, faced with the same sluggish market, have shown no inclination to cut prices." [14]

Questions

1. What did the Norge spokesman mean by "a realistic appraisal of the home laundry industry"?
2. Why didn't the other manufacturers follow the price cut? Do you think they eventually did?

CASE 4-17   Paradoxical copper

"Custom smelters raised their copper prices yesterday by a half-cent a pound to 38 cents—after the major producers [15] had just cut prices 6 cents a pound to 40 cents.

---

[13] Jules Backman, *Administered Prices*, privately published pamphlet, 1957, p. 5.
[14] New York *Times*, June 9, 1954. © 1954 by The New York Times Company.
[15] Major producers of copper customarily process their own ore. Small ore producers who cannot afford to operate their own processing facilities utilize custom smelters, who will either purchase the ore directly or process it for a fee. (Authors' note.)

Here's the way several copper traders explained the paradox: the big mine producers sat tight for more than three months while the custom smelters and foreign sellers trimmed prices repeatedly in search of customers. A week ago the smelters, who are estimated to account for less than 15 per cent of copper sold in this country, were down to 37½ cents a pound. That was low enough. Last Monday some buyers re-entered the market.

By last Monday also, the producers apparently felt they had withheld price action long enough. One after another during the next three days, they all cut to 40 cents.

The smelters, with sales revived and a slightly firmer trend noted in London copper prices, decided they could inch their prices up a half-cent to 38 cents." [16]

Questions

1. Do copper producers set any price that they wish?
2. How is it possible that some sellers are raising their price at the same time that others are lowering theirs? How can you explain a difference of price among sellers?

CASE 4-18   Sellers' market for cars

In the years following World War II the demand for automobiles was very strong, and the quantity demanded at official prices was greater than the quantity which the industry could supply. As a result, some dealers engaged in "under-the-counter" deals at prices above the levels designated by the car makers, while elsewhere long waits were required in order to buy a new car at the regular price. The following exchange, which took place during a Senate committee hearing investigating corporate profits, touches on this situation.

"*Mr. Vance* (of Studebaker Corp.): Our selling prices for cars and trucks —wholesale to dealers—today average 110 per cent more than in 1940. Our actual costs for material, labor, and factory overhead, exclusive of fixed charges, average 111 per cent more than in 1940. . . .

Our pricing policy since the war has been that prices should be increased only in proportion to the increase in actual costs. We have not charged all that the traffic would bear. The best evidence of this is the black market—one of industry's greatest headaches—where new cars have been selling at a considerable premium over our retail prices. . . .

Senator Flanders: Although your prices are up substantially, the rate of increase has not exceeded that of your costs. . . . That is your statement. Now, that leaves out of consideration, if that is your policy, any refer-

[16] New York *Times*, June 9, 1954. © 1954 by The New York Times Company.

ence to the competitive price position as between your cars and other cars. Does that mean that during this period there have been no competitive influences which would have affected your pricing?

Mr. Vance: No, sir. . . . It is perfectly obvious, Senator, that the competitive pressure today is less than it is normally, and less than it was and less than it will be.

But I might say in that connection that we are conscious of it even in these times, because, in our business, clientele is important just as it is to the doctor or the grocer, and it is the friends we make today who determine the kind of business we do when competition returns.

As a matter of fact, our experience in the past has been that two-thirds of our sales are repeat sales, made to people who are already driving or operating our product.

Senator O'Mahoney: Now, you said that the Studebaker Corporation has not attempted to charge all that the traffic would bear, and you spoke also of the black market, headache of the manufacturer. What steps do you take, and what steps does the industry take so far as you know, to persuade dealers to maintain the level of prices less than what the market will bear which you try to state?

Mr. Vance: So far as dealers' delivered prices are concerned, we check them carefully and urge our dealers not only to sell cars at a normal markup, but we try to point out to them, as we know so well ourselves, that the time will come when the friends they make today will be valuable to them. We have on a few occasions, where dealers have flagrantly violated the policies that we have laid out for them, canceled their contracts. . . .

Senator O'Mahoney: In other words, you have taken punitive action to enforce upon the dealer adherence to a pricing policy, a price ceiling, to use a word which has been very much used in recent years, which you have set down?

Mr. Vance: Yes, sir.

Senator O'Mahoney: Now that means, does it not, Mr. Vance, that wherever the automobile industry has done that, it has abandoned the so-called free market?

Mr. Vance: No, sir; I don't follow you.

Senator O'Mahoney: Well, the free market, as I understand it, is the market in which supply and demand will fix the price, in which the price will not be fixed by the government or by any private agency.

Mr. Vance: I would like to say very definitely that we think it is bad business for our dealers to try to take advantage of the kind of situation that has existed during the past couple of years, and in the long run it will hurt them and hurt us.

Senator O'Mahoney: I think that you are quite right.

Mr. Vance: Now, if that is fixing prices, then my answer to your question is 'yes.' " [17]

Questions

1. Who sets the price of automobiles? Does the same answer apply to manufacturers' prices to dealers and dealers' prices to consumers?
2. Why were automobile prices below their equilibrium level?
3. Is price a means of rationing goods? What other means are there?
4. In what sense was there a "sellers' market" for automobiles? How could this have been avoided?

CASE 4-19   Why we need unions

"Finally, in our industrial system there are gradually more and more wage and salary earners who must seek to sell their services, but few employers available as buyers. Except in abnormal circumstances the supply usually exceeds the demand. Without collective bargaining through labor unions, working people would have little choice but to accept whatever price is offered for their services.

Because of these tremendous advantages of the employer over the worker in the absence of unions and collective bargaining, isn't it the sheerest nonsense to talk about the benefits of 'pure competition' in a so-called 'free' labor market?

At every work place the foreman would merely auction off the jobs and the lowest bidder would set the prevailing 'market price.' The depressed wages which would result not only would injure working people; they would cause insufferable damage to the national economy, as well." [18]

Questions

1. Do you agree or disagree with the above? Give reasons for your answer.
2. What does the writer mean when he says "the supply usually exceeds the demand"? Can you show this graphically?
3. Are wage rates a good example of administered prices? Explain.

CASE 4-20   Administered prices in the oil industry

"Price-fixing in the oil industry is made possible largely through the machinery set up by the states and the federal government to control crude oil production, rather than through collusion.

---

[17] Statement of Harold S. Vance, Chairman and President of Studebaker Corp., Joint Committee on the Economic Report of the President, Hearings on Corporate Profits, 80th Congress, December 6–21, 1948, pp. 242–60.

[18] "Why We Need Unions," *Labor's Economic Review*, AFL–CIO, February 1956, p. 15.

No collusion is needed. As long as the regulatory authorities function efficiently and keep production within market demand, the oil companies have no fear of a surplus, and may set the prices they pay for crude oil and then charge the prices for their products at what the traffic will bear.

In the case of the price increases now being investigated in Washington, it is unlikely that any collusion in the strictest sense of the word existed. No meetings of top executives were needed to bring about the advance.

All that was necessary was for one leading company to raise crude oil prices [i.e., to offer to pay more for crude oil] and the others had to follow, if they were to obtain the necessary crude oil to process. With the refinery margin of profit at a level where the higher price crude oil could not be absorbed, petroleum products had to be raised.

ETHICS AND EARNINGS

When the Humble Oil and Refining Company, an affiliate of the Standard Oil Company (New Jersey), raised crude oil and product prices last month, it did not take the other companies long to follow suit.

Humble Oil is a leading producer as well as refiner. In 1955 it produced an average of 357,300 barrels of crude oil a day and refined 247,800 barrels a day. Thus the price advance simply meant that it would get that much more for its output in excess of its own refinery needs. When it subsequently raised the price on refined products to absorb the rise in crude oil, it obtained a higher price for its entire output.

About the only thing the oil industry can be charged with is that it took advantage of the situation resulting from the control of oil production and the Suez crisis.

The increase added some $1,250,000,000 to the nation's oil bill, and was calculated to add greatly to the earnings of the companies, which have been increasing steadily for the past several years.

In testimony last week before the House Commerce Committee, M. J. Rathbone, president of the Jersey Standard, said that as a result of the rises in prices and sales his company expected to increase net earnings this year by $100,000,000 more to $900,000,000.

CALL RISE OVERDUE

The contention of the industry generally is that the price rise was long overdue, since the price of crude oil had been unchanged since mid-1953. During that period, prices of steel and other items entering into oil operations, including wages, advanced substantially.

However, there must have been some offsetting factors, such as improved efficiency, or earnings could not have increased so greatly during the period.

The price of crude oil must have been maintained in that interval at a level that encouraged drilling despite the fact that output of existing wells was kept far below their most efficient rate of output. In fact, since 1953, drilling has reached new peaks each year, and several billion barrels have been added to oil reserves in the face of record production.

During this period of price stability, from mid-1953 to 1956, supplies of crude oil were abundant both here and abroad. At the close of last year, the excess idle productive capacity in this country was estimated at 2,000,000 barrels a day.

To hold production down to market demand, the state regulatory bodies were keeping this oil in the ground under conservation laws aided by the Federal Interstate Oil Compact and the Connally 'Hot Oil' Act.

The oil compact among other things gives the producing states authority to set up conservation agencies to prevent the physical waste of oil and gas from any cause.

This is rather broad, and it has been interpreted to mean that excess stocks cause waste. One reason why the Texas Railroad Commission, the oil authority in that state, refused at first to increase the allowable production to as much as purchasers were willing to buy was that gasoline stocks were excessive. The agency held that more crude oil production would be wasteful, since gasoline in storage would evaporate.

The 'Hot Oil' Act specifically prohibits the shipment in interstate commerce of any oil produced in violation of state conservation laws. This means that any producer who extracted more oil than permitted by the state would be subject to federal penalty.

In both the oil compact and the Connally Act, there are clauses to the effect that production of oil and gas must not be limited for the purpose of stabilizing or fixing prices. However, the question arises as to how production can be limited without influencing prices.

TEXAS IN THE SADDLE

All leading oil states except California regulate output. But Texas, which produces about 46 per cent of the nation's oil and has almost the same percentage of known reserves, is the key to the effectiveness of the control program. So long as it can limit production to the market demand which it determines from buyers before it sets the allowable each month, there is not much of a chance of a drop in the price of crude oil. If prices should drop, a cut in production could be ordered and kept in effect until prices were restored.

Under such a set-up, the oil companies can put prices at almost any level they want, with assurance that they will not be called upon to buy more crude oil than they need to maintain prices. If any producer should refuse to comply with the production limit, he would be dealt with under Texas laws, and if he should attempt to sell any 'hot oil' in interstate commerce, he would be in violation of federal laws.

Ernest O. Thompson, chairman of the Texas Railroad Commission, acknowledged before a House Committee recently that since the program started, the price of East Texas crude oil had advanced from 10 cents a barrel to more than $3.00.

Of course 10 cents a barrel, posted by at least one major buyer for East Texas crude oil in the depression, was ridiculously low. Whether the present price of $3.25 is justified is a matter on which there is some doubt by many economists and government officials." [19]

Questions

1. Show graphically what would have happened to the price of crude oil from mid-1953 to 1956 if the state regulatory bodies had not restricted supply.
2. To what do you attribute the recent rise in the price of crude oil? Was there any way that the increase in price could have been avoided?
3. In your opinion, should oil prices be permitted to find their own level in an unregulated market? Why or why not?

GENERAL EQUILIBRIUM

As we have seen, partial equilibrium analysis deals with a limited number of economic variables under "controlled" conditions; i.e., all other factors are treated under *ceteris paribus* while we work out the results of a limited number of forces. In determining the equilibrium price for a particular commodity, for example, we assumed that no change occurred in either the position of the demanders (i.e., in their incomes or preferences) or of the suppliers (i.e., in their costs). We also assumed that the prices of all other commodities and services remained fixed. Under these assumptions, we observed the interaction of supply and demand for the particular commodity and arrived at an equilibrium solution.

The general equilibrium concept, developed by Leon Walras (1834–1910), makes use of mathematics to handle many variables in many equations simultaneously. It is concerned with relationships throughout the entire economic system, and with the interdependence of all economic units. Thus, in dealing with the determination of prices

---

[19] J. H. Carmical, "No Plot Is Needed: Law Rigs Oil Price," New York *Times*, February 24, 1957. © 1957 by The New York Times Company.

and quantities, the general equilibrium approach emphasizes the inter-relationship of all prices and quantities, and specifies that the equilibrium position for all commodities and services can and should be determined simultaneously.

Walras' proof that the economic system could be described by a set of equations with all prices and quantities as a determinate solution was an outstanding theoretical achievement. General equilibrium analysis has not, however, proven to be of great value for practical problems. In most real life situations it is neither necessary nor feasible to take into account the fact that every part of the economy is related to every other part. It is usually sufficient to isolate the most important variables and treat all others under *ceteris paribus*. The concept is useful, though, in reminding us that changes in one market may have important repercussions in other and even seemingly unrelated markets.

One fairly recent development which may prove to be a means of applying a type of general equilibrium analysis to real world problems is the input-output table developed by Professor Wassily Leontief of Harvard. Such a table is compiled by dividing the entire national econ-

FIG. 4-6   Hypothetical Input-Output Table

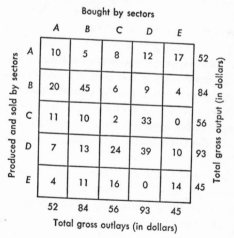

Explanation

Reading across the matrix tells us the destination of the output of each sector; e.g., sector A uses up 10 units of its own output, and sells 5 units to B, 8 units to C, 12 units to D, and 17 units to E.

Reading down the matrix tells us the source of inputs for each sector; e.g., sector D buys 12 units of A's output, 9 units from B, 33 units from C, 39 units from itself, and none from E.

omy into sectors. These sectors usually consist of industry groups, a sector for households, a sector for government, and a sector representing the rest of the world. The table indicates how much each sector buys from every other in dollar terms, and how much each sells to every other sector. For each sector, total outlays or purchases must equal total production or total receipts. Since the sectors include government and households, payments to these sectors in the form of taxes, wages and salaries, dividends, etc. are treated as purchases by the sector making such payments, and as receipts by the sectors receiving such payments. Once the values in the table are filled in, the table is used to predict how changes in the output or purchases of any one or more sectors will affect the output and purchases of every other sector of the economy. In Fig. 4-6, for reasons of simplicity, we have shown the economy divided into five sectors. In the actual input-output tables which have been compiled, the economy is divided into several hundred sectors. This, however, does not change the underlying structure of the table.

CASE 4-21   Cigars and pickles

"Go into tobacco growing areas and you will hear a lot of talk about 'synthetic' or 'homogenized' tobacco. To most people who talk about it—mainly growers and warehousemen—it's somewhat of a mystery. They don't know very much about the process involved. They know even less about the impact it is going to have on them, though they feel it will be considerable. Some say it spells disaster for them. . . .

One thing is certain. There has been a tremendous shift toward purchases of lower-grade tobacco leaf by cigarette makers. This is reflected in prices for low- and high-grade tobacco. Tobacco prices are supported by the government. But even though growers of top leaf are selling more of their crop to the government, prices have sagged below the support level. . . .

Actually, the use of the word 'synthetic' is misleading. The manufacturers have not come up with an ersatz tobacco. What they have done is to develop a process for reconstituting tobacco into pliable sheets (synthetic leaves) that can be shredded into thin strands much the same way as natural leaf.

The big advantage of the process is that you can utilize stems, broken leaves, and inferior leaves. You can't do this with natural leaf, so you waste a lot of tobacco. In the reconstituting process, all the tobacco is ground up into small particles, then rolled into sheets somewhat the same way paper is made out of wood pulp. Some companies are experimenting with the use of adhesives or fiber mats to bind the scrap tobacco in forming the sheets. In this form the processed tobacco can be used as an outside binder for cigars or can be shredded and blended in with higher grade tobacco for cigarette filling. . . .

One area that already has felt the pinch of processed tobacco is the Connecticut Valley. A good deal of the top grade tobacco used as an outer binder in cigar making is grown here. And processed tobacco leaf is taking a big bite out of its market. It's estimated that 40% less binder grade leaf will be needed to produce the same number of cigars as today when processed tobacco leaf comes into wider use by cigar makers." [20]

"Preliminary reports indicate that cucumber pickles are going to be a more important Connecticut Valley crop, replacing much of the acreage that formerly was devoted to tobacco. . . .

The stimulus to utilize the land for cucumbers has come largely from D. M. Jewett, Inc., of South Deerfield, Mass., a nationally known pickle manufacturer." [21]

Questions

1. Do you see any connection between the tobacco industry innovation described here and the price of pickles? If so, show it graphically.
2. Can you think of any other commodities or services which might be affected by the developments described above?

CASE 4-22   Cutbacks bring on the jitters

"U.S. industry continues to shudder as the Pentagon continues to whack away at military spending. The queasiness stems from two factors:

1. The Defense Dept.'s efforts to cut back military expenditures to $38-billion is playing havoc with many companies that have depended on defense work.

2. There's a sudden fear that the prop of defense spending is being sawed off just when the economy had lost its zip, and that perhaps this heralds the end of the 'gravy train.'

Just how long the current attack of shakes will last is not certain. It could endure through the fourth quarter, even into the first quarter of 1958, if Pentagon officials have their way. According to Defense Dept. planners, the fourth quarter should find military spending at the $38-billion target.

At first blush, Defense's intent to stay within its designed budget

[20] "New Trend in Cigarettes," *Business Week*, May 26, 1956, pp. 198–202. Copyright, 1956 by McGraw-Hill Publishing Company, Inc. Reprinted by permission.

[21] New York *Times*, March 10, 1957. © 1957 by The New York Times Company.

doesn't sound too exciting. But defense spending is running at a $42-billion-a-year clip, and a cutback means a drop of $4-billion. If the Pentagon is to achieve a $38-billion annual average, it will have to shear spending to a $34-billion rate in the first quarter of 1958. With this in mind, industry has just cause for worry.

Already, the current round of cuts and stretchouts—contracts rescheduled for later delivery—is having a visible impact on business:

Labor layoffs are cropping up in the aircraft industry, which has had a terrific jolt from canceled projects and stretchouts. General Dynamic's Convair Div., for example, has laid off 4,000 men since the end of June.

Many companies are beginning to shift from defense work to commercial business. . . .

Prime contractors are beginning to study each new job, to determine whether they can do it themselves instead of farming it out to subcontractors. Some subs who haven't the setup to change to other jobs if prime concerns pull back work could be backed right out of business.

Signs of these strains appear all over the nation. The West Coast, of course, heart of the aircraft industry, is hit the hardest. The Southwest with its complex of aircraft, oil, and electronics companies also has suffered. Uneasiness is evident, too, in the big cities of the East and Midwest. It's a rare instance when a manufacturer praises Defense for its pruning.

Within this general framework, however, each defense contractor has been affected differently, depending upon the amount of defense business he carries and his product. . . ." [22]

Questions

1. Explain why this case involves general equilibrium rather than partial equilibrium analysis.
2. Show how the input-output analysis could be helpful in analyzing the effects of the cutback in defense spending.
3. Can you think of any other recent occurrences which raise problems requiring this type of analysis?

[22] *Business Week*, August 24, 1957, p. 29. Copyright, 1957 by McGraw-Hill Publishing Company, Inc. Reprinted by permission.

CHAPTER FIVE

Elasticity, Part I

THE CONCEPT OF ELASTICITY

General Definition

The statement $y = f(x)$, as we have observed, tells us that the two variables, y and x, are related. This signifies that changes in y are dependent upon or related to changes in x. What it does not reveal, however, is the extent to which these relative changes take place in any given situation. The concept of elasticity provides us with a measure of such relative changes. We define elasticity as the proportional change in y per unit of proportional change in x. The most important application and development of the elasticity concept has been in economics, but it may be used in any field which studies and measures changes in related variables.

Applications in Economics

In the chapters on demand and supply, we noted that the quantity of a commodity that is demanded or supplied varies with changes in the price of the commodity. And we also noted that the quantity demanded of a commodity varies with changes in income and with changes in other prices. It is sometimes important to know more, however, than the mere fact that these relationships exist. We may want to know, for example, *how much* more of a commodity will be demanded at a lower price, or how much more will be demanded if the consumer's income should rise. Similarly, it may be important to ascertain the quantity which will be supplied at different prices. The concept of elasticity is used by economists to measure these relationships. In this chapter we will investigate the elasticity of demand schedules. In the following chapter we will study the elasticity of supply schedules; the elasticity of income demand schedules; and the relationship between the quantity demanded of one commodity and the price of another, referred to as cross elasticity of demand. These are not the only applications of the elasticity concept in economics, but they are by far the most important.

PRICE ELASTICITY OF DEMAND

The general law of demand, as we have seen in Chapter 3, states that (other things being equal) the lower the price of a commodity, the larger the quantity demanded. This is illustrated by the following schedule:

PRICE	QUANTITY DEMANDED
$9	1
8	2
7	3
6	4
5	5
4	6
3	7
2	8
1	9

As its name indicates, the general law of demand expresses the relationship between price and quantity demanded only in general terms. If we were engaged in selling, we could expect, on the basis of the law, to sell more of a product if we lowered the price. We would soon discover, however, that under varying circumstances, and for different products, the consumer reaction to a change in price might vary tremendously. For some commodities, such as bread or potatoes, a drop in price might not have much effect on the quantity demanded. But would the same be true for automobiles? Or for television sets? What would happen, for example, to the sale of chocolate bars if the price were raised or lowered? Or to put the problem in a slightly different form, suppose a clothing merchant suddenly finds himself with an over-stock of raincoats. What price would he have to charge in order to dispose of his surplus wares? In all of these cases, the answer depends upon what is called the *price elasticity of demand*.

By price elasticity of demand we mean the proportional change in quantity demanded relative to the proportional change in price. If the proportional change in quantity is greater than the proportional change in price, we say demand is elastic. If it is smaller, we say demand is inelastic. If the proportional change in quantity is exactly equal to the proportional change in price, we say that demand has *unitary elasticity*. If, for example, a decrease of 10 per cent in the price of bread produces only a 5 per cent increase in the quantity demanded, the demand for bread is inelastic. If an increase of 10 per cent in the price of automobiles leads to a decrease of more than 10 per cent in the quantity demanded, the demand for automobiles is elastic. In the case of the clothing merchant, if the demand for his raincoats is elastic, he will need only a relatively small decrease in price in order to get a relatively large increase in his rate of sales. If demand is inelastic, however, relatively large decreases in price will yield only relatively small increases in the number of raincoats sold.

The most important factor determining elasticity in these and other cases is the extent to which substitutes are available for the commodity in question. When the price of a commodity rises, buyers would naturally like to switch to something else whose price has not risen. Whether this will occur on a large scale or not depends upon the availability of substitutes.[1] Similarly, if the price of a commodity falls, buyers will want to switch to it and will do so to the extent that the commodity in question is a good substitute for goods that they have been buying. The more unique a commodity is, the less likely it is that a price increase will drive buyers to other goods, or that a price decrease will attract buyers away from other goods—i.e., the more inelastic will be the demand.

One manifestation of the relation between substitutability and elasticity is the frequent observation that demand is more elastic in the long run than in the short run. The long run, by definition, is a period in which the rigidities of the short run are removed, and, therefore, substitution may take place with greater ease.

You will observe that price elasticity of demand is a measurement of relative changes along a given demand schedule. It is concerned only with the relationship between price and quantity; all other variables which may affect the quantity demanded are treated under the rule of *ceteris paribus*. When the quantity demanded changes as a result of a *shift* in the demand schedule, the concept of price elasticity does not apply.

Another simple way to define price elasticity of demand is in terms of the impact of changes in price and quantity on the total revenue received by sellers (or the total amount spent by buyers, which is of course the same thing). Total revenue is calculated by multiplying price by quantity. If total revenue increases as price decreases, demand is elastic. If total revenue decreases as price decreases, demand is in-

---

[1] I.e., from the point of view of the buyer. Physical similarity is neither necessary nor sufficient to establish substitutability. The crucial question is whether the buyer himself considers alternative products to be satisfactory.

elastic. If total revenue does not change as price changes, then demand
has unitary elasticity.

PRICE	QUANTITY DEMANDED	TOTAL REVENUE
$9	10	$ 90
8	30	240
7	45	315
6	60	360
5	72	360
4	90	360
3	110	330
2	140	280
1	180	180

The above schedule tells us that for the range of prices from $9 to $6,
demand is elastic, and for the range from $4 to $1, inelastic. It also tells
us that for the range of prices from $6 to $4, demand has unitary elasticity. As the above example clearly indicates, it is not necessary for
the elasticity of demand for a commodity to be the same at all points
on the demand schedule. When people say that "the demand for salt
is very inelastic," or that "the demand for air freight is very elastic,"

FIG 5-1   Elasticity and Total Revenue

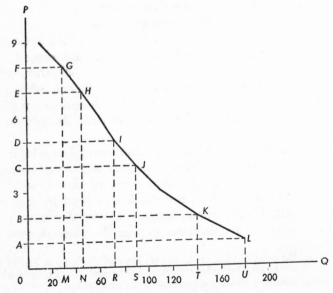

they are presumably referring to demand conditions at about present price levels. There may very well be some portions of the demand curves for salt and air freight in which the situation would be quite different.

The difference between elastic and inelastic demand may also be observed graphically. The above demand schedule has been plotted as a demand curve in Fig. 5-1. Total revenue at any point is equal to the rectangle formed by the two axes and the dotted lines drawn from the point to the axes. This follows from the fact that total revenue is equal to quantity multiplied by price, and the area of a rectangle is equal to the height (in this case the price) multiplied by the width (in this case the quantity). Total revenue at point *G*, therefore, is equal to the area of the rectangle *OMGF*. If we move down the schedule, from point *G* to point *H*, we may draw another rectangle, *ONHE*, and observe whether it is larger or smaller than the first. If it is larger, as in this case, total revenue has increased with a decrease in price, and demand is elastic between *G* and *H*. A comparison of the rectangles drawn at points *I* and *J* shows that *ORID* and *OSJC* are of equal size, indicating that demand has unitary elasticity between these two points. However, a comparison of the rectangles drawn at points *K* and *L* shows that *OTKB* is larger than *OULA*, indicating that demand is inelastic between these two points.

FIG. 5-2   Varying Elasticities Along a Straight Line Demand Curve

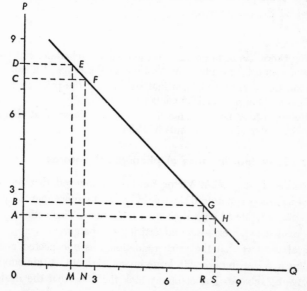

We have thus observed that elasticity may change from one point to another along the demand curve. This is equally true if the demand curve is a straight line. In Fig. 5-2, you will note that the rectangle *ONFC* is larger than the rectangle *OMED*, indicating that demand is elastic between the points *E* and *F*. The rectangle *OSHA*, however, is smaller than the rectangle *ORGB*, showing that demand is inelastic between points *G* and *H*.

The relationship between elasticity and total revenue may be summarized as follows.

Demand is *elastic* if:

   TR (total revenue) rises as you move down the curve

   TR falls as you move up the curve

Demand is *inelastic* if:

   TR falls as you move down the curve

   TR rises as you move up the curve

Demand has *unitary elasticity* if:

   TR is unchanged as you move up or down the curve

CASE 5-1   Change in the supply of peanuts

Under the headline "Peanut Shortage Sends Up Prices," a newspaper story reported that a summer drought resulted in a peanut crop of about one billion pounds in 1954, compared with a crop of one and a half billion pounds in 1953. The report also stated that the price for peanuts received by farmers was 12.5 cents per pound for the 1954 crop, compared with 11.1 cents for the crop of the previous year.

Questions

1. Assuming there has been no shift in the demand schedule, can you show that the demand for peanuts was elastic over the range studied?
2. If demand for peanuts had been inelastic, would the price in 1954 have been higher or lower than 12.5 cents per pound?
3. Would your answer be the same if it could be shown that there was a change in the demand for peanuts in 1954?

CASE 5-2   Lowering the price of phonograph records

In December 1954, R.C.A. Victor Records announced that retail prices on 33⅓-revolutions-per-minute disks would be cut by more than 30 per cent. Other companies followed with their own reductions. This action by R.C.A. was accompanied by an extensive advertising campaign.

In spite of the fact that the price reduction was unexpected and found many dealers and distributors with large inventories, R.C.A. announced that it would give no rebates. The company took the view that the dealers and distributors would experience so great an increase in business that they would more than make up for any mark-downs they would have to take.

In the spring of 1955, surveys were conducted to ascertain the effects of the price cut. The findings were in part as follows:

a. R.C.A.'s dollar volume on long-playing records in the first three months of 1955 was up 30 per cent from the level of the preceding quarter.

b. Retailers in New York City had experienced increases of 10 to 15 per cent in dollar volume. Other cities reported comparable gains.

c. In cities where there had been heavy competition from discount houses, merchants reported they had won back some of their lost customers.

d. Many dealers reported they were selling more accessories and related merchandise as a result of the increase in customers created by the lower prices.[2]

Questions

1. In the situation described, is demand elastic or inelastic? How would you judge?

2. In the absence of competition from the discount houses, under what circumstances would it have been to the advantage of the regular dealers to cut prices?

3. The year 1954 was a recession year, while 1955 was a year of generally rising incomes. How would this information affect your analysis of the above case?

4. R.C.A. and a number of other record companies *raised* the list price of many of their $3.98 records to $4.98 in February 1958. Why do you think this action was taken?

CASE 5-3   Lowering of price by T.V.A. to increase consumption of electricity

One of the broad objectives fixed for the Tennessee Valley Authority when it was established in 1933 was to promote the wider and better use of electric power for domestic use. The Authority believed it could accomplish this purpose, and at the same time dispose of its large quantity of surplus power by selling this power at rates substantially below that of private concerns. After putting its new rates into effect, the Authority, in December 1935, made a before-and-after study of consumption in seven localities. The results are summarized in the table on page 134.

Questions

1. On the basis of this summary, can it be said that the demand for electricity was elastic?

2. Did the T.V.A. accomplish its purpose?

[2] Reported in the *Wall Street Journal*, December 28 and 29, 1954, and the New York *Times*, April 24, 1955.

Average Consumption, Number of Customers, Total Revenue, and Average Revenue per Kilowatt-Hour, Before and After Introduction of T.V.A. Rates [3]

CONTRACTOR	DATE T.V.A. SERVICE BEGAN	MONTHS T.V.A. RATES IN EFFECT AT JUNE 30, 1935	AVERAGE CONSUMPTION PER CUSTOMER (kilowatt-hours)		NUMBER OF CUSTOMERS		TOTAL CONSUMPTION (kilowatt-hours)		TOTAL REVENUE		AVERAGE REVENUE (cents per kilowatt-hour)	
			Month prior to T.V.A.	June 1935	Month prior to T.V.A.	June 1935	Month prior to T.V.A.	June 1935	Month prior to T.V.A.	June 1935	Month prior to T.V.A.	June 1935
Tupelo, Mississippi	February 7, 1934	17	49	112	955	1,241	46,398	138,570	$3,436	$2,849	7.4	2.1
Alcorn County Electric Power Association	June 1, 1934	13	49	101	1,180	1,519	58,288	153,880	3,129	3,298	5.4	2.1
Athens, Alabama	June 1, 1934	13	51	112	521	712	26,589	79,667	1,464	1,655	5.5	2.1
Pontotoc County Electric Power Association	June 1, 1934	13	33	71	311	450	10,158	31,985	648	781	6.4	2.4
New Albany, Mississippi	November 12, 1934	7	43	75	539	577	22,896	43,021	1,553	1,028	6.8	2.4
Pulaski, Tennessee	January 4, 1935	6	49	84	477	531	23,581	44,431	1,370	991	5.8	2.2
Dayton, Tennessee	February 1, 1935	5	40	53	451	480	17,995	25,457	1,132	680	6.3	2.7

[3] Tennessee Valley Authority, Department of Electricity, Division of Rates, Research, and Economics, *Statistical Bulletin No. 7*, reprinted in Malcolm P. McNair and Richard S. Meriam, *Problems in Business Economics*, McGraw-Hill, N.Y., 1941, p. 94.

3. Could private concerns *profitably* have followed T.V.A.'s example? What further data would be needed to answer this question?

CASE 5-4   Elasticity as a basis for price determination

"The strategic decision in pricing a new product is the choice between (1) a policy of high initial prices that skim the cream of demand and (2) a policy of low prices from the outset serving as an active agent for market penetration. Although the actual range of choice is much wider than this, a sharp dichotomy clarifies the issues for consideration.

Skimming price. For products that represent a drastic departure from accepted ways of performing a service, a policy of relatively high prices coupled with heavy promotional expenditures in the early stages of market development (and lower prices at later stages) has proved successful for many products. There are several reasons for the success of this policy:

1. Demand is likely to be more inelastic with respect to price in the early stages than it is when the product is full grown. This is particularly true for consumers' goods. A novel product, such as the electric blanket . . . is not yet accepted as a part of the expenditure pattern. Consumers are still ignorant about its value as compared with the value of conventional alternatives. Moreover, at least in the early stages, the product has so few close rivals that cross-elasticity of demand is low. Promotional elasticity is, on the other hand, quite high, particularly for products with high unit prices, such as television sets. Since it is difficult for the customer to value the service of the product in a way to price it intelligently, he is by default principally interested in how well it will work.

2. Launching a new product with a high price is an efficient device for breaking the market up into segments that differ in price elasticity of demand. The initial high price serves to skim the cream of the market that is relatively insensitive to price. Subsequent price reductions tap successively more elastic sectors of the market. This pricing strategy is exemplified by the systematic succession of editions of a book, sometimes starting with a $50 limited personal edition and ending up with a 25-cent pocket book.

3. This policy is safer, or at least appears so. Facing an unknown elasticity of demand, a high initial price serves as a 'refusal' price during the stage of exploration. How much costs can be reduced as the market expands and as the design of the product is improved by increasing production efficiency with new techniques is difficult to predict. One of the electrical companies recently introduced a new lamp bulb at a comparatively high initial price, but with the announcement that the price would be reduced as the company found ways of cutting its costs.

Penetration price. The alternative policy is to use low prices as the principal instrument for penetrating mass markets early. This policy is the reverse of the skimming policy in which the price is lowered only as short-run competition forces it. The passive skimming policy has the virtue of safeguarding some profits at every stage of market penetration. But it prevents quick sales to the many buyers who are at the lower end of the income scale or the lower end of the preference scale, and who, therefore, are unwilling to pay any substantial premium for product or reputation superiority. The active approach in probing possibilities for market expansion by early penetration pricing requires research, forecasting, and courage.

A decision to price for market expansion can be reached at various stages in a product's life cycle: before birth, at birth, in childhood, in adulthood, or in senescence. The chances for large-volume sales should at least be explored in the early stages of product development research, even before the pilot stage, perhaps with a more definitive exploration when the product goes into production and the price and distribution plans are decided upon. And the question of pricing to expand the market, if not answered earlier, will probably arise once more after the product has established an elite market.

Quite a few products have been rescued from premature senescence by pricing them low enough to tap new markets. The reissue of important books in the 25-cent pocket-book category illustrates the point particularly well. These have produced not only commercial, but intellectual renascence as well to many authors. The pattern of sales growth of a product that had reached stability in a high-price market has been known to undergo sharp changes when it was suddenly priced low enough to tap new markets. A contrasting illustration of passive policy is the recent pricing experience of the airlines. Although safety considerations and differences in equipment and service cloud the picture, it is pretty clear that the bargain-rate coach fares of scheduled airlines were adopted in reaction to the cut rates of nonscheduled airlines. This competitive response has apparently established a new pattern of traffic growth for the scheduled airlines.

An example of penetration pricing at the initial stage of the product's market life, again from the book field, is Simon & Schuster's recently adopted policy of bringing out new titles in a $1, paper-bound edition simultaneously with the conventional higher priced, cloth-bound edition." [4]

[4] Joel Dean, "Pricing Policies for New Products," *Harvard Business Review,* Vol. 28, No. 6, November 1950, pp. 49–51. Copyright, 1955 by The President and Fellows of Harvard College. Reprinted by permission.

Questions

1. In connection with the so-called "skimming price," can you think of other cases where markets have been divided according to price elasticities?
2. Can you think of any example of the use of penetration pricing in recent years?
3. How can you account for the fact that a product, such as a book, can be sold at two different prices at the same time? Does the fact that the paper-bound edition has a larger sale than the cloth-bound edition show that there is an elastic demand for the product?

CASE 5-5 Effect of price changes upon cotton consumption

The following table shows the estimated effect of both a price rise and a price decrease on the domestic consumption of cotton in various uses.[5]

	SMALLER CONSUMPTION IF PRICE IS 40¢ INSTEAD OF 25¢ (*thousands of 478-lb net wt. bales*)	GREATER CONSUMPTION IF PRICE IS 12¢ INSTEAD OF 25¢ (*thousands of 478-lb net wt. bales*)
	Amount of decrease	*Amount of increase*
Men's clothing	339	59
Women's clothing	140	57
Children's clothing	31	6
Bedding and other household furnishings	286	105
Bags	242	140
Cordage and twine	118	35
Awnings, tents, tarpaulins	29	39
Plastic laminates	85	177
Tire cord	87	501
Thermal insulation	88	109
All other	358	156

Questions

1. On the basis of the information given, is it possible to calculate elasticity of demand for cotton? Explain your answer.

MEASUREMENT OF PRICE ELASTICITY OF DEMAND

Until now, we have been concerned only with determining whether demand is elastic or inelastic, and we have observed the rela-

[5] Adapted from *Proceedings of the Eighth Cotton Research Congress.*

tionship of elasticity to total revenue. We are now prepared to give greater precision to our measurement, and to determine the actual extent of elasticity in any given situation.

We have defined price elasticity of demand as the proportional change in quantity relative to the proportional change in price. More precisely, we can say:

$$e = \frac{dQ}{Q} \div \frac{dP}{P}$$

where e means the coefficient of elasticity, Q means quantity demanded, dQ means the change in quantity demanded, P means price, and dP means the change in price. Thus, if we have a change in price from 51 cents to 50 cents, and an accompanying change in quantity demanded from 100 to 101, the coefficient of elasticity will be:

$$e = \frac{1}{100} \div \frac{-1}{50} = -.5, \text{ or simply } .5$$

We will usually omit the minus sign, since it is understood that the elasticity of demand with respect to price is always negative. (This is true because quantity and price always change in opposite directions, in accordance with the general law of demand.) We may observe from the formula that the greater the relative change in quantity demanded compared to the relative price change, the larger will be the coefficient of elasticity, and vice versa. If the coefficient is larger than 1, demand is elastic; if it is smaller than 1, demand is inelastic; if it is exactly 1, we say demand has unitary elasticity.

The coefficient of elasticity gives us a much more accurate identification of a demand schedule as elastic or inelastic than does the apparent slope (i.e., the relative steepness or flatness) of a demand curve. The steepness or flatness of any plotted curve depends upon the scales against which the curve is plotted. But scales are chosen arbitrarily; furthermore, the same relationship can frequently be stated in different units. For example, if a fall in price from \$5 to \$4 is accompanied by an increase in quantity demanded from 5 to 6 units, the absolute rate of change is $(6 - 5) \div (5 - 4)$, or $\frac{1}{1}$. However, if we had used cents instead of dollars as the unit of price in our schedule, the ratio would become $(6 - 5) \div (500 - 400)$, or $\frac{1}{100}$. The demand curve would now have a different slope, although no actual change in quantity demanded would have occurred. The same kind of confusion could be introduced if quantity demanded were expressed in ounces instead of pounds, cases instead of bottles, etc. A true measure of the effect of a price change must, therefore, be independent of any particular unit of

measurement chosen for price or quantity. The formula for the coefficient of elasticity is appropriate because it compares relative changes,
not absolute changes.

Fig. 5-3 illustrates the danger of drawing conclusions from the appearance of the curve. The two demand curves shown in Fig. 5-3 are
identical, and have identical elasticities, even though they appear to be
different because of the different scales.

FIG. 5-3 Effect of Scale upon Appearance of a Curve

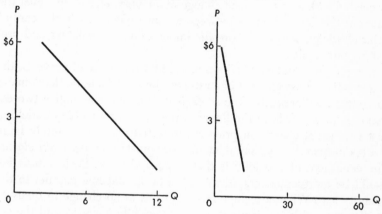

The formula for elasticity given above is useful when the changes
in price and quantity are extremely small. What we are doing, in effect,
is measuring the elasticity around a single point of the demand curve
by permitting the price and quantity demanded to vary by a very small
amount around that point. For this reason, this measure of elasticity is
known as point elasticity. When we consider a substantial change in
either price or quantity demanded, or both, however, our formula for
point elasticity must be modified.

To measure the elasticity between two points, economists use the
concept of arc elasticity. The formula for arc elasticity is:

$$e = \frac{Q_1 - Q_2}{\left(\dfrac{Q_1 + Q_2}{2}\right)} \div \frac{P_1 - P_2}{\left(\dfrac{P_1 + P_2}{2}\right)}$$

where Q_1 is the original quantity, Q_2 the quantity after the change,
P_1 the original price, P_2 the price after the change. Here we are actually

measuring the average elasticity between the two points, rather than the elasticity at either the first or the second point. Thus, if a decline in price from \$8 to \$5 results in a change in quantity demanded from 100 to 210 units, we calculate arc elasticity as follows:

$$e = \frac{100 - 210}{\left(\dfrac{100 + 210}{2}\right)} \div \frac{8 - 5}{\left(\dfrac{8 + 5}{2}\right)} = \frac{-110}{155} \div \frac{3}{6.5} = -1.54$$

We may interpret this to mean that a 1 per cent change in price will be associated with a 1.54 per cent change in quantity, on average, over the range of the demand curve between the two points. As in the case of point elasticity, we may ignore the minus sign in calculating and presenting our results.

As we have indicated, the more elastic the demand curve is, the larger will be the coefficient of elasticity; the more inelastic the demand curve, the smaller will be the coefficient. We may now notice two extreme cases which form the limits to the range of possible elasticities. If a very small change in price is associated with an infinitely large change in quantity, we say demand is completely or *perfectly elastic*. The coefficient of elasticity is then expressed as ∞. Such a situation would be represented graphically by a horizontal line parallel to the quantity axis. When a change in price leads to no change in quantity at all, we say demand is completely or *perfectly inelastic*, and the coefficient is zero. This is represented graphically by a vertical line parallel to the price axis (see Fig. 5-4).

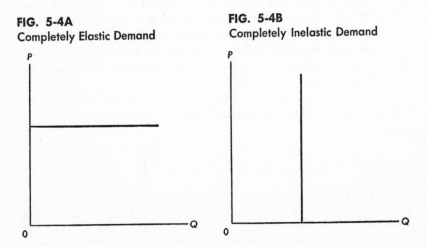

FIG. 5-4A
Completely Elastic Demand

FIG. 5-4B
Completely Inelastic Demand

We may now summarize the possibilities in terms of elasticity co-efficients as follows:

If *e* is	Demand is
∞	Completely elastic
above 1	Elastic
1	Unitary elasticity
below 1	Inelastic
0	Completely inelastic

CASE 5-6 Calculating arc elasticity

Given the following demand schedule,

P	Q
$6	3
5	7
4	9
3	15
2	20

calculate the arc elasticity of demand:

Between $6 and $5
5 and   4
4 and   3
3 and   2
6 and   4
4 and   2

CASE 5-7 Drawing demand curves

1. Draw a demand curve which has unitary elasticity throughout.
2. Draw a demand curve which is inelastic at high prices and becomes elastic at low prices.
3. Draw a demand curve which is elastic at high prices and becomes inelastic at low prices.
4. Draw a demand curve which has a different elasticity at each and every point on the curve.

CASE 5-8 Farmer Brown's corn

William Brown is a corn farmer in Iowa. Last year Mr. Brown had 2,000 bushels of corn to sell. On the day that he decided to market his crop the going price for corn was $1.35 per bushel. The local grain merchant told

Brown that he could sell part or all of his crop at that price. Brown's offering was such a small part of the total corn crop that, regardless of how much he decided to sell, he could have no influence on the price.

Questions

1. How would you describe the elasticity of demand for Mr. Brown's corn? Show it graphically.
2. Does the demand curve for the entire United States corn crop also look like this? Why or why not?

CASE 5-9   The Jones family's demand for salt

The Jones family has an annual income of about ten thousand dollars. In an average year it consumes about 4 pounds of salt at a total cost of 20 cents (five cents per pound). This past year all the suppliers of salt in the city where the Jones family lives raised the price of salt to 10 cents per pound. Mrs. Jones continued to buy about 4 pounds per year in spite of the price rise.

Questions

1. How would you describe the elasticity of demand for salt as discussed above? Show it graphically.
2. Do you think the elasticity would be the same regardless of the income of the family?
3. Do you think the elasticity would be the same regardless of the price of salt?
4. Suppose one manufacturer had raised the price to 10 cents and the others had kept theirs at 5 cents a pound. Would the demand curve for his salt look the same as the demand curve for salt in general? Explain why or why not.

CASE 5-10   Diverse uses of salt

The demand for salt for household use is usually regarded as being highly inelastic. Salt, however, has many other uses, and the demand for salt has shown a marked increase over the years.

The tremendous increase in salt production in the United States is shown in Table 1. From 1880 to 1949, salt has increased 1,970 per cent in quantity, and 1,100 per cent in value. The great variety of uses for salt is shown in Table 2. It has been estimated that there are about 1,400 direct uses for salt as sodium chloride, and that larger quantities are used as a source material for other products. The use of salt is particularly important in the chemical industry, where it is frequently indispensable as a raw material for which there are no substitutes.[6]

TABLE 1   U.S. Salt Production and Prices, 1880–1949

YEAR	SALT PRODUCED (thousand short tons)	VALUE (thousands of dollars)	AVERAGE PRICE (per ton)
1880	835	4,830	$5.78
1890	1,243	4,752	3.82
1900	2,922	6,945	2.38
1910	4,243	7,900	1.86
1915	5,352	11,748	2.20
1920	6,840	29,894	4.37
1925	7,398	26,162	3.54
1930	8,054	25,009	3.11
1935	7,927	21,838	2.75
1940	10,360	26,475	2.56
1945	15,394	36,069	2.34
1949	15,590	54,048	3.47

TABLE 2   End Uses of Salt, 1948 (in short tons)

Chlorine, bleaches, chlorates, etc.	2,838,028
Soda ash	7,392,248
Dyes and organic chemicals	183,274
Soap (as a precipitant)	44,202
Other chemicals	615,266
Textile processing	115,393
Hides and leather	230,811
Meat packing	710,300
Fish curing	35,348
Butter, cheese, and dairy products	102,356
Canning and preserving	144,811
Other food processing	213,175
Refrigerant (car icing)	216,627
Livestock	792,518
Railroad and highway dust and ice control	468,934
Table and household	672,987
Water treatment (zeolite system of water softening)	446,956
Metallurgy	65,777
Not classified	1,144,502

[6] Based on Arthur E. Inman, *Salt, An Industrial Potential For Kansas*, University of Kansas Research Foundation, Lawrence, Kansas, 1951, pp. 13–14, 27–28. Tables 1 and 2 have been adapted from the same source.

Questions

1. Can the figures in Table 1 be used to confirm (or refute) your answers to the questions in the preceding case?
2. Would you expect to find any difference in the price charged for salt for household use as compared with the price for commercial use? Explain your answer.

CASE 5-11   Elasticity of railroad passenger traffic

In July 1956, the two largest passenger railroads, the Pennsylvania and the New York Central, applied to the Interstate Commerce Commission for large increases in first-class fares ranging from one-third to one-half of the existing first-class fares. If a 50% increase were to go into effect, the New York-Chicago Pullman fare, with roomette, would rise to $85.63. The present first-class *airline* fare is $49.61.[7]

The amount of the proposed increase in first-class passenger fares has led to considerable speculation as to what the railroads have in mind. Some observers feel that the railroads, confronted by steadily falling volume in first-class travel, fast growing airline traffic, and the inevitability of bigger and faster planes, have decided to avoid further expense in supplying adequate first-class accommodations by driving the first-class passengers away from the railroads to the airlines. This the railroad companies deny, claiming that they are merely attempting to bring fares into a more realistic relationship with costs.

Questions

1. What considerations would bear out the contention of the railroad companies? Of the other observers? What do you think would be the response of passengers to the proposed changes in fare? Why?
2. Assuming that first-class railroad fares are increased by 50%, what percentage of change in passenger miles would indicate that the elasticity of demand was unitary?

CASE 5-12   Effect of an increase in subway fares

The threat of a deficit on New York City's Rapid Transit System led to a reconsideration in 1951–52 of the structure of Rapid Transit fares. In order to evaluate the relative merits of various fare proposals, it became necessary to know the probable effect of various fare changes on the volume and patterns of traffic.

The available data on elasticity for New York consisted primarily of the experience at the time of the change from the 5-cent fare to the 10-cent fare on July 1, 1948. Data were obtained for the period July 1947 to February

---

[7] Data as reported in *Business Week*, August 4, 1956, p. 31.

1951, representing twelve months before, and thirty-two months after the change. The results were classified according to the different types of traffic. Taking the average level of traffic for the three years 1947–49 as 100, these results showed the following:

1. Downtown weekday traffic fell immediately after the fare change from a previous level of 106 to 98, or a drop of 1.6% for each 1-cent rise in fare. There was a slight tendency to drop off further to a level of 97, or perhaps 96, after a short lapse of time, contrasting with the slightly rising trend of the data for the twelve months preceding the change.

2. Traffic originating in outlying areas on weekdays appeared to have a considerably greater short-run elasticity. In addition there appeared to be a substantial "delayed action" effect. Traffic dropped after the fare change from a previous level of 110 to 97, and finally fell further to a level of 92 by 1950. Since some of the traffic originating in outlying areas was destined for the downtown area, there was some duplication between this classification and the previous one. It was estimated that the traffic originating in outlying stations and not destined for the central zone had an elasticity of at least 4.3% per 1-cent fare change. As some of this was long-haul traffic of low elasticity (e.g., the traffic through the central zone to the other side) it was further estimated that the elasticity of the short-haul traffic in the outer zone was at least 5% for each 1-cent change in fare.

3. The data for nonworking days showed little difference in the immediate impact of the fare on traffic from outlying areas and on traffic from the central zone; in both cases the indicated change was 4% per 1-cent change in fare. In the subsequent trend, however, the outlying traffic showed a further decline of 12% by 1950, whereas the traffic at downtown stations showed a further decline of only about 6 or 7%.

Putting all these indications together, and with some degree of hunch and guesswork, a table showing a general pattern of elasticity was constructed. (See page 146.) The levels of elasticity shown assume that about half of the decline in traffic from the summer of 1948 to 1950 was attributable to a delayed reaction to the fare increase.[8]

Questions

1. On the basis of these calculations, how would you decide whether the response of traffic to changes in fare was elastic or inelastic?
2. Assuming that the per cent increase in traffic indicated in the table is consistent for each 1-cent decrease in fare from 10 cents to 0 cents, is there any change in elasticity over this range of fares?

---

[8] Adapted from William S. Vickrey, *The Revision of the Rapid Transit Fare Structure of the City of New York*, Technical Monograph No. 3, Finance Project, Mayor's Committee on Management Survey of the City of New York, February 1952, pp. 74–88. The table has been adapted from the same source.

Estimated Percentage Response of Various Types of Traffic to Fare Change

PERCENTAGE OF INCREASE IN TRAFFIC OVER THE PRESENT TEN-CENT LEVELS
RESULTING FROM EACH ONE-CENT DECREASE IN FARE

| | TRAFFIC ORIGINATING DURING WEEKDAYS | | | | | Saturday, Sunday, & holidays |
	Rush hour	Near rush	Midday	Evening and night	Total	
From Central Zone:						
Local	2.1	2.2	4.0	3.0	2.9	5.5
Medium haul	1.5	1.5	2.6	1.4	1.7	4.0
Long haul	1.4	1.4	2.5	1.3	1.6	4.0
Total	1.6	1.5	3.0	1.6	1.9	4.7
From Middle and Outer Zones:						
To Center Zone:						
Medium haul	1.5	1.5	2.6	1.4	1.7	4.0
Long haul	1.4	1.4	2.5	1.3	1.6	4.0
To Middle and Outer Zones:						
Local	7.5	7.5	9.1	5.0	7.5	8.0
Medium haul	3.3	3.4	6.0	4.0	4.0	6.0
Through downtown	1.7	1.9	2.5	2.5	2.0	4.0
In and out	7.5	7.5	7.5	7.5	7.5	9.0
Total	2.9	3.0	4.6	2.6	3.3	5.5

3. To what extent is it valid to attribute the delayed response to changes in fare to elasticity? Can you think of factors other than the change in fare that might bring about this response?

4. Will the answers to the foregoing questions be appreciably affected if you allow for changes in the value of the dollar from 1947 to 1952?

CASE 5-13 Elasticity of demand for automobiles, I

It is frequently claimed that the lowering of the price of automobiles as the result of mass production has been responsible for the great increase in automobile consumption. This contention, however, would be difficult to prove.

A study by C. F. Roos and Victor von Szeliski in 1939 throws some light on this question.[9] On the basis of their study of available data, Roos and von Szeliski concluded that price has not been a very important factor in determining automobile sales. Their findings in regard to elasticity of demand for automobiles are summarized in the table on page 147.

---

[9] Roos and von Szeliski, *The Dynamics of Automobile Demand*, General Motors Corp., N.Y., 1939, p. 94.

Elasticity of Demand for Automobiles with Respect to Price, 1919–1938

1919	1.03	1929	1.41
1920	1.04	1930	1.51
1921	1.04	1931	1.46
1922	1.05	1932	1.44
1923	1.05	1933	1.30
1924	1.15	1934	1.34
1925	1.22	1935	1.34
1926	1.26	1936	1.33
1927	1.33	1937	1.38
1928	1.37	1938	1.53

Questions

1. How would one describe the price elasticity of demand for automobiles on the basis of this study?
2. If the findings in this study are correct, would it be in the interest of automobile manufacturers to lower prices?

CASE 5-14   Elasticity of demand for automobiles, II

The following is taken from the 1958 testimony of a vice president of the Ford Motor Company before a subcommittee of the United States Senate:

"The elasticity of demand for automobiles is necessarily involved in Mr. Reuther's proposal that each manufacturer reduce prices by $100 a car. The proposal was first publicized last August. . . .

Mr. Reuther argues that a $100 reduction in price would not cost the manufacturers anything, because it would increase volume sufficiently to compensate them for the reduction in price. Our appraisal of Mr. Reuther's proposal is that it was nothing more than an effort to divert attention from his own highly inflationary demands. But accepting his proposal at face value, let us examine it on its merits. In doing so, let us bear in mind that the proposed reduction would apply across the board, and would not be limited to any one car line, and that it would be permanent, not temporary, in nature. Mr. Reuther asserts that in such a reduction 'there would be little risk' for the automobile manufacturers.

Mr. Reuther's proposed price cut of $100 per vehicle would wipe out, we estimate, about half our 1957 car and truck profits, assuming no increase in volume. If the proposed price reduction would have such an effect on Ford Motor Company's profits, what effect would it have on the profits of our smaller competitors?

But Mr. Reuther asserts that this loss of profits would be largely offset by gains from our Company's share of a one million car increase in industry sales. What is the basis of this assertion? It is a statement by Mr. Carl E. Fribley, then head of the National Automobile Dealers Association, to the effect that if there had been no price increase on 1957 models, a million more units would have been sold. From this, Mr. Reuther has derived his assumption that a $100 reduction in car prices, about 4%, would have increased sales by 16%. This would indicate an elasticity of demand of −4.0.

Mr. Fribley was, I am sure, voicing his honest opinion. But unless his opinion was based on objective analysis, it is likely to have been biased by his special interests. There is in the record no indication of how Mr. Fribley arrived at his conclusion, or to what extent, if at all, his opinion was shared by others.

Mr. Fribley's opinion is at odds with the serious, scholarly attempts to measure the elasticity of demand for automobiles. These studies indicate a much smaller increase in units sold in response to a price reduction. They show that the elasticity of demand for new cars produced by the industry probably is in the −.5 to −1.5 range—that is, only about 12% to 40% as large as Mr. Reuther's interpretation of the Fribley guess.

I do not profess to know just what the elasticity of demand for an automobile is. But in the light of the findings of those who have made the studies, and in the light of everything else we know about the character of the demand for automobiles, Mr. Reuther's assertions do not make sense.

The elasticity of demand for automobiles can have many different meanings, depending on the frame of reference. In this discussion, it refers to the responsiveness of sales to a permanent price change made by all manufacturers. The relative response of sales to a temporary price cut may be greater than if the cut is permanent. But as I have said, in the problem before us, we are concerned not with a price cut over a few months or over a single year, but with one that is permanent and across the board. . . .

In previous testimony, attention was called to the range of discretion that a seller may have in establishing a price. In the case of an automobile manufacturer, the range of discretion in setting prices on a car line is small. We have not found it possible to price much above the most nearly comparable models of competition; to do so would entail heavy loss of sales volume. We have found it impossible to price substantially below competition and still make a reasonable profit for our shareholders. . . ." [10]

---

[10] Statement by Mr. Theodore O. Yntema, Vice President–Finance, Ford Motor Company, before the Subcommittee on Antitrust and Monopoly of the Committee on the Judiciary, U.S. Senate, February 4–5, 1958.

Questions

1. Do you agree that Mr. Fribley's figures indicate an elasticity of demand of −4.0? Can you calculate the indicated elasticity more accurately?
2. Do you agree that a temporary cut in price might produce a greater response of sales than would a permanent cut? Why or why not?
3. If prices above those of competitors "entail heavy loss of sales volume," would prices below those of competitors result in a heavy increase in sales volume and therefore in profits? Why or why not?

CASE 5-15   Elasticity of demand for tobacco

"The introduction of tobacco to Spain was followed in the succeeding century by its spread to all the principal parts of Europe. By 1560 it was generally accepted on the Continent as a specific remedy for most ailments. Tobacco was still unfamiliar in England at this time but was soon adopted by Sir Walter Raleigh and recommended with almost missionary zeal. Within a few years the custom of 'drinking' smoke had spread from the sea captains to the court and to such other classes as could afford the new dissipation. . . .

Aversion to the weed, aversion to Sir Walter Raleigh, and the fact that hated Spain was the principal source of supply led King James to attempt to suppress tobacco use by admonition and by raising the import duty from 2d. to 6s., 10d. per pound. Opposition to tobacco did not acquire such strength on the continent of Europe, but in Turkey, Persia, India, and China savage penalties were intermittently visited upon the users or purveyors of tobacco.

Prohibitions and objections were fruitless then as later both because of the difficulty of enforcement, and because of the financial sacrifice which enforcement demanded. The effect of King James's tariff was to drive tobacco into illegal channels, to stimulate home cultivation, and to deprive the fisc of revenues which it could well use. The possibility of securing supplies from Virginia rather than from Spain removed one mercantilist objection. The fiscal argument was probably controlling. It was early discovered that the demand for tobacco would support any price within a wide range, if only that price could be enforced, and the possibilities for taxation were too attractive to miss.

In England the easiest way of collecting this levy was through the ports. Accordingly, duties were reduced somewhat to lessen the premium on smuggling, cultivation was prohibited within the British Isles and encouraged in the American colonies. All colonial tobacco regardless of ultimate destination was routed through English ports, where a heavy duty was collected. Virginia might indeed be a colony 'founded upon smoak,' but the foundation was solid enough. The first successful English settlement in North America survived by virtue of the weed, and, until the end of the colonial era when Whitney's cotton gin gave a new direction to agriculture, tobacco remained the principal export staple of Virginia, North Carolina, and Maryland, and the chief support of successful colonization in those latitudes.

Other countries than England found other ways to profit from tobacco. Tariffs, excise, or the exploitation of monopoly have been used in different places and in different times to enrich the treasury or to profit private interests. But always and everywhere, from the first days, men have appreciated the inelasticity of tobacco demand and the consequent capacity of tobacco to bear heavy charges.

In this country the cultivation of tobacco was for a long time of greater importance than manufacture or consumption, and the conditions of demand were looked at from the point of view of the farmer. All through the colonial era and later, growers were aware of the high prices which short crops would bring, and there were constant efforts to limit production. Intercolonial jealousies, the powerlessness of government, and the large number of producers combined to thwart most of these plans, but the continuous complaints of 'overproduction' show that colonial farmers were familiar with problems which have since become general in agriculture and that they were well aware of the price insensitivity of tobacco.

Excise taxes were introduced in this country to fight the Civil War, and subsequent imposts have been added repeatedly without decreasing the use of tobacco or even, so far as can be seen, effectively slowing its growth. Private interests were aware of the possibilities and established monopoly as soon as it was practicable to do so. So long as tobacco manufacture was in the hands of hundreds of small firms, nothing could be accomplished. But when the cigarette industry developed with only a few firms, and when cigarette machinery made technically possible the indefinite expansion of those firms, combination was effected. Monopoly profits from cigarettes were used to extend control over most other parts of the tobacco industry. Once control was established, the profit history of the old American Tobacco Company was adequate testimony to what men had long known: that the demand for tobacco is peculiarly insistent and unresponsive to price." [11]

Questions

1. Why is demand for tobacco so "insistent"?
2. If demand is as inelastic as is indicated, why is it that prices have not gone up much higher?

[11] Richard B. Tennant, *The American Cigarette Industry*, Yale U. Press, New Haven, 1950, pp. 115–17. © 1950 by Yale University Press.

CASE 5-16   Taxation of tobacco in the United States

Cigarettes are taxed by the federal government, by 42 states, and by the District of Columbia. In the six states not levying a cigarette tax, the federal tax of 8 cents per pack of 20 applies. In the other 42 states, an additional average of about 3¾ cents applies, or a total of 11¾ cents per pack. It was estimated that federal and gross state taxes from cigarettes in the fiscal year ending June 30, 1956, would total about $2.1 billion—approximately $100 million more than in the previous fiscal year.[12]

Questions

1. Why, in your opinion, is such a heavy tax levied upon cigarettes? Do you agree that cigarettes should be taxed heavily?
2. Assume that the federal tax on cigarettes is doubled and completely passed on to the consumer. If the quantity purchased falls by less than 50 per cent, does this prove that demand is inelastic?

CASE 5-17   Elasticity of demand for tobacco—the British experiment

1. The British government, in an effort to raise revenue to finance war and postwar needs, progressively raised the tax on tobacco from 9s. 6d. per pound in 1938 until it amounted to 35s. 6d. per pound in 1947. At the latter rate, a package of 20 cigarettes cost 2s. 4d. (48 cents at the then current rate of exchange). . . . Expenditure on tobacco rose from 177 million pounds sterling in 1938 to 603 million pounds sterling in 1947; consumption rose from 190 million pounds to 250 million pounds in the same period. The London *Economist* reported that huge additional revenue was secured by increases in the tobacco duty since 1939 without affecting consumption.

2. In 1947, the Labor government increased the duty by another 50 per cent to 54s. 10d. per pound, which raised the price of cigarettes to 3s. 4d., or 68 cents per package of 20. Here the purpose was not to raise revenue, but to decrease consumption in order to save dollars spent for importing tobacco. The government had hoped to reduce consumption by 25 per cent. This hope was not realized. Tobacco consumption totaled 225 million pounds in 1947, or 10 per cent less than the 250 million pounds used in 1946. Finally, in 1952, it became necessary to cut down expenditures for dollar tobacco by imposing quota restrictions on imports.[13]

---

[12] Based on U.S. Department of Agriculture, "The Tobacco Situation," Agricultural Marketing Service, June 26, 1956.

[13] Data based in part on reports in *The Economist*, London, February 26, 1944, pp. 277–78, and April 17, 1948, p. 648.

Questions

1. Can you calculate the elasticity of demand for tobacco in Great Britain from the information given in the first paragraph?
2. Using the information given in paragraphs 1 and 2, and assuming all other things remained unchanged, calculate the arc elasticity of demand for tobacco in Great Britain between the prices of 48 cents and 68 cents per package of cigarettes.
3. If British demand is as indicated what effect will the quota restrictions have on the price? Who stands to profit?

CASE 5-18   Elasticity of demand for tobacco—competition among brands

"There have . . . been three occasions on which different retail prices prevailed among the 'Big Three,' and the reaction in two cases indicates a high degree of elasticity in brand demand.

On October 1, 1918, the net wholesale price of Lucky Strike cigarettes was raised to $6.77 per thousand. Prices of Camel and Chesterfield were unchanged at $5.29. On November 11, Lucky Strike prices were cut back near the level of the other two. The effect on monthly sales is shown in Table 30.

TABLE 30   Lucky Strike Sales and Share of the Market, August 1918–January 1919

MONTH	LUCKY STRIKE SALES (millions of cigarettes)	NATIONAL TAX-PAID WITHDRAWALS (millions of cigarettes)	LUCKY STRIKE SHARE OF THE MARKET (per cent)
August 1918	414.8	3,442	12.1
September	406.4	3,403	11.9
October	321.8	3,027	10.6
November	279.8	2,987	9.4
December	220.1	2,788	7.9
January 1919	188.7	3,079	6.1

In four months the relative importance of Lucky Strike cigarettes declined by half. The price differential amounted to 3¢ a pack and was in force for only five weeks. It is not apparent what other influences may have been at work. If this development resulted from price differences alone, it bespeaks a very high degree of demand elasticity.

In March 1922, prices of Lucky Strike and Camel were cut from $6.62 to $6 net. Chesterfield reduced only to $6.35. Retail prices were a cent higher than those of the other brands, and sales declined. At the end of two months, Liggett and Myers began giving an allowance off invoice of 30¢ a thousand. This reduced the wholesale differential to 5¢, which was not enough to be reflected generally in a difference at retail.

On July 30, 1946, Chesterfield net prices were briefly raised from $6.25 a thousand to $6.45. Camel and Lucky Strike were unchanged, and in two weeks Liggett and Myers rescinded their increase. In the absence of information as to the effect on Chesterfield sales, one cannot draw conclusions regarding the elasticity of brand demand. In such a short time the effect was probably small, especially as many retailers did not raise the price of Chesterfield relative to the other brands." [14]

Questions

1. Is the decline in Lucky Strike sales from August 1918 to January 1919 attributable to a movement along the demand curve or to a shift in demand?

2. Is the continued decline in Lucky Strike sales after November 11, 1918, consistent with the explanations offered in the case?

3. How do you account for the elasticity in brand demand in the face of the known inelasticity of demand for tobacco products as a whole?

4. Can you conceive of a situation in which a price rise in one brand would not have a serious effect on sales volume for that brand?

CASE 5-19   Elasticity of demand facing different suppliers

In his book on international economics, Professor Charles P. Kindleberger states that countries which supply a considerable proportion of the world's exports of a commodity—e.g., Brazil in coffee (55%), India in tea (49%), Australia in wool (43%), Cuba in sugar (49%), the Philippines in copra (54%), and Malaya in tin (58%) and rubber (47%)—face a demand curve almost as inelastic as the demand for the commodity as a whole. The reason he gives is that attempts to substitute for these commodities in the various importing countries would cause national repercussions. On the other hand, demand is said to be highly elastic for countries whose output of these commodities is small relative to total supply—Costa Rican coffee (1%) and Guatemalan coffee (3¾%). Colombian coffee falls in between (18%).[15]

Questions

1. Why do the demand curves differ in elasticity for suppliers of different sizes?

2. Can you think of cases of exports where even large suppliers (in relation to the total supply) face an elastic demand?

[14] Richard B. Tennant, *op. cit.*, pp. 160–61.
[15] Charles P. Kindleberger, *International Economics,* Richard D. Irwin, Inc., Homewood, Ill., 1953, p. 135.

3. If Brazil should cut its coffee production by 25%, would the total revenue of Brazilian coffee growers increase? Why or why not?
4. In your opinion, what type of "national repercussions" might occur in the various importing countries if it became necessary to find substitutes for the commodities listed above?

CASE 5-20   Elasticity of demand for automotive steel

"AN ANALYSIS OF THE DEMAND
FOR STEEL IN THE AUTOMOBILE INDUSTRY

PURPOSE

The purpose of this study is to review the factors which determine the demand for steel as a raw material in the automobile industry, and to appraise particularly the relative significance of the price of steel as one of these factors.

SUMMARY OF THE FINDINGS

The quantity of steel consumed as a raw material by the automobile manufacturing industry depends directly upon (1) the number of cars produced; (2) the quantity of steel used per car; and (3) the production of replacement parts and related equipment. The price of automotive steel can affect the quantity sold only by influencing one or more of these three factors.

The demand for automobiles has recently been the subject of an exhaustive study by C. F. Roos and Victor von Szeliski. They found that the number of new passenger cars sold in any year was dependent on (1) national income; (2) the number of cars in operation; (3) the age distribution of cars in operation; (4) the scrapping rate; (5) the price; and (6) other factors including used-car allowances, financing terms, operating costs and dealers' used-car stocks. After making proper allowance for the influence of national income, number of cars in operation, age distribution, and scrapping rate, they concluded that the elasticity of demand for new passenger cars was approximately 1.5; or in other words, that a 1% reduction in the price of cars would cause a 1.5% increase in the number of cars sold.

A change in the price of steel could affect the number of automobiles sold only if it were passed on to the ultimate consumer as a reduction in the price of cars. The cost of steel in a car is, however, only approximately 13% of the f.o.b. price, or approximately 10% of the delivered price of the car. A reduction of 10% in the price of automotive steel would, therefore, permit a reduction of only 1% in the delivered price of the car if it were passed on entirely to the consumer. Since this 1% reduction in automobile prices would give rise to only 1.5% increase in the number of cars sold, it follows that a 10% reduction in the price of steel would give rise to an increased consumption of steel of but 1.5% through its effect on the number of cars sold. Thus changes in the price of steel are far from effective in raising the consumption of steel through increasing the volume of car sales.

From the evidence available, the price of steel appears to have an even less significant effect on the quantity of steel used per car. The increased use of steel per car over the past fifteen years is mainly attributable to the increased popularity of enclosed models and heavier cars, and intense competition among motor companies in the improvement of their product. The conclusion that the price of steel is a minor influence in the quantity of steel consumed per car is supported by the absence of a relationship between the weight of passenger cars and the price of steel after the series have been adjusted for secular trends.

Replacement parts and accessories have a value only about one-seventh as great as new cars produced. It seems reasonable to conclude that the elasticity of demand for these products is not greatly different from the elasticity of demand for new cars. But even if parts and accessories had an appreciably higher elasticity of demand, because of their relatively small value they could not have much effect on the elasticity of demand for all automotive steel.

The total effect of a reduction in price upon the consumption of steel by the automobile industry, through increase in the volume of car production, increase in the use of steel per car, and increase in the production of replacement parts and accessories, is therefore relatively slight. Combining these elements, the elasticity of demand for automobile steel is probably not in excess of .2 or .3. In other words, a 10% reduction in the price of such steel could not increase the consumption of steel in the motor vehicle industry by more than 2 or 3%.

The price of steel is therefore a minor factor in determining the quantity of steel consumed as a raw material in the automobile industry.[16]

Questions

1. Do you agree with this analysis?
2. On which of the following two contentions would you place the greatest importance: (a) that the high cost of steel can be passed on to the consumer without any substantial decrease in the purchase of automobiles, or (b) that the cost of steel is a relatively unimportant part of the cost of producing automobiles? Explain your answer.

---

[16] United States Steel Corporation, *An Analysis of Changes in the Demand for Steel and in Steel Prices, 1936-1939*, T.N.E.C. Exhibit No. 1412, pp. 11-13.

3. Would you come to the same conclusions in regard to increasing wages in the automobile industry? What factors would you take into account in advising the industry whether or not it could safely grant such an increase?

CASE 5-21   Elasticity of demand for labor

In a recent study of the pulp and paper industry, the elasticity of demand for pulp and paper was described in the following terms:

"The demand for pulp and most types of paper is relatively inelastic in the short run. While demand varies directly with fluctuations in business activity, cyclical fluctuations in paper consumption are moderate compared with those in many other industries. Most studies of the industry have emphasized the relatively high degree of stability which characterizes demand (and output). The consumption of paper has shown spectacular growth in recent decades as a result of population increase, the development and exploitation of new markets, and the more widespread adoption of paper in its manifold uses. In other words, demand in the industry is characterized by low price elasticity, moderate sensitivity to cyclical fluctuations, and a rising growth trend."

The demand characteristics of the industry were further discussed as follows:

". . . relative stability of output and the phenomenal growth of consumption in recent decades have combined to create a favorable employment situation in the industry. The effect of these factors is revealed in the comparative employment indices (1923–25 = 100) that follow.

YEAR	PULP AND PAPER	ALL MANUFACTURING	NONDURABLE MANUFACTURING
1929	106.1	106.0	105.9
1932	81.9	66.3	79.2
1937	114.3	108.8	112.6
1938	106.1	92.6	103.8
1943	132.7	188.6	133.4
1946	154.8	152.0	139.6
1948	175.0	159.7	142.2
1949	164.2	145.7	134.6
1950	170.0	154.0	138.1

It is clear that employment in the pulp and paper industry has been stable and expanding compared with employment in general.

. . . consideration of the part played by labor in the production of pulp and paper suggests that the demand for most types of labor is quite inelastic. Several factors point in this direction: the demand for the industry's products is relatively inelastic; labor requirements are largely fixed by the nature and size of mill equipment; and labor costs are a relatively small proportion of total costs—10 to 25 per cent, depending on the type of mill. The demand for common labor is perhaps less inelastic than that for other types of labor because of the possibilities of substitution. It is at this level—the handling of materials in woodyards and pulp mills —that the greatest opportunities would seem to exist for the installation of labor-saving devices. To the extent that substitution does occur, however, it is a long-run rather than short-run process; and any displacement of labor is likely to be more than offset by the expansion of job opportunities due to increasing product demand.

The above conditions underlying the demand for labor in the industry suggest that the unions are in a strong bargaining position with respect to wage matters. This view is essentially correct; though . . . it requires some modification in the light of other considerations." [17]

Questions

1. In what respect would the development of substitutes for paper and pulp have an effect upon the elasticity of demand for labor in this industry? Explain your answer.

2. Can you think of other industries in which labor costs are likely to constitute only a small percentage of total costs? Where they are a large part of total costs? Does the elasticity of demand for labor seem to vary with this factor?

3. Common labor in the pulp and paper industry represents even a smaller percentage of total costs than does all labor in the industry. Can we conclude that the demand for common labor is more inelastic than the demand for all labor?

---

[17] Robert M. MacDonald, "Pulp and Paper," in Lloyd G. Reynolds and Cynthia H. Taft, *The Evolution of Wage Structure*, Yale U. Press, New Haven, 1956, pp. 100–03. © 1956 by Yale University Press.

CHAPTER SIX

Elasticity, Part II

INCOME ELASTICITY OF DEMAND

As we indicated in Chapter 2, the relationship between quantity demanded and income may be shown by means of an income demand schedule and curve. To measure the reaction of quantity demanded to changes in income we use the concept of income elasticity of demand.

The formula for measuring the coefficient of income elasticity is similar to that used for price elasticity. At any point on the income demand curve the coefficient of income elasticity (n) is given by:

$$n = \frac{dQ}{Q} \div \frac{dY}{Y}$$

where Q means quantity demanded, Y means income, and dQ and dY indicate a very small change in each of these variables. In order to calculate the coefficient of elasticity between two points we use our formula for arc elasticity:

$$n = \frac{Q_1 - Q_2}{\left(\dfrac{Q_1 + Q_2}{2}\right)} \div \frac{Y_1 - Y_2}{\left(\dfrac{Y_1 + Y_2}{2}\right)}$$

Income elasticity is thus measured by the percentage change in quantity demanded divided by the percentage change in income. If the coefficient is greater than 1, the quantity demanded is sensitive to changes in income, and demand is elastic. If it is less than 1, demand is inelastic with respect to income. A coefficient of exactly 1 means that the income elasticity of demand is unitary. There is usually a positive correlation between changes in quantity demanded and changes in income. With respect to some goods, however, the correlation between changes in quantity demanded and changes in income is negative, i.e., quantity demanded will change in an opposite direction to changes in income (see Fig. 6-1). We have noted that such goods are designated "inferior." Where the correlation between changes in quantity demanded and changes in income is positive, the coefficient of income elasticity is also a positive number. In the comparatively rare instances when the correlation is negative, the degree of elasticity is generally not considered important. On a purely formal basis, however, elasticity in such a situation can be calculated in the usual way. The coefficient of elasticity would then be a negative figure, and the negative sign should be retained.

FIG. 6-1   Income Elasticity of Demand

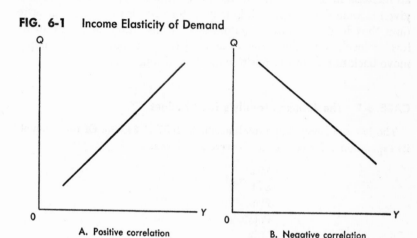

A. Positive correlation   B. Negative correlation

You may recall that in Chapter 2 we indicated that the quantity demanded in the income demand schedule could be expressed either in physical units or dollar amounts. Regardless of which method is used, the income elasticity will be the same, as may be seen by referring to Figs. 2-4 and 2-5. A change in income from $2,000 to $3,000 results in a change in quantity demanded from 10 to 20, or a change in dollar amount demanded from $50 to $100. The coefficient of income elasticity between those two points is 1.67 in either case.

Just as in the case of price elasticity, there is no basis for assuming that the coefficient of income elasticity for a commodity is the same at all points on the income demand schedule. On the contrary, it is highly likely that it is different at different levels of income.

Similarly, the time element must also be considered when discussing income elasticity of demand. If we are interested in the effect on the quantity demanded of a change from one level of income to another, we must recognize that the answer may depend in part upon whether the new level of income has just been reached or has prevailed for some time.

Finally, we may note that income elasticity of demand measures movement along a given income demand schedule, with other variables impounded in *ceteris paribus*. Once we permit changes in taste or relative prices, we are no longer dealing with the pure income effect. For example, time series data which show the quantity of a commodity bought in various years, and also show the level of income in those years, may or may not indicate the income elasticity of demand. Also, an increase in income which leads to changes in expenditure within a given income demand schedule may in turn result in changes in taste (and thus lead to a new schedule). If income then decreases to its former level, we cannot always assume that expenditure will simply move back to the former position on the old schedule.[1]

CASE 6-1   The Johnson family's food budget

The Johnson family had a total income in 1957 of $4,000. Of this amount, its expenditures for certain foods were as follows:

Meat	$110
Salt	1
Fruit	24
Potatoes	10
Milk	140

In 1958, the family's income rose to $5,000, and its expenditures for the same items were as follows:

Meat	$150
Salt	1
Fruit	30
Potatoes	9
Milk	155

Questions

1. What assumptions must be made in order to use the above data to show income elasticity of demand?
2. Having made these assumptions, show the relations between income and demand in the above situations graphically.
3. Calculate the income elasticity of demand of the Johnson family for the various foods listed.
4. Can we assume that the Johnson family's income elasticity of demand for these foods would be the same at all levels of income?

---

[1] This problem of irreversibility may sometimes arise in connection with price demand schedules as well.

CASE 6-2   Income elasticities for farm products, I

In an article attempting to project future demand for farm products, the following coefficients of income elasticity of demand were used. These coefficients were ". . . approximations . . . based on consumer-purchase surveys, time-series analysis, and judgment of commodity specialists. . . ." [2]

Tomatoes	.40	Wheat and flour	−.20
Potatoes and		Dry beans and peas	−.20
sweet potatoes	−.25	Sugar	−.07
All vegetables	.25		
Citrus fruits	.65	Beef	.40
All fruit	.32	Pork	.20
		All meat	.25
Chicken and turkey	.30	Fluid milk and cream	.12
Eggs	.15	Fats and oils	.06

Questions

1. How would you explain the meaning of the above figures in nontechnical terms?
2. On the basis of these results, what predictions would you make concerning the future per capita demand for farm products if income rises? If income falls?

CASE 6-3   Income elasticities for farm products, II

"Neither population increases nor prospects in per capita consumption of agricultural products will cause large premiums to be placed on prices and incomes in agriculture. The income elasticity of demand for agricultural products in aggregate is too low at the U.S. stage of economic development for any great increase in per capita consumption of the aggregate farm product. Economic development and a growing national income can cause sizable increases in per capita intake of food in nations such as Asia where hunger is often widespread. However, the elasticity coefficient declines with economic growth and a rise in family incomes. The high stage of economic development in the U.S. causes consumers to place more food at a low level in their ordering of wants. The elasticity coefficient for food in aggregate for the U.S. is somewhat less than 0.3. . . . It is only slightly higher for all farm products (including nonfood commodities). The coefficient will decline further as per capita in-

[2] Rex F. Daly, "The Long-Run Demand for Farm Products," *Agricultural Economics Research*, Vol. 27, No. 3, July 1956, p. 80.

comes increase. This low elasticity, and the inability of our growing economy to spiral food consumption to any great level, is emphasized by the fact that food intake in pounds per person in the United States has not increased in 45 years. . . . There are more Americans who worry about overeating than there are who suffer hunger pangs. The period of economic growth ahead will cause the greatest relative increase in demand in nonagricultural industries where products have elasticity coefficients ranging upwards from 1.0 and characterize consumption patterns of a wealthy society. Statements to this point merely emphasize that foreseeable growth of the U.S. economy will neither (1) be restricted by agricultural output in the sense of a Malthusian restraint on the size and quality of the labor force or (2) call for any greater increase in aggregate output than is now in sight from changes occasioned by the present rate of investment in capital and innovation for agriculture. Just as predictions of aggregate outcome may rest largely on the income elasticity of demand, this same coefficient can be used to suggest differential changes in the make-up of the aggregate agricultural product. . . ." [3]

Questions

1. Is the argument in this case based on income elasticity of demand, or on a shift in the income demand schedule? Explain.
2. If income elasticity of demand is to be used to predict changes in the make-up of the aggregate agricultural product, what other factors would have to be considered?
3. In 1929 consumer expenditures for food and tobacco were 25.5% of disposable personal income, while in 1953 they were 30.8%. Real per capita disposable income was approximately 50% higher in 1953 than in 1929. How do you reconcile these facts with the arguments of the preceding cases?

CASE 6-4   Changing number and kind of retail shops

According to the findings of two British economists, in both the U.S. and Canada there appears to have been a historical tendency for the number of shops engaged in selling the staples or necessaries of consumption to decline relative to the population. By contrast, in both countries the relative number of shops selling luxury goods has generally increased. The findings of the study are summarized in the table on page 163; on the basis of this study and of a previous study which showed a similar pattern of development in Great Britain, the tentative conclusions given here were advanced.

[3] Earl O. Heady, "Adjustments in Production to a Growing Economy," *Journal of Farm Economics,* Vol. 37, December 1955, pp. 1062–63. Reprinted by permission.

United States and Canada: Retail and Service Trades—Historical Changes in Numbers of Shops Relative to Population, by Major Kinds of Business Groups

KINDS OF BUSINESS BY MAJOR GROUPS	NUMBER OF SHOPS PER 10,000 POPULATION				GENERAL CHARACTERISTICS OF GOODS RETAILED
	U.S.A.		Canada		
	1929	1948	1930	1951	
Grocery group and other food retailer	42.9	36.1	46.6	36.4	Necessaries
Confectioners, tobacconists, and news agents	8.8	3.7	11.7	8.3	Necessaries
Clothing group	12.7	10.2	13.3	14.4	Intermediate
Hardware group	4.6	5.2	4.8	5.5	Luxuries
Booksellers and stationers	0.6	0.5	0.4	0.5	Luxuries
Chemists' goods and photographic goods group	4.8	4.0	3.5	3.2	Intermediate
Furniture group	3.3	4.1	1.9	2.2	Luxuries
Jewelry, leather, and sports goods group	2.3	2.9	2.0	2.9	Luxuries
General group	1.3	1.6	0.6	1.5	Intermediate
Coal, builders' materials, and corn group	7.0	5.3	4.5	2.8	Not consumers' goods
Other nonfood retailers	4.5	3.5	3.1	2.4	Luxuries
Catering group	11.0	13.3	5.5	10.0	Luxuries
Hairdressers	—	11.6	9.9	9.1	Luxuries
Funeral furnishers	—	1.3	0.8	0.8	Luxuries
Portrait photographers	—	0.8	0.7	0.8	Intermediate
Repairers group	—	6.3	6.1	5.4	Luxuries
Motor vehicles, cycles, and accessories group	5.9	6.1	3.6	4.8	Luxuries
Motor vehicle repairers and garages group	—	18.8	11.2	12.1	Luxuries
Total number of shops	—	135.2	130.2	123.1	
Total population	121,770,000	146,045,000	10,208,000	14,009,429	

"In view of the similarity between these patterns of development and the British, it is tempting to speak of what might be called the 'Ford effect.' This would reflect the fact that wherever productivity in distribution and the real income of the community both increase over fairly long periods of time, the relative number of shops selling necessaries will tend to decline, and the relative number of shops selling luxuries will tend to increase. This result would be the outcome of the joint action of two forces on the number of shops; first, the influence of increasing productivity, which tends to reduce the number of shops; and secondly, the influence of the increasing scale of real consumption as income rises, which tends to raise the number of shops. Both these forces operate on all trade groups, but the influence of increased real consumption on numbers of shops will be asymmetrical because of the tendency for a diminishing proportion of income to be spent on necessaries as income increases. Consequently, it is possible for the net result of the operation of the two forces we have distinguished to be consistent with our own and Professor Ford's findings for Great Britain, the United States, and Canada, even when the increase in productivity bears uniformly on all trades and, *a fortiori*, if there is a tendency for the increase in productivity to be larger in trades retailing staple articles of consumption." [4]

Questions

1. Do the argument and the table on page 163 bear out the contention that income elasticity of demand is higher for luxury goods than for necessaries? Why or why not?
2. What factors other than elasticity may account in part for the changes that are shown?
3. Have the major groups of businesses listed in the table been properly classified? How would you define a necessity and a luxury?
4. Does the level of income have any bearing on whether a commodity or service is a necessity or a luxury?

CASE 6-5   Income elasticity of demand for utility services

"Just as most small buyers seem to have a price inelasticity of demand for utility services, so they seem to have an income inelasticity of demand for the same services. Being unwilling to forego consumption of utility services, these buyers, as their incomes decline, are willing to spend increasing proportions of their incomes for such services. They reduce or eliminate expenditures on household furnishings, clothing, and even some kinds of foods before they pare down their expenditures on water, electric, gas, and possibly telephone services. The small monthly bills of domestic utility consumers, as well as personal dependence upon the services, account for the income inelasticities of demand. A family apparently can forego the purchase of high-price items such as an automobile, a rug, or fine clothing more easily than it can cut down expenditures of $10 to $15 a month on gas, electric, water, and telephone services. Families apparently consider utility services a basic part of their lives, something akin to a subsistence quantity of food. Income inelasticity of demand is an objective measurement of the indispensability of utility services.

Because the domestic consumers and other small buyers have an income inelasticity of demand for most utility services, utility firms enjoy

---

[4] Lady Hall and J. Knapp, "Number of Shops and Productivity in Retail Distribution in Great Britain, the United States, and Canada," *Economic Journal,* Vol. 45, No. 257, March 1955, pp. 86–87. Reprinted by permission.

a greater stability of revenue and earnings than do nearly all nonutility companies. During the thirties, for instance, the decrease in revenue of electric, gas, telephone, and water companies was not so great as that of the national income. Only the urban transportation industry experienced a great depression decrease in revenue and earnings. Substitution of private automobiles for street railway and bus service was a special reason, however, for the decrease of urban transportation revenue." [5]

Questions

1. Draw a typical income demand curve for utility services. Explain the shape of the curve.

2. Would you expect the utility industry to expand during a period of rising incomes? Why or why not?

3. One of the reasons given for the inelasticity of demand is that monthly bills for domestic utility consumers are small. Is this a valid reason? Why or why not?

CASE 6-6 Income elasticities of family expenditures

On the basis of a study of wage-earners' budgets for 1901 and 1918–19, and of farm-family budgets for 1922–24, two economists reached the following conclusions as to the effects of changes in family income upon family expenditures for various groups of goods and services:

1. Elasticity of expenditures upon food: In both the 1901 and the 1918–19 studies the coefficient of income elasticity at approximately average income was found to be near 0.6. The 1922–24 farm study, which used total expenditure as an independent variable instead of income, yielded comparable results. The authors state that, in their opinion, the fact that the income elasticity of expenditure is appreciably less than unity is one of the most important causes for the decline in the proportion of the working population engaged in agriculture.

2. Elasticity of expenditures upon clothing: In all three studies, the coefficient of income elasticity of expenditures upon clothing was somewhat greater than unity, being 1.1 or 1.2. The proportion of the total expenditures of the average farm family which went for clothing (approximately 15%) was somewhat less than the proportion of total income spent in 1918–19 by the average urban working-class family (approximately 16%). However, this difference in average expenditures was not so much caused by differences in income (an average of $1,632 for working-class families as opposed to an average of $1,600 for farm families) as by the fact that in rural life less emphasis is placed on clothing than in cities. In both cases, however, the

[5] Emery Troxel, *Economics of Public Utilities*, Rinehart, N.Y., 1947, pp. 43–44.

percentage spent for clothing was higher than was true of working-class families in 1901, when the proportion of total income spent by families with an average income of $750 was between 12 and 13 per cent. This increase, the authors state, was in part caused by the higher real incomes enjoyed by the average families in the later period, but may also have been caused by a shift through time of the demand curve for clothing by families of a given income level.

3. Elasticity of expenditures upon rent: All three studies showed that expenditures upon rent do not increase as rapidly as total income. This tendency, however, was far more marked in the case of the two earlier urban studies than in the later farm study. The income elasticity of expenditures for rent was from .70 to .75 for the middle-income group in 1901, and from .64 to .68 for the middle-income group in 1918–19. The elasticity of expenditures for rent for the 1922–24 middle-income group of farm families was close to, but slightly less than, unity.

4. Elasticity of expenditures upon fuel and light: The coefficient of elasticity for fuel alone for the 1901 middle-income group was found to be somewhere around .40, and for fuel and light combined approximately .50. In 1918–19 the coefficient for the combined group was also found to be approximately .50. There was thus a marked degree of constancy over time in the relative elasticity of expenditures for these purposes. The authors conclude that the very low income elasticity of expenditures for fuel is one of the reasons for the relative decline in the proportions of the working class engaged in coal mining. As real income has risen, the amounts spent upon fuel for domestic use have not increased correspondingly, and this has operated to squeeze workers out of this industry into other fields.

5. Elasticity of expenditures upon furniture and furnishings: The 1918–19 study showed expenditures for these purposes to have an elasticity of something greater than unity, ranging between 1.14 and 1.23. The 1922–24 set of farm families similarly showed coefficients for a similar but not identical group of "furniture and portable equipment" of somewhere between 1.24 and 1.36.

6. Elasticity of expenditures for miscellaneous purposes: Expenditures for other miscellaneous items tended to increase more rapidly than either total expenditures or income. In 1901, the coefficient of income elasticity for these purposes for the middle-income group was only between 1.0 and 1.19. In 1918–19, it was close to the latter figure. In 1922–24, among the middle-income farm families the elasticity of expenditures was as high as 1.74. This high degree of elasticity was particularly marked in the case of expenditures for advancement (e.g., education).[6]

---

[6] Based on H. Gregg Lewis and Paul H. Douglas, "Studies in Consumer Expenditures, 1901, 1918–19, 1922–24," *The Journal of Business of the University of Chicago*, Vol. 20, No. 3, October 1947, Part 2.

Questions

1. Can you suggest reasons why the different types of expenditures have different income elasticities?

2. How would you describe the impact of income elasticity of expenditure upon the growth of particular industries? What other factors would play an important part in such growth?

3. How do you account for the change or the lack of change in the coefficient of elasticity between the earlier and the later periods? Would it have made any difference if the studies had covered the same group of families at three different periods instead of three separate groups?

CASE 6-7   Income elasticity of consumer expenditures, I

The following chart shows how expenditures on four consumer items varied by income groups in 1950: [7]

FIG. 6-2   Consumer Expenditure at Various Levels of Income, 1950

Per cent of total income

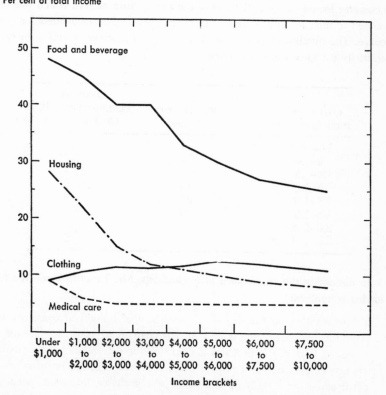

Income brackets

[7] Based on *Study of Consumer Expenditures, Incomes, and Savings*, Vol. 2, *Summary of Family Expenditures for Current Consumption*, Wharton School of Finance and Commerce, University of Pennsylvania, Philadelphia, 1956, p. 10.

Questions

1. To what extent does this chart substantiate the findings in the previous case?
2. Calculate the income elasticity of demand for the different types of expenditure between incomes of $3,500 and $4,500.

CASE 6-8   Income elasticity of consumer expenditures, II

In 1945 Mr. Louis J. Paradiso, Chief of the Business Statistics Unit of the Bureau of Foreign and Domestic Commerce, U.S. Department of Commerce, classified 174 items of consumer expenditure according to their sensitivity to changes in disposable income. The basis for the classification was the coefficient of income elasticity of demand, which was calculated in the following manner. Consumer expenditure for each good was plotted separately as a function of disposable income for the period from 1929 through 1940. Curves were then fitted to this data, with an allowance made wherever necessary for any long-term trend in the expenditure pattern which was unrelated to income. The coefficient of elasticity was then calculated for each curve. The number of goods and the extent of consumer spending in each elasticity category were as follows:

COEFFICIENT OF INCOME ELASTICITY	NUMBER OF GOODS	CONSUMER EXPENDITURES, 1939 (*billion dollars*)
Less than 0	5	.2
0– .4	24	6.2
.4– .8	49	21.4
.8–1.2	53	29.5
1.2–1.6	25	5.6
1.6–2.0	8	1.2
2.0–3.0	6	2.2
3.0 and over	4	.2

In discussing the significance of his findings, Mr. Paradiso made the following comments:

"Information on the degree of sensitivity of individual consumer expenditure items or groups of items to changes in consumer income is useful in that (1) it provides a yardstick for determining the probable change in demand for a product with the change in the business cycle, (2) it serves as a basis for estimating the probable maximum potential demand for consumer goods, and thus throws light on policies relating to production, employment, and capital expansion, and (3) it meets the need for information to appraise changes in raw material requirements, import requirements, and other problems related to supply and demand for consumption goods." [8]

Questions

1. Does Mr. Paradiso's method yield an income demand curve as defined in the text? Why or why not?
2. What is the purpose of allowing for a long-term trend?
3. To what extent do you agree or disagree with Mr. Paradiso's conclusions concerning the usefulness of his findings?

CASE 6-9   Income elasticity of demand for imports

According to government statistics, the national income of the United States in 1937 was $73.6 billion. In 1938 it fell to $67.6 billion. In 1937 the index of the quantity of imports into the United States stood at 93 (1948 = 100); in 1938 it fell to 67.

Questions

1. Assuming that there were no changes other than income which affected the volume of imports, calculate the income elasticity of demand for imports over the range indicated.
2. What does this result suggest as to the nature of United States imports?
3. If we assume that prices of imports fell more than did domestic prices from 1937 to 1938, but that tastes remained constant, would the *true* income elasticity of demand for imports be greater or smaller than the coefficient calculated from the figures given above?

CROSS ELASTICITY OF DEMAND

We have seen that the concept of elasticity is used to describe the relationship between quantity and price or between quantity and income. Another interesting application of the concept is with respect to changes in quantity demanded as a response to one of the other determinants of demand, namely, the price of some other good. This measure is known as cross elasticity of demand; it is given by the percentage change in quantity demanded of good A divided by the percentage change in the price of good B, other things being equal.

For example, consider the impact of changes in the price of butter on the demand for margarine. We assume a fixed price for margarine and unchanging tastes. The quantity of margarine demanded will

<hr>

[8] Louis J. Paradiso, "Classification of Consumer Expenditures by Income-Elasticity," *Survey of Current Business*, January 1945, pp. 7–8.

then vary with changes in the price of butter, as illustrated by the following schedule:

PRICE OF BUTTER	QUANTITY OF MARGARINE DEMANDED AT PRICE $.30
$1.00	500
.90	480
.80	460
.70	430
.60	350
.50	250
.40	100
.30	50
.20	10

We may calculate the cross elasticity of demand of margarine with respect to butter (e_{mpb}), using the formula for arc elasticity, as follows:

$$e_{mpb} = \frac{Q_{m_1} - Q_{m_2}}{\left(\dfrac{Q_{m_1} + Q_{m_2}}{2}\right)} \div \frac{P_{b_1} - P_{b_2}}{\left(\dfrac{P_{b_1} + P_{b_2}}{2}\right)}$$

where Q means quantity, P means price, the subscripts m and b refer to margarine and butter, and the subscripts 1 and 2 refer to the two points on the schedule or curve.

If the two commodities are good substitutes for one another, the cross elasticity of demand will be high; if they are not, it will be low. If the two goods bear a complementary relationship to one another, the coefficient of cross elasticity will be negative. This means that increases in the price of one good (e.g., golf clubs) will lead to decreases in the quantity demanded of the second good (e.g., golf balls) and vice versa. If two goods are completely unrelated, the coefficient of cross elasticity would be about zero.

CASE 6-10   Which bus do you ride?

The Fifth Avenue Bus Company and The Fourth Avenue Bus Company are owned and managed by different groups. A few years ago the Fifth Avenue Company increased its fare from ten cents per ride to twelve cents. The Fourth Avenue Company did not change its fare, and found that, as a result of the increase by its rival, the number of fares collected increased from 40,000 to 50,000 per day.

Questions

1. Calculate the cross elasticity of demand for Fourth Avenue bus rides with respect to Fifth Avenue bus prices.
2. Is the relationship one of complements or substitutes? How can you tell?
3. Suppose the Fourth Avenue line had raised its price from ten cents to twelve cents, and the Fifth Avenue line had kept its fare at ten cents. Would the coefficient of cross elasticity of Fifth Avenue with respect to Fourth Avenue necessarily have been the same as in Question 1?

CASE 6-11   The du Pont cellophane case

In a civil action brought in the courts by the Department of Justice against the du Pont Company, the government charged that the company had monopolized interstate commerce in violation of the Sherman Act in the production and sale of cellophane. The evidence showed that during the period from 1923 to 1947, the du Pont Company produced almost 75% of the cellophane sold in the United States. It was also true, however, that cellophane constituted less than 20% of all flexible packaging materials sold in the U.S. during this period. One of the important questions that the courts had to decide was whether the relevant market for determining the extent of du Pont's market control was that of cellophane alone, or of all flexible packaging materials.

On June 11, 1956, the Supreme Court of the United States decided in favor of the du Pont Company. In the opinion of the majority of the Supreme Court Justices, cellophane's interchangeability with numerous other materials sufficed to make it a part of the market for flexible packaging materials in every one of its uses. Cellophane, it was pointed out, furnished less than 7% of wrappings for bakery products, 25% for candy, 32% for snacks, 35% for meat and poultry, 27% for crackers and biscuits, 47% for fresh produce, 34% for frozen foods, and 75 to 80% for cigarettes. Cellophane thus shared the packaging market with others. Measured by wrapping surface, cellophane accounted for only 17.9% of flexible wrapping materials. The majority were also of the opinion that there was great "sensitivity" of customers in the flexible packaging markets to price or quality changes in cellophane, which they regarded as further proof that the market was broader than cellophane alone.

A minority of the Supreme Court Justices took another view. In a dissenting opinion, three of the nine Justices expressed the opinion that the market for cellophane was a distinctive one. They found it hard to believe that buyers who were practical businessmen would have bought cellophane in increasing amounts over a quarter of a century if other packaging materials, selling at from one-seventh to one-half cellophane's price, were really close substitutes. They also found confirmation of their views in the conduct of sellers other than du Pont. They noted that Sylvania, the only other cellophane producer, absolutely and immediately followed every du Pont price change, even dating back its price list to the effective date of du Pont's change. On the other hand, they found that producers of other types of flexible packaging materials displayed apparent indifference to du Pont's repeated and substantial price cuts. During the period 1924 to 1932, it was pointed out, du Pont dropped the price of plain cellophane 84%, while the price of glassine remained constant; moreover, during the period 1933 to 1946 the prices for glassine and wax paper actually increased in the face of a further 21% decline in the price of cellophane. If "shifts of business" due to "price sensitivity" had been substantial, it was argued, glassine and wax paper producers who wanted to stay in business would have been compelled by market forces to meet du Pont's price challenge. The fact that producers of glassine and wax paper remained dominant in the flexible packaging materials market without meeting cellophane's tremendous price cuts convinced the three Justices that cellophane was not in effective competition with these products.[9]

Questions

1. Show how the concept of cross elasticity of demand is implicit in the reasoning in both the majority and minority opinions of the Court.
2. On the basis of the facts that are given, do you agree with the majority or the minority opinion? Why?

CASE 6-12 Cross elasticity of demand for cigarettes

"The principal factors which determine whether there is a willingness to make a substitution are the price and quality of the products and the taste preferences of the purchasers. . . . The cigarette 'war' of the 1930's, with its oscillating demand for burley blend cigarettes, provides an excellent example of the dynamic interplay between price, quality, and taste. At the start of the battle popular cigarette consumption was almost entirely limited to the 'big-name' burley brands, which retailed for fifteen cents per pack, but when a number of independent companies produced a different blend to sell at ten cents per pack, a substantial portion of smokers switched to the newer, cheaper brands. Admittedly, the cheaper cigarettes were less desirable. That almost all smokers preferred the 'big-name' brands for taste is evidenced by the fact that when these companies reduced their cigarettes to thirteen cents per pack, they drove the independents out of the market. Thus to the average smoker, the five

---

[9] Based on United States v. E. I. du Pont de Nemours and Company, 351 U.S. 377.

cent saving made up for the difference in quality and taste; the three cent saving did not." [10]

Questions

1. Indicate how the cross-elasticity concept is used in this situation.
2. Can you say whether the cross elasticity of demand was elastic or inelastic?
3. What additional information would you need to calculate the coefficient of cross elasticity?
4. In your opinion, why haven't mass distributors, such as grocery chains or large department stores, put out their own brands of cigarettes at lower prices, as they have done for other commodities, such as liquor, drugs, and canned goods?

ELASTICITY OF SUPPLY

The elasticity concept is also applicable to the supply schedule, i.e., the relationship between the price of a commodity and the quantity that will be produced or offered for sale at that price. Elasticity of supply is the measure of the percentage change in the quantity supplied relative to percentage change in price. If the quantity supplied is highly responsive to changes in price, supply is elastic. If a change in price results in a relatively small change in the quantity supplied, supply is inelastic. If the change in price is accompanied by a proportionately equal change in quantity supplied, elasticity is unitary. As in the case of elasticity of demand, we may measure elasticity of supply either at a point on the supply curve, or between two points, depending on whether we treat the variables as continuous or discontinuous.

The formula for point elasticity of supply is:

$$\frac{dQ}{Q} \div \frac{dP}{P}$$

while the formula for arc elasticity of supply is:

$$\frac{Q_1 - Q_2}{\left(\dfrac{Q_1 + Q_2}{2}\right)} \div \frac{P_1 - P_2}{\left(\dfrac{P_1 + P_2}{2}\right)}$$

Since price changes and changes in quantity supplied generally move in the same direction, the coefficient of elasticity of supply is usually positive. The size of the coefficient may vary from 0 to infinity. A co-

[10] "The Market: A Concept in Anti-Trust," 54 *Columbia Law Review* 580, pp. 588–90, 1954. © by the Directors of the Columbia Law Review Association, Inc.

efficient of 1 is unitary elasticity. If the value of the coefficient lies between 0 and 1, supply is inelastic, while a value of greater than 1 but less than infinity denotes an elastic supply. An elasticity coefficient of infinity signifies that supply is perfectly elastic, which means that any amount will be supplied at the existing price. A coefficient of 0, on the other hand, means that supply is perfectly inelastic and that the same quantity will be supplied at any price.

CASE 6-13   The supply of fresh strawberries

During the season as many as 1,400 dozen cases of fresh strawberries can arrive at the New York City produce markets in a single day. These strawberries are highly perishable, and if not sold within a day of arrival must be discarded. Once the owners have consigned them to New York, they must be sold at the best price obtainable.

Questions

1. How would you describe the supply situation in the above case? Show it graphically.
2. Would the long-run supply curve look the same? Why or why not?

CASE 6-14   The supply of cashmere

"Cashmere, 'the wool of emperors,' stands in danger of pricing itself out of a new-found American market. . . .

[One leader in the field] credits higher incomes, suburban living, and air conditioning for rising demand over the past half-dozen years for cashmere sweaters and shawls, coats, suits and skirts. . . .

For years, cashmere was largely a British monopoly. One company, Joseph A. Dawson, Ltd., did most of the business, purchasing the fiber in China, removing the coarse outer 'garde' hair, and selling the soft inner down to spinners who in turn sold yarn to Scottish knitters.

During World War II, the Russians began sending cashmere from Outer Mongolia to the United States in the empty bottoms of Liberty ships returning from the Murmansk run. One American says he purchased some of this fiber at 46 cents a pound, which compares with $6 a pound today.

After the war, one or two companies began purchasing cashmere from Iran. Although admittedly of coarser texture than the Chinese or Mongolian cashmere, and hence unsuitable for knitting, the Iranian product was well adapted to weaving. . . .

Iranian cashmere, priced then at 90 cents to $1 a pound brings $4 today—if a buyer can be found. Manufacturers say they are staying out of the market until the price situation improves. If necessary, they add, they are prepared to lose part of their season. . . .

The Chinese clip has been diverted to Britain and Japan. And since for a time the Chinese cashmere was sold cheaper, the British and Japanese were able to sell knit goods in the American market at prices below those of American mills.

Today, this differential has been eliminated. Prices have risen because supplies can't be increased. Cashmere is combed or plucked from the goats in their spring moulting season by seminomadic people, who use the animals also for milk and for meat.

The fact that the goats live at great heights in regions of extreme winter cold, wide day-and-night temperature variations, and sparse vegetation makes it difficult to expect a great increase in their numbers. . . .

Although statistics are vague, these persons estimate that production has averaged 1,500 long tons a year from China, 1,000 tons a year from Outer Mongolia, and 2,000 tons a year from Iran. There has been no increase in a generation, they say. . . .

Manufacturers say they do not expect to see cashmere sweaters, priced now at $25, back at the $15 level they held before the war.

But makers who have seen their products climb from one price level to the next are beginning to be concerned." [11]

Questions

1. How would you describe the supply situation for cashmere? Show this on a graph.
2. Why have cashmere prices risen to such heights? What part has supply played in this rise?
3. Is the supply curve for cashmere likely to change in the long run? Why or why not?

CASE 6-15   Elasticity of supply for agricultural products, I

"The tendency of agriculture in modern economic society to maintain a high level of production in depression periods has never failed to receive attention at such times. . . .

In terms of conventional equilibrium analysis, the factors which cause agriculture to maintain its output must have to do with the supply curve. Certain popular discussion runs in terms of a 'stable' demand for agricultural products during depression, which is met in turn by a stable flow of supplies. But such an argument is tenable only if the demand is effective in maintaining stable prices. Actually farm prices tend to fall more

---

[11] Albert L. Kraus, "Price Rises Imperil Sales of Cashmere," New York *Times*, September 16, 1956. © 1956 by The New York Times Company.

quickly and farther than the prices of other products; it is in the face of this that supplies tend to remain fairly constant. . . .

In dealing with the supply curve we must keep forcibly in mind at all times that we are dealing with a curve of aggregate agricultural output. Much of the confused discussion of supply responses . . . has arisen from simple failure of the expositors to state whether they were speaking of one product or all farm products. . . . For most individual farm products, the evidence is that their output is highly responsive to price changes if a little time is allowed for adjustment. . . . But if the response in question is that of the total output of a given group of farms, then it is indeed slow. . . ." [12]

Questions

1. On the basis of the above discussion, how would you describe elasticity of supply for agricultural products as a whole? For individual products?
2. Can you explain why this difference exists?
3. Show the two situations on a graph.

CASE 6-16 Elasticity of supply for agricultural products, II

YEAR	RELATIVE FARM PRICES (1910–1914 = 100)	CROP ACREAGE PLANTED (in millions)
1919	112	363
20	121	359
21	88	358
22	85	354
23	101	353
24	101	353
25	106	364
26	100	359
27	99	358
28	102	367
29	101	363
30	106	368
31	73	372
32	62	376
33	67	372
34	73	339
35	86	360
36	91	360
37	90	364
38	78	356
39	78	344

[12] J. K. Galbraith and J. D. Black, "The Maintenance of Agricultural Production During Depression," *Journal of Political Economy*, Vol. 47, No. 3, June 1939, pp. 305–08. © 1939 by the University of Chicago.

The table on page 176 shows relative farm prices (i.e., prices received by farmers relative to prices paid by farmers) and total crop acreage in the U.S. for the period from 1919 to 1939.[13]

Questions

1. Is "crop acreage" a good measure of farm output for the purpose of calculating elasticity? Why or why not?
2. To what extent do these figures bear out the statements made in the previous case?

CASE 6-17   Elasticity of supply for agricultural products, III

In an article which sought to determine the response of the production of cotton and cottonseed to changes in price, the following coefficients of elasticity of supply were derived: [14]

	COEFFICIENTS OF ELASTICITY OF SUPPLY	
	1910–1924	*1925–1933*
1. Acreage related to composite price of cotton and cottonseed	0.24	0.22
2. Acreage related to price of cotton	.25	.22
3. Acreage related to price of cottonseed	.11	.22

Questions

1. To what extent do these results bear out the statements made in Case 6-15? How would you explain this?

CASE 6-18   The supply of labor in a one-company town

The ABC Woolen Company is the only large employer in a small town in New England, and most of the people in the town work for the company. Recently the company found it necessary to reduce wages by 20 per cent. As a result, 75 men and women out of a total force of 850 quit their jobs.

[13] D. Gale Johnson, "The Nature of the Supply Function for Agricultural Products," *American Economic Review*, Vol. 40, No. 4, September 1950, p. 549. © 1950 by the American Economic Association.

[14] Robert M. Walsh, "Response to Price in Production of Cotton and Cottonseed," *Journal of Farm Economics*, Vol. 26, No. 2, May 1944, p. 366. Reprinted by permission.

Questions

1. Is the supply of labor facing the ABC Woolen Company elastic or inelastic? What reasons can you suggest to explain this situation?
2. Calculate the coefficient of elasticity of supply using the above figures.
3. Would the situation be more or less elastic in the long run? Why?

CASE 6-19   The supply of chemical engineers

The XYZ Chemical Corp., a very large producer of industrial chemicals, was faced with the problem of doubling the number of chemical engineers employed in its research laboratories. In order to accomplish this the company found it necessary to raise the salaries paid to chemical engineers by 25 per cent.

Questions

1. Would you describe the supply of chemical engineers facing the XYZ Chemical Corp. as elastic or inelastic? Explain your answer.
2. Using the above figures, calculate the coefficient of elasticity of supply.
3. In your opinion, would the supply of chemical engineers facing all chemical companies combined be more or less elastic? Why?

CASE 6-20   Elasticity of supply for labor

In an article discussing the labor force in the United States, Professor Clarence D. Long raises the following question concerning the response of the labor force to increases and decreases in real wages:

"A primary question has always concerned whether the supply of all labor to all employers might actually decline as average real wages rise; and, conversely, as real wages decline, whether a larger aggregate stream of labor might pour into the market from workers struggling to maintain their standards of life.

This question concerns also the magnitude of the response. Suppose it turns out to be certain, as many economists perhaps from occupational cynicism have surmised, that more pay brings really less work to market. How great relatively might be the fall in supply that accompanies a given rise in real incomes? Could it be so great that labor may be said with some truth to desire only a constant living standard and to show no more gratitude to the industrial system than to reduce its availability for work in equal proportion to the rise in its wages? This position was taken by the ancient mercantilists. It is still defended by some employers of native labor in areas remote from civilization. . . .

In partial contrast, might modern labor, while substantially reducing its offerings, nevertheless temper its desire for leisure by withdrawing labor in smaller proportion than the real wage increase? A statistical conclusion of this sort was reached by Paul Douglas in a pioneer study of several years ago, and has been accepted generally by economists as showing that the short-run supply curve of labor is mainly inelastic and yet does have considerable (negative) slope. If that conclusion were sound, it would mean that increases in income would be accompanied by declining percentages of the population in the labor force. . . ." [15]

Questions

1. Show the short-run supply curve for labor as described by Paul Douglas.
2. How does this supply curve differ from that of the supply curve for labor for a particular firm or industries? What is the reason for this difference?

CASE 6-21   Wheat on Central Island

Central Island is a small Pacific island which grows no wheat of its own, but must import all the wheat requirements for a population of 10,000. The price of wheat imported into Central Island was $2.37 per bushel. Then the Central Island government imposed an import duty of 50 cents per bushel on wheat. Subsequently, the price on the island rose to $2.87 per bushel, the pre-duty price remained constant at $2.37, and the amount of wheat imported declined.

Questions

1. In your opinion, why did the quantity of wheat imports decline?
2. How would you describe the supply of wheat facing Central Island? Show it graphically.
3. Does the supply of wheat facing the world as a whole also look like this? Explain.
4. Why did the price on Central Island rise by the full amount of the duty? Under what circumstances does the price of an imported article rise by less than the amount of the duty?

CASE 6-22   The supply of land, I

"The eastward expansion of Long Island suburbs may be slowed down by home builders' recovery of marginal meadowland in areas nearer to New York City. Most of this land has been previously passed over by builders seeking solid ground for home developments.

---

[15] Clarence D. Long, "The Labor Force and Economic Change," in Richard A. Lester and Joseph Shister, eds., *Insights Into Labor Issues,* pp. 331–32. Copyright, 1948 by The Macmillan Company, N.Y. Reprinted by permission.

Now they are turning back to reclaim land they once shunned. These developments in the recent housing market have caused the shift:

1. Having penetrated deeply into Suffolk County in search of land for sizable projects, developers now find that land costs there have risen to heights that make medium-priced homes almost prohibitive to build.

2. The Long Island suburbs have spread so far to the east that new dwellings are becoming unattractive to prospective purchasers who face daily commuting to the city. Many builders concede frankly that they must sell homes in Suffolk primarily to persons who work on Long Island.

The once-shunned sites are on the south shore of Nassau County between Lawrence and Bellmore. They are marginal because they do not rise sufficiently above sea level for simple construction projects.

But developers now find that, at current prices, these sites can profitably be turned into prime land. . . .

Developers of marginal areas agree that one of their biggest tasks is that of educating the home-seeking public to the value of such land. This means that they have to overcome a certain amount of prejudice resulting from public unfamiliarity with the situation.

The builders contend that, once such land is created, sometimes at the rate of two acres a day, it is as good or better than conventional sites. . . ." [16]

(Note: Nassau County adjoins New York City; Suffolk County occupies the eastern portion of Long Island.)

Questions

1. The supply of land is often spoken of as being completely inelastic. Does the above support or refute this view?
2. Illustrate your conclusions graphically.
3. Once the land has been reclaimed, could you use the same curve to predict the effects of a decrease in the price of land?

CASE 6-23   The supply of land, II

"A tax on land values does not add to prices, and is thus paid directly by the persons on whom it falls; whereas, all taxes upon things of unfixed quantity increase prices, and in the course of exchange are shifted from seller to buyer, increasing as they go. If we impose a tax upon money loaned . . . the lender will charge the tax to the borrower, and the borrower must pay it or not obtain the loan. If the borrower uses it in his business, he in his turn must get back the tax from his customers, or his

---

[16] Walter H. Stern, "Builders Turning West on L.I.; Reclaim Meadows in Nassau," New York *Times*, April 14, 1957. © 1957 by The New York Times Company.

business becomes unprofitable. If we impose a tax upon buildings, the users of buildings must finally pay it, for the erection of buildings will cease until building rents become high enough to pay the regular profit and the tax besides. If we impose a tax upon manufactured or imported goods, the manufacturer or importer will charge it in a higher price to the jobber, the jobber to the retailer, and the retailer to the consumer. . . . In this way all taxes which add to prices are shifted from hand to hand, increasing as they go, until they rest upon consumers, who thus pay much more than is received by the government. Now, the way taxes raise prices is by increasing the cost of production, and checking supply. But land is not a thing of human production, and taxes upon rent cannot check supply. Therefore, though a tax on rent compels the land owners to pay more, it gives them no power to obtain more for the use of their land, as it in no way tends to reduce the supply of land. . . ." [17]

Questions

1. What assumptions must be made about elasticity of supply for land and for other goods in order to justify the above statements in regard to the shifting of taxes?

CASE 6-24   Forward and backward shifting of taxes

1. "The shifting of a tax will involve a change in the price of something from what it otherwise would have been. When the tax is shifted *forward*, the price which constitutes the vehicle for shifting will increase. If completely shifted the price will be higher than it otherwise would have been by the amount of the tax. . . .

When a tax is shifted *backward*, the price which constitutes the vehicle for shifting will decrease as compared with what it would have been. There are some situations in which the buyer of the product upon which taxes will be levied at a subsequent stage can shift a part or all of it backward to the seller in the form of a lower buying price. It is essential to distinguish real backward shifting from inability of a seller to shift the tax forward. . . . To determine whether the tax was partially shifted forward from seller to buyer, or partially shifted backward from buyer to seller, we must know upon whom government originally imposed the tax. If originally imposed upon the seller, we conclude that it was partially shifted forward; if originally imposed upon the buyer it was partially shifted backward." [18]

2. "A tax can be shifted only if the taxpayer can alter the supply of his

---

[17] Henry George, *Progress and Poverty*, Walter J. Black, N.Y., 1942, pp. 348–49.
[18] Philip E. Taylor, *The Economics of Public Finance*, pp. 302–03. Copyright, 1948 by The Macmillan Company, N.Y. Reprinted by permission.

goods or services, or his demand for some other product or factor of production. This he can do only if he is in a position to enter into a subsequent price transaction. Shifting may be forward or backward, and the extent of shifting will be determined by the resistance on the part of those to whom it is attempted to shift the tax. . . . The less elastic the supply of the goods or factors bought by the taxed individual, the more easily the tax can be passed backward. The less elastic the demand for the goods or services sold by the taxpayer, the more easily the tax can be passed forward. . . ." [19]

Questions

1. Assume that the government levies a tax upon a producer, thereby adding the amount of the tax to the cost of production. Show the effect of this on price and quantity sold in the following situations:
   a. Where supply and demand are both relatively elastic
   b. Where supply is elastic but demand is completely inelastic
   c. Where supply is completely inelastic but demand is elastic
   d. Where supply and demand are both relatively inelastic

2. In each of these situations, indicate the extent to which the tax has been shifted.

[19] Kenyon E. Poole, *Public Finance and Economic Welfare*, Rinehart, N.Y., 1956, pp. 145–46. © 1956 by Rinehart and Company, Inc.

CHAPTER SEVEN

Maximization and Marginal Analysis

MAXIMIZATION

Economics has been defined as the "science which studies human behavior as a relationship between ends and scarce means which have alternative uses." If means are scarce, not all the ends can be attained. One acts "economically," however, by using the scarce means to obtain as much of the ends as possible, i.e., to *maximize* the ends. In formal economics, economic behavior is maximizing behavior. This may take many forms. A student, for example, may try to maximize his average grade; a small boy may try to maximize the pleasure of a trip to an amusement park. In the one case, the scarce resource is time available for study; in the second, it is the limited size of the allowance. The act of maximizing implies doing the best you can, given the circumstances in which you find yourself.

In studying a private enterprise economy, we are most interested in two chief types of maximizing behavior: consumer behavior as an attempt to maximize satisfaction, and business behavior as an attempt to maximize profit. These two aspects of maximization are discussed in detail in this chapter. State planning and public policy in general are presumably designed to maximize the welfare of the state or the welfare of the people as a group. The logic and analysis of such maximization are more complicated than that of the consumer or the firm, and are generally treated in more advanced works on economic theory and welfare economics.

The concept of maximization is closely related to another concept we have already encountered, that of equilibrium. We have seen that various parts of the economic system are in equilibrium when the forces which act upon them are in balance. The equilibrium of quantity and price in a particular market is based on a balance of supply and demand. This balance, in turn, requires that each demander and supplier in that market be at a position where he has no desire to change. Unless each demander and each supplier has achieved individual equilibrium, the forces of demand and supply cannot be said to be in perfect balance. A consumer is said to be in equilibrium when, given his income, his tastes, and the prices of goods, he allocates his income in a manner which he believes maximizes his satisfaction. A business firm is said to be in equilibrium when, given the state of technology, the demand for its product, and the supply schedules of the factors of production, it chooses a rate of output and a combination of factors which will maximize profit (or minimize loss).

What has been said about the usefulness of the concept of equilibrium applies as well to maximization. The concept is important, not because all consumers and all business firms are always at their maximum positions, but because it shows us the direction toward which they are trying to move. By assuming a desire to maximize, we can deduce theories or hypotheses about how people will react to changes in tastes, technology, prices, etc. The test of the concept, therefore, does not depend upon whether maximization is a perfect description of reality, but upon whether the hypotheses we can derive by using this concept do in fact offer reliable guides for prediction.

Our general law of demand, for example, is based in part upon maximization. When the price of a good decreases, a consumer who is trying to maximize satisfaction will normally find that this can be accomplished by buying more of the good whose price has decreased, and less of certain other goods which might serve as substitutes for the first good. Likewise, when the price of a good rises, he will tend to buy less of that good and to substitute others in its place. Note that the concept of maximization does not imply that the consumer is as well off after a price increase as before it. It only suggests that, given the new price situation, he will try to adjust his spending so as to obtain as much satisfaction as possible.

Similarly, our theories about the reactions of businessmen to changes in demand, changes in technology, or changes in the prices of factors of production depend partly upon the assumption that the businessman is trying to make as much profit as he can. As these variables change, he will usually respond by increasing or decreasing output, changing the size of his plant, or substituting one factor of production for another. This response will normally be in the direction of greatest profit (or least loss) rather than the reverse. While all businessmen may not maximize at all times, the predictions based on such an assumption usually turn out to be far better than those based on any other simple model. We may observe that in very highly competitive industries, the businessman has no alternative to trying to maximize profit if he wishes to stay in business. In less competitive situations, the businessman has a somewhat greater range of possible behavior.

THE MARGIN

In studying maximizing behavior, a related concept of great importance is that of the margin. It is assumed that people or firms who seek to maximize their position generally start from a position that has already been established, and move gradually and experimentally to a new position. This type of change is said to take place *at the margin*. A producer may thus decide to add an extra worker to the payroll, or to increase production by a slight amount. We would refer to the extra worker as the marginal worker and to the increase in production as the marginal product. By making small changes of this kind, a person or firm can determine whether the change is in the direction of, or away from, maximization. Further adjustments can then be made in the light of this information.

According to many economists, the concept of the margin is the single most important tool of economic analysis. Neoclassical as distinct from classical economics dates from the 1870's when three great economists, William Jevons in England, Carl Menger in Austria, and Leon Walras in France and Switzerland, developed and refined the marginal concept. Applications of this concept may be found in every field of economics. In this chapter we will be mainly concerned with four applications: the concepts of marginal revenue, marginal cost, marginal product, and marginal utility.

We can define the marginal concept more technically by stating it in terms of the relative rate of change in economic variables. We know from the expression $y = f(x)$ that changes in the variable y are related to changes in the variable x. One aspect of this relationship has already been described in our treatment of elasticity (Chapter 5), where elasticity was defined as the proportionate change in y related to the proportionate change in x, i.e., $\frac{dy}{y} \div \frac{dx}{x}$. We may now define a marginal magnitude as the ratio of the *absolute* change in y to the *absolute* change in x. It is simply dy/dx, where dy means a change in y, and dx means a change in x.

MARGINAL REVENUE

We can illustrate by using the concept of marginal revenue. A business firm's total revenue is obviously the quantity sold multiplied by the price of the goods sold. Marginal revenue, then, may be defined as the change in total revenue per unit change in the quantity sold. If we know the demand schedule for the firm's commodity, we can construct a table showing both total revenue and marginal revenue at various levels of sales, as is done in Table 7-1.

TABLE 7-1

PRICE	QUANTITY DEMANDED	TOTAL REVENUE	MARGINAL REVENUE (dTR/dQ)
$10	1	$10	$ 6
8	2	16	2
6	3	18	2
5	4	20	0
4	5	20	−2
3	6	18	−11
1	7	7	

Note that Table 7-1 has been set up so that in each case the quantity changes by exactly one unit. If such figures are available, calculation of marginal revenue is a very simple process; for each change in price and quantity, the marginal revenue is simply the difference in total revenue divided by 1. If the quantity changes by more (or less) than one unit for each change in price, however, it is necessary to divide the change in total revenue by the change in quantity to arrive at marginal revenue. Thus, if quantity in the schedule above had changed from 1 to 3 when the price changed from $10 to $8, marginal revenue would have been calculated as follows:

PRICE	QUANTITY DEMANDED	TOTAL REVENUE	MARGINAL REVENUE $(dTR/dQ = 14/2 = \$7)$
$10	1	$10	$7
8	3	24	

You should note one important fact about the two tables we have just presented: the marginal revenue figures are placed *between* successive total revenue figures, rather than on a line with them. This is done in order to indicate that the marginal revenue we are measuring is an average rate of change between two points on the schedule, rather than the rate of change at one point or the other.

We must bear in mind that although the marginal concept is most frequently stated as the rate of change in one variable per unit of a second related variable, what it really measures is the *ratio of the rates of change in the two variables*. As we have already seen, changes in two related variables can be tabulated in a single schedule or plotted as a single curve. We may think of the rate of change between two points on a schedule or curve, or we may think of the rate of change at a single point on the schedule or curve. The former involves finite changes, the latter infinitely small changes. The distinction is similar to the one between arc elasticity and point elasticity. As in the case of elasticity, the rate of change at a single point offers a more precise definition of the concept, but the rate of change between two points is more fruitful in practical application.

The application of the marginal concept can easily be visualized graphically. If we wish to measure the marginal revenue *between* points A and B on the total revenue curve in Fig. 7-1, we simply find the point at which a horizontal line from A (the old price-quantity relationship) intersects a vertical line from B (the new price-quantity relationship). In Fig. 7-1 this is indicated by point C. The distance BC gives us the change in total revenue; the distance AC gives us the change in quantity sold; and the ratio BC/AC gives us the marginal revenue produced by moving from point A to point B.

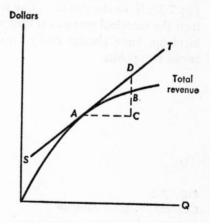

FIG. 7-1
Marginal Revenue as the Slope of the Total Revenue Curve

But (as hinted above) we can also apply the marginal concept to any single point on the curve. Thus the marginal revenue *at* point A on the total revenue curve is given by the slope of a line drawn tangent to the curve at that point. This last statement, however, requires a little explanation.

The slope of any straight line drawn on a graph is defined as the ratio of the vertical distance between any two points on the line to the horizontal distance between the same two points. These distances can be obtained by dropping a vertical line from the higher point, extending a horizontal line from the lower point, and measuring off the distances to the point where the two lines intersect. If we extend our line BC in Fig. 7-1 up to meet the tangent line at point D, we have one of these distances; the horizontal line AC gives us the other. The slope of the tangent line is thus expressed by the ratio DC/AC. Now if we want to consider a change along the total revenue curve much smaller than that expressed by movement from A to B, our reference point will shift to the left from the present point C, and the equivalent point D will shift downward and to the left. This means, however, that the new distance BC will be closer to the new distance CD than was true for the old situation. The closer we get to point A, the more nearly do the two distances approach each other. At an infinitely small distance from point A, the difference between BC and DC will be infinitesimally small, and we can therefore say that the slope of the tangent line expresses the marginal revenue of the total revenue curve at point A.

You will observe that if the curve has the same slope at all points, i.e., if it is a straight line, then the marginal revenue is the same at each point, and is the same for finite or infinitely small changes (see Fig. 7-2). If the slope of the curve is constantly changing, as in Fig. 7-1, then the marginal revenue is different at each point, and calculations involving finite change really yield the average rate of change between two points.

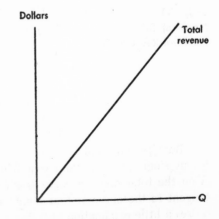

FIG. 7-2
Constant Marginal Revenue

CASE 7-1 State liquor stores in Norway

Liquor sales in Norway are a government monopoly under a government corporation, Vinmonopolet. The corporation was originally created in 1922 as an alternative to a 1916 prohibition law which became difficult to enforce due to smuggling and illicit distilling.

The corporation is forbidden by law to advertise its products. Instead, it runs advertisements in periodicals warning the public of the terrible consequences of imbibing, and exhorting people not to purchase liquor. Of its profits of 26,000,000 kroner in 1953, 600,000 kroner was expended for this purpose. About 1,500,000 kroner (just over $200,000) was used to assist alcoholics. The remainder went into the state coffers.

The stores themselves have no display windows (the windows being painted black), and arrangements are made inside the stores to discourage loitering. Clerks are forbidden to give sales talks or to offer advice except at the customer's request. Customers remain between railings as they place their order, pay for their purchase at the cashier's window, pick up their liquor in exchange for their sales slips, and finally leave the store.

Liquor stores can be established only by community majority vote. Communities under 4,000 population cannot have stores. Once a vote is taken, the question cannot come up again for eight years.

Liquor prices are kept high. There is a 10% sales tax, a 25% spirits tax, and a 150% emergency tax. The price of a bottle of Johnny Walker Red Label, for example, is $8.92—in a country where the average factory worker earns around $1,500 a year.[1]

Questions

1. How does this pattern differ from maximizing behavior?
2. Where profit maximization does not exist as a goal, do you think there can be suitable guides for making business decisions and suitable objective criteria for judging a business's performance?

CASE 7-2 Calculation of optimum level of rail freight rates

In an article in the *Journal of Farm Economics*, the author seeks to determine the best rate policy from the viewpoint of the railroad. He states that the two main factors to consider are elasticity of demand for rail freight service and the costs of transportation. For a commodity with an elastic demand for rail service, lower rail freight rates result in both higher volumes of rail traffic and higher gross revenues. The higher volume of traffic entails higher variable costs. In certain cases, the possibility exists that the increase

---

[1] Adapted from "Norway's State-Run Liquor Stores Do Their Best to Push Down Sales, Profits," by Mitchel Gordon, *Wall Street Journal*, November 3, 1954.

in variable costs will exceed the increase in gross revenues resulting from rate reductions. For other commodities, increases in gross revenue will exceed any increase in variable costs.

In calculating his results, the author considered the "optimum rate" for each commodity to be the rate yielding the maximum amount of revenue in excess of variable (out-of-pocket) costs. As shown in the table below, the author compared the current average rail charges for eight commodities with the charges estimated to yield the highest possible revenues in excess of variable costs. In every case tested the current average charges would have to be reduced in order to maximize net revenue.

Actual Railroad Charges Compared with Charges Maximizing Net Revenue above Out-of-Pocket Costs, 1952

(AVERAGE CHARGES, INCLUDING REFRIGERATION, FOR FLORIDA FRESH FRUITS AND VEGETABLES IN MAJOR EASTERN MARKETS)[2]

COMMODITY	ACTUAL CHARGES (*dollars per 1,000 pounds*)	CHARGES MAXIMIZING INCOME ABOVE OUT-OF-POCKET COSTS	PERCENTAGE DECREASE IN ACTUAL RATES NEEDED TO ATTAIN MAXIMUM NET INCOME
Beans, snap	2.12	1.95	8.0
Cabbage	1.51	1.45	4.0
Celery	1.78	1.72	3.4
Corn, green	2.01	1.99	1.0
Grapefruit	1.26	1.14	9.5
Oranges	1.16	1.09	6.0
Potatoes	1.25	1.22	2.4
Tomatoes	1.82	1.74	4.4

Questions

1. If demand is inelastic, will it ever pay to lower rates?
2. Assuming that total variable cost is zero, what rates should be set by the railroad seeking to maximize its income?
3. In your opinion, why were the actual rates charged different from the rates which would maximize net revenue?

CASE 7-3   The basis of union power

"It is not commonly recognized . . . that control of wages *is* control of entry [into an occupation], especially where seniority rules are in force,

---

[2] Adapted from "Elasticity of Demand for Railroad Transportation of Florida Produce," by Ezekiel Limmer, *Journal of Farm Economics*, Vol. 37, No. 3, August 1955, pp. 452, 458.

and, even failing such rules, where qualitative selection is important and turnover itself very costly to firms. If able to enforce standard rates, experienced, established workers can insulate themselves from the competition of new workers merely by making their cost excessive, that is, by establishing labor costs and wage expectations which preclude expansion of production or employment in their field. . . .

Frankly, I can see no reason why strongly organized workers, in an industry where huge investment is already sunk in highly durable assets, should ever permit a return on investment sufficient to attract new capital or even to induce full maintenance of existing capital. If I were running a union and were managing it faithfully in the interest of the majority of its members, I should consistently demand wage rates which offered to existing firms no real net earnings but only the chance of getting back part of their sunk investment at the cost of the replacement outlays necessary to provide employment for most of my constituents during their own lifetime as workers. In other words, I should plan gradually to exterminate the industry by excessive labor costs, taking care only to prevent employment from contracting more rapidly than my original constituents disappeared by death and voluntary retirement.

If I were operating, as labor leader, without the valuable hostages of large sunk investment, I should be obliged to behave more moderately. But I should still seek, controlling prices via labor costs, to restrict production as rapidly as consistent with decline of my membership by death and retirement and, while permitting some return to investors, should try always to induce only as much employment and production as my original constituents could take care of without new members. . . ." [3]

Questions

1. If unions behaved as indicated in the above statement, what would they be maximizing?

2. Do unions in fact behave in the manner described above? Can you think of other things unions might want to maximize?

3. Are the maximization goals of unions always inconsistent with the maximization goals of employers? Explain.

CASE 7-4 Marginal tax rates

The federal income tax in 1956 for single taxpayers and married persons filing separate returns is given in the table on page 192.

---

[3] Henry C. Simons, *Economic Policy for a Free Society*, U. of Chicago Press, Chicago, 1948, pp. 131–32. © 1948 by the University of Chicago.

TAXABLE INCOME (after exemptions and deductions)	TAX
$ 0	$ 0
2,000	400
4,000	840
6,000	1,360
8,000	1,960
10,000	2,640
20,000	7,260
32,000	14,460
50,000	26,820
70,000	42,120
100,000	67,320
150,000	111,820
200,000	156,820
250,000	202,320
500,000	429,820
1,000,000	884,820

Questions

1. Calculate the average tax rate and the marginal tax rate at various levels of income.
2. On the basis of the above schedule, estimate the tax on a taxable income of (a) $6,750; (b) $133,500.

CASE 7-5   Cramming for exams

Laura Jackson is a sophomore at State U. She is cramming for final exams and only has six hours of study time left. Her goal is to get as high an *average* grade as possible in three subjects: economics, French, and English, and she must decide how much time to spend on each. According to the best estimates that she can make, her grade in each subject will vary depending upon how much time is devoted to it according to the following schedule:

ECONOMICS		FRENCH		ENGLISH	
Hours of study	Grade	Hours of study	Grade	Hours of study	Grade
0	20%	0	40%	0	57%
1	45	1	52	1	67
2	65	2	62	2	75
3	75	3	71	3	81
4	83	4	78	4	85
5	90	5	83	5	88
6	92	6	86	6	89

Questions

1. How much time should Laura devote to each subject?
2. Can the answer be found without resorting to trial and error? How?

Marginal Revenue and Total Revenue as Related to Price Elasticity of Demand

As we saw earlier in the chapter, marginal revenue may be defined as the change in total revenue per unit change in quantity demanded (or sold). We are now ready to draw some general conclusions about the possible relationships between marginal revenue and total revenue as the quantity demanded varies.

If total revenue rises as quantity increases, marginal revenue is positive. If total revenue remains constant as quantity changes, marginal revenue is zero. If total revenue declines as quantity increases, marginal revenue is negative. We may thus note a connection between marginal revenue and elasticity of demand. If demand is elastic, marginal revenue is positive; if demand is inelastic, marginal revenue is negative; and if demand has unitary elasticity, marginal revenue is zero. It should also be noted that the greater the elasticity, the more nearly the marginal revenue approaches the price. In the special case of completely elastic demand, the marginal revenue is exactly equal to the price. This follows from the fact that when demand is completely elastic, additional units can always be sold without any decrease in price, and therefore each unit sold will increase total revenue by the amount of the price. This is illustrated as follows:

COMPLETELY ELASTIC DEMAND			
Price	Quantity	Total revenue	Marginal revenue
$5	1	$ 5	
5	2	10	$5
5	3	15	5
5	4	20	5
5	100	500	5

The following charts (Figs. 7-3 to 7-5) illustrate the relationships between marginal revenue, average revenue, and total revenue under varying conditions of demand elasticity.

(Note: To save space we have halved the vertical scale in the right-hand portion of each chart.)

FIG. 7-3 Revenue with Varying Elasticity of Demand

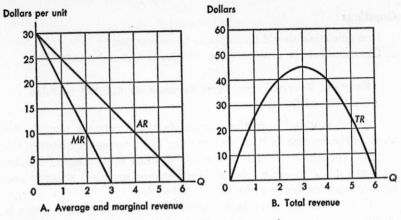

A. Average and marginal revenue

B. Total revenue

FIG. 7-4 Revenue with Completely Elastic Demand

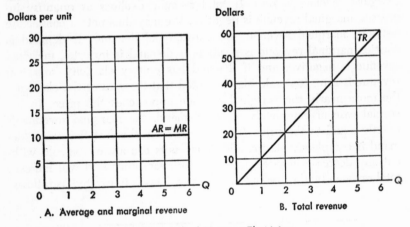

A. Average and marginal revenue

B. Total revenue

FIG. 7-5 Revenue with Demand of Unitary Elasticity

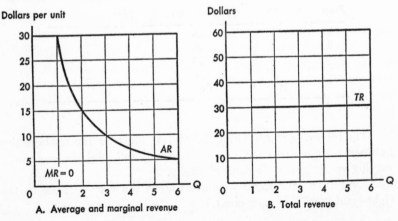

A. Average and marginal revenue

B. Total revenue

CASE 7-6   Calculating total and marginal revenue

Questions

(Refer to Case 2-12, Tropicade Soda, I):
1. Calculate total revenue at the various quantities.
2. Calculate marginal revenue at the various quantities.
3. Plot total, average, and marginal revenue curves.

MARGINAL COST

In Chapter 3 we discussed cost as a function of the rate of output (i.e., quantity supplied) and learned to distinguish between fixed and variable cost and between total and average cost. In this section we will add the concept of marginal cost to our kit of analytical tools.

Marginal cost may be derived from total cost in the same manner that marginal revenue is derived from total revenue. We define it as the change in total cost per unit change in quantity, or dTC/dQ. Using the same cost schedule as in Table 3-1 (p. 84), we may calculate marginal cost as follows:

RATE OF OUTPUT (*units per week*)	TOTAL FIXED COST	TOTAL VARIABLE COST	TOTAL COST	AVERAGE FIXED COST	AVERAGE VARIABLE COST	AVERAGE TOTAL COST	MARGINAL COST
0	$300	$ 0	$300	$ ∞	$ 0	$ ∞	
1	300	80	380	300	80	380	$ 80
2	300	150	450	150	75	225	70
3	300	210	510	100	70	170	60
4	300	280	580	75	70	145	70
5	300	375	675	60	75	135	95
6	300	540	840	50	90	140	165

From our previous knowledge of costs and from this table we can draw the following conclusions:

1. Marginal cost is practically always a positive figure. In order for marginal cost to be zero, additional output would have to be obtained without any increase in cost; and in order for marginal cost to be negative, increased output would have to result in a decrease in total cost. Such possibilities are extremely remote, if not impossible.

2. Although we defined marginal cost in terms of total cost, exactly the same results could be obtained from measuring the rate of change in total variable costs alone. Fixed cost has absolutely no effect on marginal cost, and may be completely disregarded in the calculation. The reason for this is fairly obvious. Fixed cost, by definition, does not change with changes in quantity. Since marginal cost is the measure

of the rate at which total cost changes as quantity changes, it depends solely upon the rate of change of variable cost.

3. If marginal cost is less than average cost, average cost will be declining. If marginal cost is larger than average cost, average cost will be rising. The student may confirm this by considering his quiz grades. If he has an average grade of 70 and then obtains a grade of less than 70 on the next (marginal) quiz, his average will fall. If he obtains a grade of more than 70, his average will rise.

Marginal Cost and the Firm's Supply Curve

With the aid of the maximization and margin concepts we can now amplify some of the remarks made in Chapter 3 concerning supply curves. Let us consider first the supply curve of a firm under pure competition (i.e., facing a demand curve which is completely elastic). We will try to answer the question, "What will be the rates of output (quantities supplied) at various prices?" To do this, we first assume a goal for the firm, i.e., that it is trying to maximize profits. We find that the most profitable rate of output will always be that at which the marginal cost is just equal to the price (and marginal cost is rising). Thus, in Fig. 7-6 if the price fixed by the market is $8, the best rate of output will be 44; if the price is $10, the best rate will be 65; and so on.

FIG. 7-6   Most Profitable Output: Pure Competition

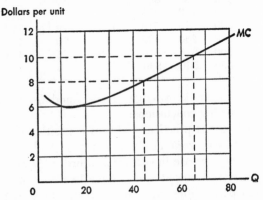

The reason for this conclusion is not too difficult to see. The firm's profit is equal to total revenue minus total cost. If the price is $8, and the demand curve is completely elastic, each additional unit that is sold will add $8 to total revenue. As long as additional units can be produced without adding $8 or more to total cost (i.e., if marginal cost is below $8), total profit will increase with increased output. Once the point is reached where further output will add more than $8 to total cost (i.e., if marginal cost is greater than $8), total profit will decrease. The most profitable rate of output, therefore, is exactly where the marginal cost equals the price. Since this is true at each and every price, it follows that the rising portion of the marginal cost curve *is* the supply curve, because it shows the quantity that will be supplied at each price.[4]

Now let us consider situations other than pure competition, where the demand curve facing the firm is not completely elastic. In such cases, the question, "What will be the quantity supplied at various prices?" is not meaningful, since the firm itself has some control over the price, and does not merely adjust output to a price which is dictated by the market.[5] Therefore, in this situation we cannot speak of a supply curve in the sense in which we have defined it above.

We can, however, ask what output *and* price the firm will choose if it wishes to maximize profit. The answer is that it will select the *output* where marginal cost equals marginal revenue, and that it will charge the highest *price* that can be obtained for this output, given the existing downward-sloping demand curve. The reasoning here is similar to that in the case of pure competition. Marginal revenue shows how much is being added to total revenue with each addition to output. Marginal cost shows the same for total cost. As long as total revenue is growing faster than total cost (i.e., marginal revenue is greater than marginal cost), then profit will increase with greater output. When total cost is growing faster than total revenue (i.e., marginal revenue is smaller than marginal cost), then profit is shrinking. Profit will be at a maximum when total revenue and total cost are changing at the same rate (i.e., marginal revenue is equal to marginal cost). This may

[4] Note that we specify that the marginal cost curve is the supply curve only if the marginal cost curve is rising. If the marginal cost curve is falling, as is true at the extreme left of the marginal cost curve in Fig. 7-6, it does not follow that the most profitable rate of output is that at which marginal cost is equal to the price, because additional units of output will add less to total cost than to total revenue. For this reason, the falling portion of the marginal cost curve does not tell us the output that will be produced, and therefore cannot be treated as a supply curve.

[5] The ability of a firm to exercise some degree of control over price is referred to as monopoly power. It should be noted that the term "monopoly" is used in various ways. Defined literally, monopoly implies a situation where there is only one seller of a commodity or service in the market, e.g., the local water supply company. This is sometimes called "pure" monopoly. In the case of "pure" monopoly the demand curve facing the firm is identical with the demand curve for the entire industry, and therefore must slope downward to the right. The monopoly firm, in the absence of government control, can choose its price. Similarly, whenever the demand curve facing any firm is not completely elastic, the firm has some control over price, and therefore we say it has some monopoly power.

FIG. 7-7   Most Profitable Output with Less Than Completely Elastic Demand

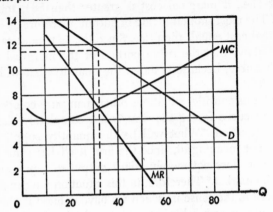

FIG. 7-8   Marginal Cost Decreasing, Then Increasing

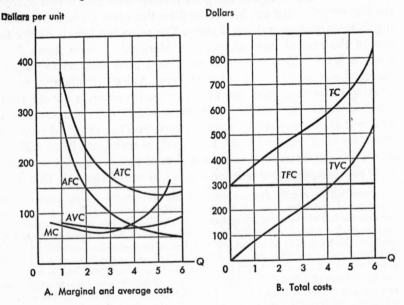

A. Marginal and average costs   B. Total costs

be seen graphically in Fig. 7-7. Given the demand curve and the marginal cost curve, the best rate of output will be at 33. But at this rate of output, the demand curve shows that the price can be set as high as $11.40. To charge less than this price would result in a decrease in possible profits; to charge a higher price would result in a lower

FIG. 7-9 Constant Marginal Cost

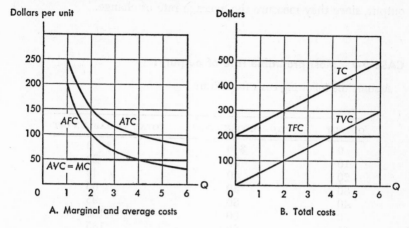

A. Marginal and average costs

B. Total costs

FIG. 7-10 Increasing Marginal Cost

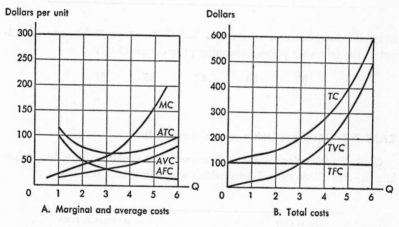

A. Marginal and average costs

B. Total costs

quantity being demanded, and therefore in lower profits. Thus, although there is no supply curve in the conventional sense, we may think of the marginal cost curve as a kind of supply curve providing we redefine it as follows: "The curve which indicates the quantity which will be supplied at various levels of *marginal revenue.*"

Marginal and Other Costs

The relationships of marginal cost and other types of cost under varying conditions of marginal cost may be seen in Figs. 7-8 through 7-10. Fig. 7-8 is plotted from the table on page 195; Figs 7-9 and 7-10 illustrate alternative patterns of marginal cost. Note that the points in the *MC* curve in each chart were plotted midway between levels of output, since they measure the average rate of change.

CASE 7-7   Most profitable rate of output, I

Assume the following costs for a firm:

OUTPUT	TOTAL FIXED COST	TOTAL VARIABLE COST
0	$30	$ 0
10	30	20
20	30	40
30	30	65
40	30	95
50	30	135
60	30	185
70	30	250

Draw the marginal cost curve, and find the most profitable rate of output at the following prices (assuming pure competition):

$5 $4 $3 $2 $1

CASE 7-8   Most profitable rate of output, II

Given the following demand and average cost schedules for a firm, calculate the rate of output and price which would maximize profit:

DEMAND		AVERAGE COST	
P	Q	Q	$\$$
$10	100	100	5.60
8	200	200	3.80
6	300	300	3.20
4	400	400	3.00
2	500	500	3.00
		600	3.30

Suppose the demand curve shifts to the right so that the quantity demanded at each price is double that shown above. Find the most profitable rate of output and price.

CASE 7-9   The cost of driving an automobile, II

Let us re-examine the Ethyl Corporation advertisement discussed in Case 3-6. The figures for average yearly driving costs are as follows:

FOR 5,000 MILES		FOR 15,000 MILES
$481.33	Depreciation	$ 481.33
104.39	Insurance	104.39
16.86	License fees	16.86
116.00	Gasoline and oil	348.00
37.00	Maintenance	111.00
25.50	Tires	76.50
$781.08	*Total*	$1,138.08

Questions

1. What is the marginal cost per mile according to these figures?
2. Plot and draw the total cost curve.
3. Plot and draw the average and marginal cost curves.
4. The advertisement says "So, as you can see quickly by the chart [meaning the table] every mile you drive costs less than the one before." Do you agree? Explain your answer.
5. Can you tell from these figures whether the marginal cost varies with the rate of output?
6. How would your answers to Questions 4 and 5 be affected if you learned that the total cost for 10,000 miles was $980? $940?

CASE 7-10   Economics of picking blackberries

"The simplest case of balance or equilibrium between desire and effort is found when a person satisfies one of his wants by his own direct work. When a boy picks blackberries for his own eating, the action of picking is probably itself pleasurable for a while; and for some time longer the pleasure of eating is more than enough to repay the trouble of picking. But after he has eaten a good deal, the desire for more diminishes; while the task of picking begins to cause weariness, which may indeed be a feeling of monotony rather than of fatigue. Equilibrium is reached when at last his eagerness to play and his disinclination for the work of picking counterbalance the desire for eating. The satisfaction which he can get from picking fruit has arrived at its *maximum,* for up to that point every fresh picking has added more to his pleasure than it has taken away; and after that time any further picking would take away from his pleasure more than it would add." [6]

---

[6] Alfred Marshall, *Principles of Economics,* 8th ed., p. 331. Copyright, 1920 by The Macmillan Company, N.Y. Reprinted by permission.

Questions

1. Using a graph showing quantity of blackberries on the horizontal axis, plot (a) total satisfaction derived from eating blackberries as a function of the quantity of blackberries; and (b) total dissatisfaction of picking blackberries as a function of the quantity of blackberries.
2. Indicate the quantity where the difference between satisfaction and dissatisfaction is greatest.
3. What relationship must exist between the rates of change of the two curves at the point where net satisfaction is greatest? Why?

CASE 7-11   Economics of subway service

"The basic consideration underlying the determination of a fare structure according to economic principles is that of insuring that the value of all the services rendered by the transportation system shall exceed by as large a margin as possible the costs of rendering that service. Of course, if the benefits derived did not exceed the costs incurred, then from a strictly economic point of view, there would be no advantage in the provision of the service. It is the excess of the value of what is produced over the costs involved that forms the essential gain from economic activity. If we are to be assured that this excess is as great as possible, we must provide service to such a degree that there remains no further possible service that carries a value to the potential user greater than its cost. Conversely, we must be sure that no service actually rendered occasions costs that exceed the value of the service." [7]

Questions

1. How would you measure "the value of all the services rendered by the transportation system"?
2. How is the concept of maximization used in this case? What is being maximized?
3. On a graph with quantity of transportation service measured on the horizontal axis, draw a curve which shows total benefit of service as a function of the quantity of service. On the same graph, draw total cost of service as a function of the quantity of service.
4. Using the graph of Question 3, find that quantity of service which would be best, according to the view expressed in the above case.
5. What must be true about the rate of increase of total benefits and total cost at this "best quantity"?

---

[7] William S. Vickrey, *The Revision of the Rapid Transit Fare Structure of the City of New York*, Technical Monograph No. 3, Finance Project, Mayor's Committee on Management Survey of the City of New York, February 1952, pp. 3–4.

CASE 7-12   How to sell Listerine

"It is my belief that when sales of a product and the advertising are both running along on a level, a company can wisely spend an *additional* dollar on advertising even if that dollar brings in net only an additional dollar and one cent. This is treason to the old-line businessman. He will tell you that in his business it is customary to spend, let's say, 13 per cent of the sales on advertising. That was good enough for his grandfather and it is good enough for him. . . .

In our case, after checking our results carefully, we plowed the money in, hoping for at least that one penny additional profit. Of course, it didn't work out that way. Every time we spent the new money much more than a penny came in." [8]

Questions

1. How is the concept of the margin used in this case?
2. Is the writer's belief sound from an economic point of view?
3. Show why it may be important to distinguish between private and social points of view in answering Question 2.

CASE 7-13   Use of resources in agriculture

"Adjustments in inputs—those facets of the supply function over which farmers do have control—have been more sensitive than examination of aggregate inputs would indicate. . . . Technical innovation and relative prices have placed different premiums on resources. They have called for increases in some resource inputs and decreases in others. These changes partially cancel each other in the aggregate index of inputs. For example, total labor inputs decreased by about 10 per cent in the period 1942–49, while fertilizer increased by 74 per cent, and annual inputs of building and machine services increased by 60 per cent. In the twenties period of contraction [sic] in agriculture, fertilizer and lime inputs decreased by 30 per cent in a single year from 1919 to 1920; power and machinery inputs declined by 18 per cent from 1920 to 1925, even though the 'technical revolution' in agriculture was beginning to press . . . for use of more of these resources." [9]

Questions

1. What reasons can you suggest for the different changes in inputs from 1942 to 1949; from 1919 to 1920; from 1920 to 1925?

[8] Gerard B. Lambert, *All Out of Step*, pp. 118–19. Copyright, 1956 by Gerard B. Lambert. Reprinted by permission of Doubleday and Co., Inc., N.Y.

[9] Earl O. Heady, "The Supply of U.S. Farm Products Under Conditions of Full Employment," *American Economic Review*, Vol. 45, No. 2, May 1955, p. 232. © 1955 by the American Economic Association.

2. Can it ever be efficient for a farmer to substitute labor for machinery? Under what conditions? Answer this question first from the point of view of the individual farmer, and then from the point of view of society as a whole.

CASE 7-14   Outlook for steel costs

The following quotation was taken from an analysis of the steel industry prepared by a Wall Street brokerage firm.

"As to the outlook for the steel industry as a whole, it should be taken into consideration that a reduction of the operating rate next year to 80–85% of capacity, as foreseen by some industry leaders, has its compensating factors. A great deal of overtime can be eliminated and labor efficiency can be increased. Production can be concentrated in the most modern units and overage plant can be retired. U.S. Steel has already undertaken significant steps in this direction by shutting down open hearth furnaces at the Homestead and Duquesne Works with a combined capacity of more than 1¼ million ingot tons." [10]

Questions

1. What does the analysis suggest regarding marginal cost of the steel industry as it approaches 100% of capacity?
2. If marginal costs are rising, does that mean that average costs must also be rising?
3. Why should a firm ever want to push output to a point where average costs are increasing?

CASE 7-15   East Hills Ice Skating Rink, I

In 1953 Larry Howard bought a popular ice skating rink in a fashionable suburb of Chicago. Shortly after taking over from the former owners, Larry realized that the rink was not as profitable as he had expected it to be. His total revenue averaged about $450 per week based on average admissions of 600 per week at a price of 75 cents. His costs, given in Table 1 on page 205, were stable in the sense that he could not lower them, and seemed to be fixed in the sense that they did not increase when attendance was heavy, or decrease when attendance was light.

Larry discussed the problem with a friend, who suggested that a change in price might help the situation. He pointed out that the previous owners had not changed the price in several years, and that there was no reason to assume that 75 cents was the best price simply because that was what they

[10] *Analysis of Steel Industry*, Loeb, Rhoades & Co., 42 Wall St., New York, N.Y., December 31, 1953. © 1953 by Loeb, Rhoades & Co.

TABLE 1   Weekly Costs

Rent	$150
Heat and electricity	35
Rink maintenance, cleaning, etc.	120
Depreciation on equipment	20
Miscellaneous	35
	360
Salary to Mr. Howard	100
	$460

had been charging. He asked Larry to estimate what his average weekly admissions would be at various prices, and following his instructions Larry prepared the following schedule:

TABLE 2   Estimated Weekly Admissions at Various Prices

PRICE	ADMISSIONS PER WEEK
$2.00	100
1.75	200
1.50	320
1.25	400
1.00	480
.75	600
.50	800
.25	1,000

Questions

1. What would be the best price for Larry Howard to charge, assuming that he wishes to maximize his profit?
2. What is the marginal revenue at that price?
3. Are there any reasons why Larry Howard might not want to charge that price?

CASE 7-16   East Hills Ice Skating Rink, II

During the summer months Larry Howard gave some serious thought to his price policy for the coming year. He had noticed that when he changed his price the previous year (see Case 7-15) most of the decline in business had been among the high school crowd, while the decrease in adult attendance had been very much smaller. He suspected that it might be wise for him to establish two prices, one for skaters under 18 years of age, and another for adults. He again went to his friend for guidance, and the friend again suggested that the first step was to prepare estimates of attendance at various prices. Larry produced the following schedules:

UNDER 18		18 AND OVER	
Price	Weekly admissions	Price	Weekly admissions
$2.00	10	$2.00	90
1.75	30	1.75	170
1.50	110	1.50	210
1.25	160	1.25	240
1.00	200	1.00	280
.75	300	.75	300
.50	460	.50	340
.25	600	.25	400

Questions

1. Which schedule seems to be more elastic? What reasons can you suggest for this?
2. What would be the most profitable price or prices?
3. Can you find the answer using the marginal revenue concept?
4. Suppose the two schedules had been reversed. Would Larry Howard have been wise to reverse the prices?

CASE 7-17   East Hills Ice Skating Rink, III

During his second year in operation Larry Howard found the two-price system working very well. Now he began to pay closer attention to his costs. He had originally believed that all of his costs were fixed, and that variable cost was zero. After a close check, however, he found that some of his costs, namely, outlays for cleaning the rink, maintenance, and refreezing, did rise somewhat when attendance was heavy and fall off somewhat when attendance was light. So far as he could determine, his costs varied about one dollar per week for each ten customers. When Larry mentioned this to his friend, the latter pointed out that this indicated a need to re-examine prices and estimated attendance. Using the same schedules as in the preceding case, the friend recommended still another change in price.

Questions

1. What price change did he recommend?
2. Show the revenue and cost situation graphically.
3. Assuming that the "friend" in this case had been a consulting firm whose fee for such advice was $500, would it have been worth while for Larry Howard to purchase this service?

CASE 7-18 The marginal cost of subway service

"It is obvious that very wide variations will take place in the costs which will be occasioned by additional traffic at different times and between different places. . . .

To determine the economically ideal rate structure, then, requires a determination of the costs of increasing the service at various times and various places, or the amounts that might be saved by decreasing the service at various times and various places. . . .

In order to form a rough picture of the way in which costs respond to various changes in service and traffic, six parameters were selected as representing in a broad over-all way the characteristics of the service supplied and the traffic handled. These categories or parameters are as follows: (1) train miles; (2) car miles; (3) maximum number of cars in service; (4) number of passengers carried; (5) number of passengers carried during the peak hours; and (6) the layout of the system, consisting of the number of route miles, number of stations, etc. An attempt was then made to develop a formula which would indicate, for any change involving an increase or decrease in one or more of these measures of the service rendered, approximately how total costs could be expected to change. . . .

These figures provide a very rough basis for estimating the costs of providing increased service at particular points. They bring out the great difference between the cost of providing additional service during the rush hours and during the nonrush hours. Additional service during the nonrush hours . . . can be provided merely by lengthening trains and by taking care of an increased number of passengers at stations. . . .

On the other hand, an increase in rush-hour traffic equal to 10 per cent of the total traffic might be impossible to take care of without an increase in the system layout, would probably require an increase in the number of train miles on most lines (since rush-hour trains are already of maximum length), would require a more than 10 per cent increase in the number of cars in service and a more than 10 per cent increase in the peak number of passengers. . . .

Even a summary examination of the data indicates that the cost of furnishing additional rush-hour service is as much as three times the cost of furnishing additional nonrush-hour service generally, and the ratio may actually be much higher than this. Indeed, if we consider the two main parameters which are used for various fare schemes—the rush hour versus nonrush hour or time parameter, and the distance-traveled parameter— it appears clear that although the distance parameter has been much more frequently used, as in setting up fares according to zones or distance, actually it is much more important to differentiate the fare according to the time of travel than according to the distance. This is particularly true in a city with a heavy concentration of traffic to and from the center as in New York. . . .

Even where distance traveled is an important factor, it appears that in almost no case is the proper fare one that varies directly in proportion to distance. It is primarily the distance traveled over congested portions of the route that should determine the fare, while the distance traveled over the noncongested portions of the route should be given relatively light weight. Direction of travel is also an important factor. . . .

The ideal economic fare system would thus vary both with time and direction, as well as according to the points of origin and destination. Almost no fare would be charged for any portion of a trip for which there are at the particular time of day normally a substantial number of vacant seats. . . ."[11]

Estimated Typical Marginal Cost, in Cents, for Various Types of Traffic

ORIGINATING IN OUTER ZONE DURING:	TRAVELING TO:							
	OUTER ZONE				MIDDLE ZONE			CENTRAL ZONE
	Out	In	In and out	Through down-town	In	In and out	Through down-town	
A.M. rush	0	2	5	30	5	5	30	25
P.M. rush	2	0	5	30	0	5	30	5
Nonrush	0	0	2	5	0	2	5	5

ORIGINATING IN CENTRAL ZONE DURING:	TRAVELING TO:		
	OUTER ZONE	MIDDLE ZONE	CENTRAL ZONE
A.M. rush	5	5	10
P.M. rush	25	20	10
Nonrush	5	5	2

Questions

1. Why is it "more important to differentiate the fare according to the time of travel than according to the distance"?

2. In your opinion, when is *average* cost lowest, during the rush hours or nonrush hours? Should this be considered in setting fares? Why or why not?

3. In your opinion, why have the subways not adopted a more rational fare structure?

---

[11] William S. Vickrey, *op. cit.*, pp. 3–4.

4. Most railroads serving commuters charge lower rates for those who ride the trains regularly every morning and evening than they do for single or round-trip fares. In the light of the above case, what is your opinion of this practice?

CASE 7-19   A.T. & T. stands in line

"Among U.S. corporations, American Telephone and Telegraph Co. looms majestically. But to the flinty-eyed bond raters of Wall Street, the giant is just another utility, and when it comes to hiring money A.T. & T. has to stand in line just like everyone else. Take a look at the company's recent $250-million debenture, which preceded the announcement of its huge stock offering. A.T. & T. sold the debentures without much strain. But it didn't get its money just by banging on the credit counter. A.T. & T. had to pay 3.76 per cent—more, in fact, than it has paid for any loan since 1930, and more than dozens of utilities have paid all summer.

Moody's rates A.T. & T. bonds only as Aa, although Standard & Poor's recently raised its rating to A1, the equivalent of Moody's Aaa. In Moody's judgment, in other words, eighty-seven utilities with Aaa ratings are better credit risks. A.T. & T., moreover, is unable to float bonds for the same price as other double-A companies; it has to pay more. That's because its issues are so large, and because pension funds, trusts, life insurance companies, etc., now have so many A.T. & T. bonds in their portfolios that they are reluctant to hold more. To get a new bond accepted, therefore, A.T. & T. has to pay a premium—in this case, at least one-tenth of 1 per cent, or $250,000 a year. These penalties for being big, it might be pointed out, are imposed not by the government but by the free money market." [12]

Questions

1. Why does A.T. & T. have to pay higher interest on its bonds?
2. If the number of bonds outstanding were smaller, would the company pay a lower interest rate?
3. What determines the interest rate?

CASE 7-20   Maximization and competition

"Further surgery, in the form of greater production cutbacks, is being prescribed to restore a healthy tone to the sluggish textile industry.

Business in the industry generally has been in the doldrums for several months. There are few signs that might be interpreted as indicating an immediate resurgence.

---

[12] "A.T. & T. Stands in Line," *Fortune*, August 1956, p. 72. © 1956 by Time, Inc.

The strongest business is centering around blends of Dacron and cotton, and nylon. As a result, some of these goods are in tight supply.

In instances where other merchandise is being sold in volume, profits are practically negligible. Market reports have indicated that some goods are being sold on a break-even basis in the hope that remaining stocks can be sold more profitably when the market stabilizes.

Prices generally have been pushed downward. For example, prices for the 80-square print cloth, the most popular unfinished cotton fabric, have been about 18¼ cents a yard in recent days. A year ago the price was about 20⅝ cents a yard.

The continuation of this generally unsatisfactory situation has caused many textile men to decide that they will not weave goods for inventory. The result has been production curtailments at several mills. Among those affected are Berkshire Hathaway, Inc., Deering Milliken & Co., and the Bates Manufacturing Company.

While this is believed to be a step in the right direction, many textile men contend that it is not widespread enough. For years most producers of print cloth yarn goods have been running their plants with three shifts working six days a week.

Some industry leaders are urging the adoption of a five-day week. Such a move, they say, would help bring production more in line with demand.

One leading executive said that the gravity of the situation demanded that the industry invoke a self-imposed, four-day work week for the second quarter of the year.

While this admittedly would run costs higher, he said the action would place producers' stocks in good shape for the final six months and enable them to recoup any earlier losses. . . ." [13]

Questions

1. In the face of declining prices, why have many producers continued to run their plants with three shifts working six days a week?
2. Draw a hypothetical demand curve for (a) the individual producer, and (b) the industry as a whole.
3. Draw a hypothetical marginal revenue curve for (a) and (b) in Question 2.

CASE 7-21   Maximization and oligopoly

"On October 5, 1929, Reynolds raised Camels from $6 to $6.40. Lorillard and Liggett & Myers followed suit the same day. American Tobacco followed on October 11. On June 24, 1931, with farmers receiving for

---

[13] Carl Spielvogel, "Textile Industry May Get Surgery," New York *Times*, February 24, 1957. © 1957 by The New York Times Company.

tobacco leaf the lowest price in a quarter of a century, manufacturing costs declining, and cigarette company profits at an all-time peak, Reynolds raised the price of Camels to $6.85 a thousand—its peak since December 1921. American Tobacco, Liggett & Myers, and Lorillard promptly followed. S. Clay Williams, board chairman of Reynolds, justified this increase because Reynolds had planned an expensive advertising campaign to popularize Camels' new moisture-proof cellophane wrapper and as an expression of 'our own courage for the future and our own confidence in our industry.'

American Tobacco gave a more realistic explanation for following Reynolds' lead. Mr. Hill admitted frankly: 'I naturally saw the opportunity to make some money.' Liggett & Myers' management thought the price increase a mistake, but nevertheless followed Reynolds' lead. Mr. Hill's hope of making money for his stockholders was immediately realized. American Tobacco's 1931 profits rose about 7 per cent above its record 1930 profits, despite a decrease in its cigarette sales. The Big Three's combined net earnings in 1931 reached the incredible amount of $105,707,939—an annual profit volume more than double that gained in 1923, on approximately the same price level, when they first called a halt to the cigarette price war." [14]

Questions

1. How is it possible that profits rose despite a decrease in sales?
2. Assuming that the firms wished to maximize profit, is it theoretically possible to set a price which is too high? Explain.
3. In view of the high cross elasticity of demand among the major brands (see Case 5-18), wasn't it dangerous for Reynolds to raise the price of Camels? What would have happened if the other companies had not followed the price increase?
4. In view of the high prices and the high profits of the cigarette makers, how do you account for the low prices received by farmers for tobacco?

CASE 7-22 Maximization and monopoly

"By the 1890's de Beers Consolidated were producing 95 per cent of the world output of diamonds and possessed complete control over the price. For the whole 40 years to 1927 their influence upon the industry was but little diminished. The discovery of diamonds in German Southwest Africa had, it is true, reduced de Beers' share by 1913 to about 76 per cent. But the growth of total sales permitted the payment of 40 per cent dividends with almost perfect regularity from 1897 to 1914.

[14] George W. Stocking and Myron W. Watkins, *Monopoly and Free Enterprise*, Twentieth Century Fund, N.Y., 1951, pp. 143–44. © 1951 by the Twentieth Century Fund.

The marketing of diamonds was comparatively early entrusted to a body known as the Diamond Syndicate which handled the whole output and disposed of it in large parcels of assorted stones. The value of the Cape output, which in 1885 had been below 20s. a carat, mounted steadily to over 31s. in 1889, was between 25s. and 30s. in 1898, and thence rose by stages to 51s. in 1906 and 57s. in 1913. The Syndicate maintained the price of diamonds by holding large stocks, which, if necessary, it increased greatly during a depression. It acted as selling agent from time to time for the majority of outside producers as well as for the South African output.

The dictatorship of the Syndicate had been threatened temporarily after 1903 by the rivalry of the Premier Mine, which at first stood outside, but it was far more seriously disturbed in the years following 1925. In that year, some 90 per cent of South African output came from the mines, the remainder from alluvial output. By 1927 the alluvial output had increased almost ten times as the result of the discovery of the new and exceedingly rich fields of Lichtenburg and Namaqualand. The share of the mines fell to just above half the Union output, and a bare third of the world's. The Syndicate tried to prevent a collapse of the market by frantic buying of alluvial stones. It is reported to have held a stock exceeding £8,000,000 in value at the end of 1927, and amounting to nearly £12,000,000 by the end of 1929.

But the Union Government could not itself afford to see the collapse of the market. It shares to the extent of 60 per cent in the profits of the Premier Mine, and derives large profits—and income taxes—from the others. A Precious Stones Act was forced through which made possible the control of alluvial diggings. It enabled the Governor-General, amongst other things, to limit the number of diggers' certificates issued, to declare that no more diggings be proclaimed, to prohibit prospecting, to limit the quantity of stones that might be recovered by individuals or by all producers, and to fix minimum prices for stones.

The first action was to prohibit for a period all diamond prospecting, but hard feeling and threats of disorder among the diggers led to its partial relaxation. Meanwhile, however, the Namaqualand discoveries were proving even richer than had been suspected. The fear that the enormous yield would ruin the market led the Government to proclaim them a State digging, to be operated by direct labour for its own profit. In ten months the Government secured some £6,500,000 worth of stones for an outlay of £105,000, a ratio of proceeds to cost that would bring tears of envy into the eye of a manufacturer of patent medicines.

Even with a substantially reduced output of alluvial stones in 1929 and subsequent years (it was scarcely more than a fifth of the 1927 output after 1932), the task of the Diamond Syndicate had become more than it could support. At the expiry of the Syndicate's five-year agreement in 1930, there was created a new body, the Diamond Corporation, with a capital of £10,000,000 which was to take over from the Syndicate the burden of holding the surplus stocks. In this de Beers has a 50 per cent interest, and shortly after its creation they took over the management of all the other large producers. The negotiations were for a long time complicated by the unwillingness of the Union Government to accept any quota restriction on its own output in Namaqualand. It was, however, finally induced to come in on terms exceptionally favourable to it, and accepted the position of one of the partners to the monopoly. The agreement assigned quotas not only to the large producers, but also to the Corporation, so that its disposal of stocks should be systematically regulated.

The liquidation of this difficult situation was further complicated by the onset of depression, which reduced the annual sales of South African diamonds from over £12,000,000 to about £1,500,000. The mines were closed down completely, and stocks slowly diminished. Finally in 1933 a new agreement negotiated between the mines, the Union Government and the Administrator of Southwest Africa gave added control. The Diamond Trading Company was to sell all diamonds for the Corporation and the producing companies, and all the various interests were to be represented on its board. These involved proceedings would appear once more to have re-established a moderately secure monopoly, with the balance of power not substantially changed, and the Union Government will henceforward collaborate with the producers in securing that the price of diamonds shall be not too closely related to their cost." [15]

Questions

1. In view of the low costs of production, why should the diamond producers ever want to restrict output?
2. Under what circumstances would it pay them to increase output?
3. If each diamond producer made his own production and marketing decisions independently, do you think prices would be higher or lower? Why?

CASE 7-23   Maximization in the automobile industry

"Automobiles will carry steadily increasing price tags in the years ahead and blistering competition will be partly responsible. This competition is demanding more frequent and broader design changes.

---

[15] Reprinted from pp. 50–53 of *Monopoly* by E. A. G. Robinson (Pitman Publishing Corp., 1941), by permission of the University of Chicago Press.

Generally past price increases have been attributed by the manufacturers to higher production costs, with competition for larger slices of the market holding the price advances down.

But the battle for buyers in the competitive market has shown the car makers that complete model changes every three years are not enough to keep up with demand for styling and engineering refinement.

So costly changes will come more often—probably every two instead of every three years. And a complete model change now can involve an expenditure of around a quarter of a billion dollars for a manufacturer like Ford or Chevrolet. A so-called major design change can cost $100,-000,000 and more.

It takes a lot of customers to balance out such an expenditure.

The Ford Division of the Ford Motor Company had a complete model change in its 1957 line. Following the industry's custom of complete changes every three years, Chevrolet was committed only to substantial changes for this year. Some sources termed them 'face lifting' alterations.

But Ford's completely new model ousted Chevrolet from the No. 1 production and retail sales spot.

Chevrolet has a completely new model coming up for the 1958 car year. It is a fair guess the change will cost Chevrolet around a quarter of a billion dollars. Chevrolet hopes the change will put it back in the top spot.

Ford, of course, likes the No. 1 place. So it is going as far as it can with styling and engineering changes for 1958, short of a complete changeover. The changes will be broader than any manufacturer ever has made for the first year following a complete revamping of its cars.

The most recent new car registration figures showed Ford running about 71,000 units ahead of its sales volume of a year ago. Chevrolet was nearly 87,000 units behind its total for the like 1956 period.

These figures are more significant than the fact that the Ford Division is slightly more than 32,000 units ahead of Chevrolet. At a certain level in sales volume, the car makers reach the point where they have back the entire investment in new model output. Then comes the profit-producing volume. The unit profit mounts as the sales volume advances in the second phase of retail distribution. Eventually it reaches the level where each unit sold is almost all 'velvet' as far as the manufacturer is concerned.

Thus it is that the car makers in the high volume field exert added effort to attain an additional 50,000 to 100,000 sales.

There is a distinction and a tremendous promotional value in the No. 1 rank in car production and retail deliveries. Some industry experts insist the Ford-Chevrolet battle still is not settled.

Some recall that in other years when the race was close the two manufacturers exchanged accusations of unfair tactics to swell registration totals. Each accused the other of registering new cars in the names of various dealers, or dealer employees.

Because the cars so registered would have to be sold later as used units or as demonstrators, the effort could become expensive. But that No. 1 spot is greatly coveted." [16]

Questions

1. "Stiff competition" usually would result in lower prices; why is that not true in this case?
2. As a general rule, when would you expect competition to result in lower prices and when in greater advertising, more style changes, etc.?
3. Do you agree or disagree with the statements made above about cost, volume, and profit? Explain, making use of the concepts of fixed, variable, and marginal cost.

MARGINAL PRODUCT

The Concept of Marginal Product

Underlying the concept of marginal cost is the concept of marginal productivity or marginal product. Marginal cost, as we have seen, is derived from the changes in total cost resulting from the addition of an extra unit of output. This increase in output is obtained through the use of some additional factor or factors of production (assuming that there has been no change in existing technology). Marginal cost may thus be regarded as the cost of the additional factor or factors required to produce an additional unit of output. If the additional factor or factors are highly productive, i.e., if a small amount will produce the specified output, marginal cost is low. If the additional factor or factors are less productive, i.e., if a large amount is necessary to produce the required output, marginal cost will be high.

The ability of a factor of production, in combination with other factors, to add to the total output is called the productivity of the factor. The marginal productivity of a factor is measured by the change in total output per unit change of input of the factor, other things remaining constant. The resulting change in total output is referred to as the marginal product.

In a manner similar to that used for marginal cost or marginal revenue, the marginal product may be derived from the changes in total product (or output) divided by the change in the input of the

---

[16] "Auto Prices Head for Steady Climb," New York *Times*, June 23, 1957. © 1957 by The New York Times Company.

factor whose productivity is being measured. The relationship between fixed and variable factors, total product, and marginal product may be seen in the following schedule:

FIXED FACTOR (e.g., acres of land)	VARIABLE FACTOR (e.g., man-years of farm labor)	TOTAL PRODUCT (e.g., bushels of wheat)	MARGINAL PRODUCT
200	0	0	500
200	1	500	700
200	2	1200	600
200	3	1800	200
200	4	2000	50
200	5	2050	

The schedule above may be considered as typical in the sense that although the marginal product increases at first, it eventually reaches a maximum and then starts to diminish. This phenomenon occurs with such regularity that it has been characterized as the *law of diminishing returns*, also called the *law of variable proportions*. The law states that if, *ceteris paribus*, we add increasing units of one factor of production to a fixed amount of another factor, there will come a point where the extra output obtained from each additional unit of input will decline or diminish. The point where this occurs is known as the point of diminishing returns.

We may now observe the relationship of marginal product to marginal cost. If the marginal product is increasing, marginal cost will be decreasing; if marginal product is constant, marginal cost will also be constant; and if marginal product is decreasing, marginal cost will be rising. The law of diminishing returns tells us that at some point marginal product will start decreasing, and therefore marginal cost will be rising. This point may be reached quite rapidly, or only after a considerable range of output has been covered. Where it occurs will depend upon the kind of productive operation being considered and the state of technology. In agriculture, for example, it is fairly obvious (as has been confirmed in many experiments) that diminishing returns set in fairly soon. In many branches of manufacturing, on the other hand, it is thought that diminishing returns do not set in over wide ranges of output. If this is true, and if the prices of the factors of production are constant, then marginal cost would be constant over a wide range. The typical break-even chart which represents total cost as a straight line is based on an assumption of constant marginal costs.[17]

---

[17] See Fig. 3-2, p. 88.

The relationship of marginal product to total product is illustrated in Fig. 7-11.

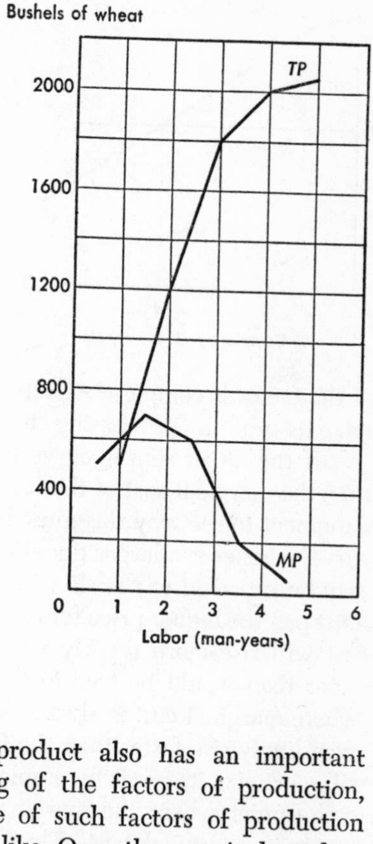

Bushels of wheat

FIG. 7-11
Marginal Product and Total Product

Marginal Revenue Product

The concept of the marginal product also has an important bearing in the theory of the pricing of the factors of production, i.e., in determining the market price of such factors of production as land, labor, capital goods, and the like. Once the marginal product of a factor has been ascertained, its value in the market may be calculated by the increase it will bring in total revenue. The sales value of the marginal product is known as the *marginal revenue product*, i.e., the marginal revenue resulting from the sale of the marginal product. If we assume that the factor supply curve facing a firm is completely elastic (i.e., that the marginal cost of a factor will be equal to its price [18]), then the firm can maximize its profit by employing additional units of that factor until its marginal revenue product (*MRP*) is just equal to its price. Thus in Fig. 7-12A we see that the best quantity of the factor for the firm to purchase would be *q*. Since the supply curve

---

[18] As in the case of the demand curve, the factor supply curve facing a firm may be completely elastic, or the price may vary with the quantity purchased.

FIG. 7-12 The Firm's Purchases of a Factor of Production

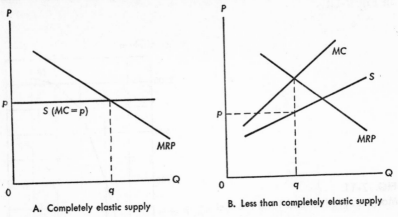

A. Completely elastic supply   B. Less than completely elastic supply

of the factor is completely elastic, MC = price, and the firm will maximize its profit by purchasing the quantity determined by $MRP = MC$.

If the factor supply curve facing a firm is not completely elastic, then the marginal cost of the factor will exceed its price. We may take a moment to see why this must be so. With an upward-sloping supply curve, whenever a larger quantity of the factor is purchased, the price may be expected to rise. But in order to secure this quantity, the firm must pay the higher price for *all* the units it purchases. As a result, total cost will rise more rapidly with an increase in the purchase of the factor than would be true in the case of a completely elastic supply (where marginal cost is always equal to price), and marginal cost will accordingly rise faster than the factor price. In this situation, the firm will maximize its profit by employing additional units of the factor up to the point where the marginal revenue product of the factor just equals its marginal cost. Thus in Fig. 7-12B we see that the best quantity of the factor for the firm to purchase would be q, and that it can obtain this quantity at price p. The price in this situation, therefore, is below the marginal revenue product.

We are thus able to lay down a rule about the quantity of a factor that will be purchased at a given price or at varying prices similar to the rule we applied to the quantity of a commodity that will be produced in relation to its price. You will recall that when we dealt with output and price, we found that profit is at a maximum when marginal revenue is equal to marginal cost. Similarly, in determining the amount of a factor to be purchased by a firm, we find that the quantity which will yield the greatest profit is that at which the marginal revenue product is equal to marginal cost (which may or may not be equal to price, depending on the elasticity of supply of the factor).

CASE 7-24   Cocoa farming in Nigeria, I

The following statistics on the relation between labor input and output of cocoa were based on the *average* results of 61 Nigerian cocoa farms: [19]

FARMS WITH MAN-HOURS PER ACRE	MAN-HOURS PER ACRE (*average*)	OUTPUT (LBS.) PER ACRE (*average*)
75 or less	70	202
76– 150	122	276
151– 300	207	309
301– 600	448	381
601–1,200	890	521
over 1,200	1,639	791

Questions

1. Calculate the marginal output per hour between different levels of labor input.
2. Show graphically total output, average output, and marginal output all plotted as functions of labor input.
3. Can you identify the point of diminishing returns?
4. Do your calculations reveal increasing returns at any point? What might explain this result?

CASE 7-25   Cocoa farming in Nigeria, II

In 1951–52 cocoa prices in Nigeria on the farm were about 160 shillings per 100 lbs. Wage rates were about 7 pence per hour. (Note: 1 shilling = 12 pence.)

Questions

1. Using the production figures given in the previous case, calculate the amount of labor per acre which would yield the greatest profit.
2. Try to solve this problem graphically using marginal revenue product and marginal cost curves.
3. Indicate how changes in the wage rate or changes in the price of cocoa would change your answer to Question 1.

[19] R. Galletti, K. D. S. Baldwin, and I. O. Dina, *Nigerian Cocoa Farmers,* The Clarendon Press, Oxford, 1956, p. 313. Reprinted by permission.

CASE 7-26   Marginal productivity of football players

"At the moment, professional footballers [20] get a maximum wage of £15 a week, plus small bonuses for wins and draws—exiguous payments by results. The marginal productivity of individual star players—easily measurable by the differences in gate receipts when they are not playing—is well up in the surtax class.[21] Inevitably, therefore, many stars get payments on the side—subsidized houses, dummy jobs, and, sometimes, straight cash payments; including these and advertisement fees, an international player can probably expect to earn around £1,500 a year. . . ." [22]

Questions

1. Show by an arithmetical example how one might measure the marginal productivity of a star player.
2. Under what circumstances would the payment received by a star player be approximately equal to his marginal productivity? Under what circumstances might it be considerably below his marginal productivity?

CASE 7-27   The effects of minimum wages

"The effects of minimum wages may in principle differ between industries in which employers do and do not have control over the wage rates they pay for labor of given skill and application. The two possibilities will be discussed in turn.

Each worker receives the value of his marginal product under competition. If a minimum wage is effective, it must therefore have one of two effects: first, workers whose services are worth less than the minimum wage are discharged (and thus forced into unregulated fields of employment, or into unemployment or retirement from the labor force); or, second, the productivity of low-efficiency workers is increased.

The former result, discharge of less efficient workers, will be larger the more the value of their services falls short of the legal minimum, the more elastic the demand for the product, and the greater the possibility of substituting other productive services (including efficient labor) for the inefficient workers' services. The discharged workers will, at best, move to unregulated jobs where they will secure lower returns. Unless inefficient workers' productivity rises, therefore, the minimum wage reduces aggregate output, perhaps raises the earnings of those previously a trifle below the minimum, and reduces the earnings of those substantially below the minimum. These are undoubtedly the main allocational effects of a minimum wage in a competitive industry.

---

[20] The players referred to here are soccer players in England. (Authors' note.)
[21] The reference here is to personal income tax rates. (Authors' note.)
[22] "Economics in Sunderland," *The Economist,* London, April 20, 1957, p. 213.

The second and offsetting result, the increase of labor productivity, might come about in one of two ways: the laborers may work harder, or the entrepreneurs may use different production techniques. . . .

If an employer has a significant degree of control over the wage rate he pays for a given quality of labor, a skillfully set minimum wage may increase his employment and wage rate and, because the wage is brought closer to the value of the marginal product, at the same time increase aggregate output. The effect may be elucidated with the hypothetical data in [the table below]. If the entrepreneur is left alone, he will set a wage of $20 and employ 50 men; a minimum wage of $24 will increase employment to 70 men. . . ." [23]

Hypothetical Data Illustrating Employer Wage Determination

NUMBER OF WORKERS	WAGE RATE	MARGINAL COST OF A WORKER	VALUE OF THE MARGINAL PRODUCT
10	$12		$36
20	14	$16	34
30	16	20	32
40	18	24	30
50	20	28	28
60	22	32	26
70	24	36	24

Questions

1. Why, under competitive conditions, does each worker receive the value of his marginal product?
2. If workers whose services are worth less than the minimum wage are forced into unregulated fields of employment, what is the impact upon wages in these unregulated fields? Why?
3. Referring to the table, explain why the entrepreneur who has control over the wage rate he pays would set a wage of $20 and employ 50 men. Also explain why a minimum wage of $24 will increase employment to 70 men.

MARGINAL UTILITY

The early theories of consumer behavior relied upon a concept known as utility, and upon a special assumption regarding the way utility increased as a consumer obtained greater amounts of a good.

[23] G. J. Stigler, "The Economics of Minimum Wage Legislation," *American Economic Review*, Vol. 36, No. 3, June 1946, pp. 358–61. The table is adapted from the same source. © 1946 by the American Economic Association.

By utility, economists mean the satisfaction or usefulness of a good to a consumer. The total satisfaction obtained from a good is treated as a function of the quantity of the good, and the *marginal utility* thus refers to the rate at which this total changes as the quantity changes.

The special assumption which earlier economists made was that of *diminishing marginal utility,* which means that the extra satisfaction obtained from each additional unit of a good is less than that obtained from the previous unit. In other words, it was assumed that utility increased at a diminishing rate.

Whether or not there is good psychological support for this assumption is a matter of much debate. The use of the concept of utility has also been criticized on the ground that it is impossible to identify and measure any specific quantity corresponding to the concept.

In recent years, economists have developed slightly more refined theories of consumer demand which do not rely on diminishing marginal utility. Instead, they assume that the more a consumer has of any one good, the less willing he will be to give up some other good in order to obtain still greater quantities of the first good. This is known as *diminishing marginal rate of substitution.*

This concept may be illustrated graphically through the use of indifference curves as shown in Fig. 7-13. Along the horizontal axis we have plotted the quantity of clothing that a consumer may be able to purchase. Along the vertical axis we have plotted the quantity of recreation. The assumption is that to acquire more clothing, the consumer must give up some recreation, and vice versa. Each point along an indifference curve represents a combination of clothing and recreation which would be equally satisfactory to the consumer, i.e., it is a matter of indifference to the hypothetical consumer whether he is at one point on the curve or another. This is not to say that he would not prefer being on a higher curve than a lower one, since the higher curves (reflecting a higher income on his part) represent greater quantities of both clothing and recreation. However, as far as the possible combinations on any one curve are concerned, he is indifferent.

The diminishing marginal rate of substitution of recreation for clothing and vice versa is indicated by the fact that the indifference curves are always convex to the origin. If they were concave with respect to the origin instead of convex, we would in effect be saying that the more of one good a consumer has, the more willing he will be to sacrifice other goods to obtain still more of the first good. This does not appear to be a reasonable assumption. It may be noted that indifference curves are seldom used in practical applications of economics, but do play an important role in theory.

FIG. 7-13 Recreation-Clothing Indifference Curve

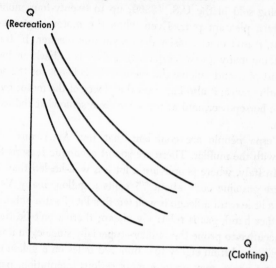

Whether we use the assumption of diminishing marginal utility or the assumption of diminishing marginal rate of substitution, the practical conclusion is essentially the same, namely, that a consumer who is trying to maximize satisfaction will buy more of a good when its price decreases and less when it increases (*ceteris paribus*).

CASE 7-28   The economics of muffling

"Among Italy's contributions to civilization, the motor scooter cannot be counted as an unmixed blessing. A visitor to Florence, for example, may be lulled to sleep by the strains of *Tosca* emanating from the municipal opera house—in Italy, opera is apt to run well past midnight—but he is in for a rude awakening when the opera lets out. Indeed, the noise made by a thousand homeward-bound Florentines, most of them riding motor scooters that sound like riveting guns, is enough to drive a tourist back to New York for a little peace and quiet.

Now it appears that Americans won't be able to escape motor scooters even by staying home. Not content with making the Italian night hideous, Piaggio & Co. of Genoa, which manufactures one of Italy's most popular scooters, the Vespa, has launched a determined assault on the American market. The prospect is, in a literal sense, disquieting.

Piaggio's American distributors, however, have reassuring news. The fact that some Vespa's make a lot of noise in Italy, they say, doesn't mean that they will be noisy here. In its pristine state, indeed, the 6-horsepower model being sold in the U.S. ($369; up to twenty-four months to pay) emits only a pleasant purr. Even when the motor is gunned with the clutch out, it isn't much noisier than a vacuum cleaner. In Italy, though, the first thing many a new Vespa owner does is to hack an inch or so off the exhaust pipe and remove the silencer. This is not for the sole purpose of generating noise; it also increases the power of the motor by about one-tenth of a horsepower, and at the same time somewhat reduces fuel consumption.

The Vespa people are confident that few Americans are likely to monkey with the muffler. There are sound economic reasons for this prediction. In Italy, where people are a lot less well-heeled than in America, and where gasoline costs about 75 cents a gallon, many Vespa owners feel that a little extra mileage is well worth a lot of extra noise. In the U.S., on the other hand, gas is relatively cheap; there won't be the same economic incentive to prune the muffler—especially since even a fully muffled Vespa will travel from eighty to a hundred miles on a gallon of gas.

The extra power may prove a more serious temptation, particularly to the hot-rod crowd. But to most Americans, accustomed to automobiles rated at 200-horsepower and up, the difference between 6-horsepower and 6.1-horsepower will probably not seem worth the bother of borrowing a hack saw.[24]

Questions

1. How is the concept of maximization used in this case?
2. Assuming that tastes are identical in Italy and the U.S., how can you explain the anticipated difference in behavior?
3. Does the behavior of Italians described above (if this behavior is the result of each individual's attempting to maximize his satisfaction) also result in maximum satisfaction for society as a whole? Why or why not?
4. Explain this case using indifference curves with miles per gallon of gas measured along one axis and absence of motor noise measured along the other.

[24] "The Economics of Muffling," *Fortune*, August 1956, p. 74. © 1956 by Time, Inc.

CHAPTER EIGHT

Aggregative Analysis: Monetary Concepts

The discussions of concepts in the preceding chapters have primarily concerned changes in the specific content of economic activity. That is, we have been analyzing the determination of prices and quantities for particular commodities and services, and the behavior of particular consumers, firms, and industries. As was mentioned in Chapter 1, however, there are also important economic problems connected with the aggregate level of economic activity. These problems involve the general price level and the over-all level of employment and output for the nation as a whole. Under conditions of relatively full employment and a stable price level, the questions of specific content are of greatest interest to economists. But when a depression grips a nation, or when inflation threatens, economists turn their attention to the aggregate level.

In order fruitfully to approach these problems, we will find it necessary to supplement the analytical tools of the previous chapters. We have seen how we may determine the price of a particular commodity or service by establishing a point of equilibrium between two functional relationships, i.e., $Q_d = f(p)$ and $Q_s = f(p)$. The same equilibrium solution also gave us the quantity of the particular commodity or service that would be exchanged in the market. When we turn to the tools and concepts which have been specifically designed to assist us in analyzing the general price level and the general level of output, we find that our knowledge of functional relationships and equilibrium analysis is still helpful. The main difference in approach is that the variables whose relationships we now analyze represent the general price level and the total quantity of all commodities and services rather than the price and quantity of any particular commodity or service.

When economists attempt to explain changes in these aggregate variables, they usually rely upon two general approaches or analytical models. One approach, closely associated with the name of John Maynard Keynes, is discussed in Chapter 9. In this chapter we will learn something about the quantity theory of money, and the so-called "transactions-velocity" approach which was given prominence by the American economist, Irving Fisher, almost a half century ago.

MONETARY CONCEPTS

The Quantity Theory of Money

One of the earliest questions which concerned writers on economic subjects was the reason for fluctuations in the price level. Some observers noted a relationship between aggregate price fluctuations and the flow of gold and silver in and out of the country. This was then elaborated into a theory called the quantity theory of money, stating that the price level (P) is proportional to the quantity of money (M). This is expressed by the equation $M = kP$, where k is a constant. What this means is that the relationship between P and M will always remain constant, i.e., if M doubles, P will double, and if M is reduced by half, P will be reduced by half. Since the time when this theory was elaborated, it has been found that the relationship between M and P is not as constant as the theory asserts; nevertheless, predictions based on the theory frequently give us useful approximations of developments in the real world.

The Equation of Exchange

Related to the quantity theory of money is the "transactions-velocity" approach, which was stated in the famous "equation of exchange." This equation may be written:

$$MV = PQ \text{ [1]}$$

where M = the quantity of money
$\quad V$ = the velocity of money
$\quad P$ = the general price level
$\quad Q$ = the quantity of final commodities and services produced and sold

In this formulation, the hypothesis $M = kP$ has been replaced by a tautology. The statement $MV = PQ$ is always true because the terms

---

[1] The equation often appears in other forms, such as $MV = PT$, where T represents the total volume of transactions rather than just the quantity of final output. Regardless of what is included in T or Q, the equation holds true, but V and P must always be redefined so as to refer to the particular version of T or Q which is being used.

of the equation $(M, V, P,$ and $Q)$ are so defined that the identity that is expressed must exist under all circumstances. As in the case of any tautology, we cannot test the validity of the equation by examining the real world. Its value consists primarily in directing our attention to the relevant variables and indicating their relationship to one another. We will examine the significance and measurement of each of these variables in turn.

THE QUANTITY OF MONEY

According to one proverb, money "makes the world go round"; while another holds that it is "the root of all evil." Economists offer a more prosaic but only slightly more specific definition. "Money," says Professor D. H. Robertson, "is anything which is widely accepted in payment for goods, or in discharge of other kinds of business obligations." [2] It follows, therefore, that what will be considered money at any given time and place will depend upon the specific laws, institutions, and habits which prevail. Cows, shells, cigarettes, and precious metals have all served as money at one time or another.

Today, in the United States, most payments for goods and other obligations are made in the form of checks drawn against demand deposits in commercial banks. Another significant fraction of payments is made with coin and currency. Most economists, therefore, say that the quantity of money in the economy is the amount of coin and currency held by the public, plus the demand deposits in commercial banks.

It is important to note that the M in the equation of exchange refers to the *stock* of money in existence at a particular moment in time. It does not refer to a *flow* of money over a period of time. For example, if someone asks you, "How much money do you make?" and you answer, "$200 a week," you are both speaking of money as a flow. But if you are asked, "How much money do you have?" and if after searching your wallet and adding your bank balance you answer, "$479.32," you are speaking of a stock of money, as the term is used in the equation of exchange. It may be helpful to think of the difference between a snapshot and a motion picture. The quantity of money can be photographed with a still camera, but the flow of money cannot.

In measuring the quantity of money in the United States, we must allow for the fact that the quantity changes from time to time. There are usually only slight changes from day to day, and larger changes from month to month and year to year. Fig. 8-1 shows changes in the

[2] D. H. Robertson, *Money*, rev. ed., Pitman, N.Y. and London, 1948, p. 2.

money supply between 1929 and 1956 on an annual basis, while Fig. 8-2 shows monthly changes during a recent two-year period. As we have indicated, the quantity of money as expressed in the equation of exchange refers to the quantity in existence at a given moment of time. Thus, when we speak of the quantity of money in a given year, we are talking about an average of all the different quantities that existed during that year. This may be approximated by calculating the average of the quantities existing at the end of each month, or at the end of each week.

FIG. 8-1   United States Money Supply, 1929–1956

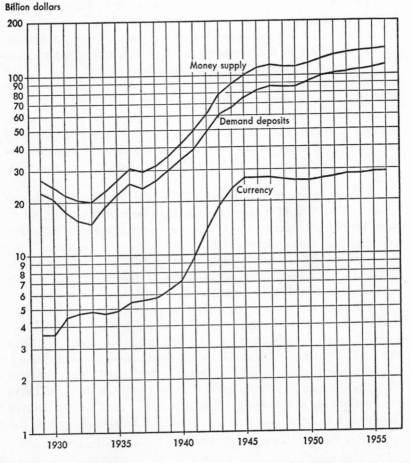

Billion dollars

FIG. 8-2   United States Money Supply, October 1955–October 1957

Billion dollars

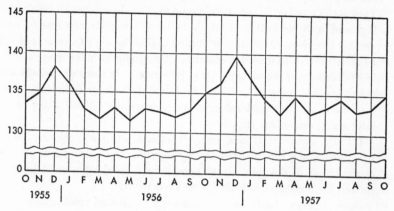

CASE 8-1   The quantity of money

As of December 31, 1956, the United States public, including all non-financial business firms, held among other assets the following (in rounded figures): [3]

U.S. government bonds and short-term loans	$100 billion
Demand deposits	111
Time deposits	82
Federal reserve notes	26
Silver certificates	2
Coins	2

Questions

1. What was the quantity of money in the U.S. on December 31, 1956?
2. How can you justify excluding some of the assets shown above from our definition of money?
3. Do you think that changes in the size of the assets you have excluded would affect *P* or *Q*? Explain.

CASE 8-2   The money supply

"Included in the list of business indicators published each month in this *Review* are statistics on 'total demand deposits adjusted' and 'currency outside the Treasury and Federal Reserve Banks.' When considered together these two figures give a simple, but adequate, indication of the size of the country's money supply, that is, the amount of money imme-

---

[3] Board of Governors of the Federal Reserve System, Division of Research and Statistics.

diately available for cash payments. Somewhat different definitions of the money supply from the one given above are used by some analysts. They include 'other liquid assets' (such as time deposits or shares in savings and loan institutions), which in normal periods are readily convertible into demand deposits or currency. The Board of Governors of the Federal Reserve System, for example, customarily includes time deposits in its definition of the money supply. However, only demand deposits and currency have been included in the table of Business Indicators, since they alone may be used for payment transactions without delay or an intervening conversion step.

On the other hand, most analysts exclude currency held by banks when estimating the available money supply. . . . These funds are not in the hands of the public, and thus, strictly speaking, cannot be considered immediately available for cash payments. . . .

Both currency and demand deposits have increased considerably since 1939. Owing to the tremendous rise in business activity, higher price levels, higher wages, and the need for higher levels of working capital, individuals and corporations have found it necessary to hold a larger volume of liquid assets. The expansion of the money supply must be related to the production of goods to determine its effect upon the economy. If production lags behind an increase in the money supply, there is a possibility of inflation, because the growing available money supply may merely be used in bidding against the relatively smaller supply of goods. However, in periods of extensive business activity and an increasing supply of goods, either an increase in the total money supply or a more intensive use of the available supply is necessary to facilitate the maintenance of a high level of activity.

The increase in the money supply in recent years has been due mainly to the increased lending activity of banks. In making a loan, a bank actually 'creates' money (demand deposits), that is, it credits the account of the borrower by the amount of the loan. Purchases of securities by the banks (unless they are purchased from the Federal Reserve Banks) also increase the money supply. Thus an increase or decline in the level of the money supply gives an indication of the aggregate lending and investing activities of the banks.

Whether a given increase in the amount of money is held in demand deposits or currency depends on the desires of people in choosing whether to deposit their funds in banks or to hold them in the form of currency. It has been estimated that currency payments probably comprise not over 10 per cent of total payments.

At different times, however, the public prefers to hold varying proportions of currency and demand deposits. . . .

The shift of funds between currency and demand deposits is affected not only by such long-run influences as the wartime needs for currency or the postwar demand for 'check' money, but also by seasonal factors working within these broader movements. For instance, although both demand deposits adjusted and currency in circulation decline somewhat in January, demand deposits usually continue to decline quite sharply in February and March, while the amount of currency outstanding tends to level off. Demand deposits begin to increase fairly rapidly in June and continue to increase throughout the fall months with a peak in December. Currency also has a December peak, but its rise does not usually become noticeable until November. . . . While the broad seasonal movements noted above usually apply, year-to-year variations arising from changed business conditions have prevented the computation of satisfactory adjustment factors for the seasonal variations of demand deposits. . . ." [4]

Questions

1. Why, in defining M, are we primarily interested in funds which are immediately available for cash payments?
2. Is the Board of Governors of the Federal Reserve System wrong in including time deposits in its definition of the money supply? Can you reconcile the different approaches taken by the Board of Governors of the Federal Reserve System and the Federal Reserve Bank of New York?
3. Why do currency payments comprise such a relatively small percentage of total payments? What are the implications of this fact for problems dealing with the money supply?
4. How would you account for the short-run changes in the quantity of currency and demand deposits?

THE GENERAL PRICE LEVEL

The P in the equation of exchange represents the general level of prices. In the real world there is no single P; there are only prices for different specific commodities and services. P, therefore, is arrived at by calculating some sort of average of the many different prices which actually do exist. This average is usually expressed in the form of an index number, i.e., the average at any given date is expressed as a percentage of the average during some specified period of time, which is referred to as the base period and is always stated as 100 per cent. If prices in 1957 are on the average twenty-five per cent higher than in 1947, and 1947 is the base period, then the index for 1957 would be 125

---

[4] "Money Supply," *Monthly Review of Credit and Business Conditions,* Federal Reserve Bank of New York, November 1951, pp. 163–65.

(i.e., 125/100). On the other hand, if 1957 were the base year, then the relationship between the earlier and the later year would be 100/125, and the index for 1947 would, therefore, be 80.

It is obvious that no index can hope to encompass the millions of different prices of commodities and services which exist at any given time in the United States. The first question to be answered in compiling an index, therefore, is what prices shall be included. A second major problem concerns the method of averaging different price changes. If automobile prices double and wheat prices decrease by half, how much importance shall be attached to each fact in computing the index?

The theoretical and practical difficulties encountered in attempting to measure P are many and exceedingly complex. We have only suggested a few as a warning to the student that no perfect measure exists, and that all price indexes should be used with caution.

The index which is probably referred to most often as representing the general price level is the Consumer Price Index compiled by the Bureau of Labor Statistics. It measures changes in the prices of about 300 different commodities and services purchased by families of urban wage earners and salaried clerical workers. The base period for this index is the average of prices during 1947–1949, i.e., 1947–1949 = 100.

Another important general index is the Wholesale Price Index, also compiled by the Bureau of Labor Statistics. This index is based upon price quotations for approximately 2,000 commodities selected to represent all commodities sold on primary markets in the United States; the base period is also 1947–1949.

CASE 8-3   The consumer price index

The following data are taken from the BLS Consumer Price Index for 1939–1957 (1947–1949 = 100).[5]

PERIOD	ALL ITEMS	FOOD	HOUSING (total)	AP- PAREL	TRANS- PORTA- TION	MEDI- CAL CARE	PER- SONAL CARE	READ- ING AND RECREA- TION	OTHER GOODS AND SERVICES
1939	59.4	47.1	76.1	52.5	70.2	72.6	59.6	63.0	70.6
1943	74.0	68.3	82.8	67.8	78.2	78.7	73.8	75.3	80.2
1948	102.8	104.1	101.7	103.5	100.9	100.9	101.3	100.4	100.5
1952	113.5	114.6	114.6	105.8	126.2	117.2	111.8	107.0	115.4
1956	116.2	111.7	121.7	105.5	128.7	132.6	120.0	108.1	122.0
1957	120.0	115.4	125.5	106.8	135.7	137.8	124.2	112.0	125.3

[5] Bureau of Labor Statistics. Figures for 1957 are January-November average.

Questions

1. To what extent do prices show similar trends? To what extent do they show different trends? Which component shows the widest variation?
2. How do you account for the variations in the price behavior of the various components of the index?
3. In view of the differences in the behavior of prices for various commodities and services, of what value is the figure for "All Items" which is sometimes used as P in the equation of exchange?

CASE 8-4   Price index for underwear

Assume that in 1900 a pair of men's long woolen underwear sold for $5 and that in 1950 the price for an identical pair was $2. Assume further that short underwear for men was $2 per pair in 1900 and $5 in 1950. Can you construct a price index for men's underwear on the basis of this information?

THE QUANTITY OF COMMODITIES AND SERVICES

Q represents the rate of real output of the nation. It is the sum of all the automobiles, wheat, haircuts, machine tools, etc., produced during a given period of time. Although all of this production is real, it is not something we can measure directly. One difficulty is that we do not have any common unit of physical measurement, such as pounds, feet, or bushels, which would be applicable to all forms of output. Moreover, even when two commodities can be measured in the same unit, the results may be devoid of economic significance. It is certainly questionable, for example, whether one pound of apples and two pounds of aluminum should be considered the same output as two pounds of apples and one pound of aluminum.

One way of attempting to measure changes in Q is to construct an index which shows the average change in output of various commodities and services. One such index which is referred to frequently by economists is the Federal Reserve Board Index of Industrial Production, which is designed to measure changes in the physical volume of output in the manufacturing and mining sectors of the economy. These sectors account for about one-third of the value of the total production of commodities and services in the United States.

Another approach to Q is through the dollar value of output. If we know the changes in the *value* of output over a period of time, and if we have a price index which reliably reflects changes in the general price level during the period, we can divide the former by the latter and form some estimate of the changes in Q (i.e., real output) over the period.

CASE 8-5   Employment and output

The following time series are all important indicators of the "real" level of economic activity in the country.[6]

	GROSS NATIONAL PRODUCT IN 1956 PRICES (*billions of dollars*)	FEDERAL RESERVE BOARD INDEX OF INDUSTRIAL PRODUCTION (*1947–49 = 100*)	CIVILIAN EMPLOYMENT (*thousands*)
1929	187.1	59	47,630
1930	169.5	49	45,480
1931	156.9	40	42,400
1932	133.5	31	38,940
1933	130.1	37	38,760
1934	143.6	40	40,890
1935	158.5	47	42,260
1936	179.5	56	44,410
1937	190.2	61	46,300
1938	181.5	48	44,220
1939	196.2	58	45,750
1940	213.7	67	47,520
1941	247.2	87	50,350
1942	278.7	106	53,750
1943	309.6	127	54,470
1944	332.6	125	53,960
1945	325.7	107	52,820
1946	290.6	90	55,250
1947	289.6	100	58,027
1948	302.7	104	59,378
1949	301.8	97	58,710
1950	329.9	112	59,957
1951	354.2	120	61,005
1952	366.6	124	61,293
1953	381.6	134	62,213
1954	374.6	125	61,238
1955	401.7	139	63,193
1956	412.4	143	64,979

[6] *Economic Report of the President,* January 1957; Board of Governors of the Federal Reserve System, *Federal Reserve Bulletin,* December 1957.

Questions

1. Explain what is meant by "Gross National Product in 1956 Prices."
2. Plot all three sets of figures on a graph.
3. Do the three indexes follow a similar pattern of change? Are there any noticeable differences in their behavior?
4. What would explain these similarities and differences?
5. Which of these indexes would be the best measure of Q? Why?

THE VELOCITY OF MONEY

V refers to the rate of turnover of money, i.e., the velocity at which money circulates. It is purely a derived measure, and there is no possibility of measuring it, even approximately, independently of the other variables in the equation of exchange. V is simply equal to the rate of spending (PQ) divided by the quantity of money (M). The tautological character of the equation is now apparent. Regardless of what values M, P, or Q may have, MV will always equal PQ because V is defined as being equal to PQ/M.

A simple analogy may help to fix the concept more firmly in the student's mind. Suppose we have a circular channel which has water continuously flowing in it. The quantity of water in the channel is comparable to the quantity of money in the economy (M). The amount of water which flows by a given check point during a specified period of time is comparable to the rate of spending of money in the economy (PQ). This amount will depend upon the amount of water in the channel (amount of money in the economy) and the velocity of the water (velocity of money). If we assume that the total length of the circular channel is one mile, that the entire channel contains 1,000,000 gallons of water, and that the water is flowing past the check point at a rate of 4,000,000 gallons an hour, we can then calculate the velocity as 4 miles per hour. Alternatively, we can say that the average drop of water makes 4 trips around the channel per hour. The velocity of money is usually expressed in this latter fashion, as the number of times the quantity of money moves around the economy during a given period of time, usually a year. Thus, if the total spending in a year is $400 billion and the average quantity of money in the economy during the year is $100 billion, then the velocity of money is 4.

CASE 8-6   Velocity of money [7]

YEAR	GROSS NATIONAL PRODUCT (PQ) (billions of dollars)	TOTAL DEMAND DEPOSITS AND CURRENCY (M) (billions of dollars)
1929	104.4	26.4
1930	91.1	24.6
1931	76.3	21.9
1932	58.5	20.4
1933	56.0	19.8
1934	65.0	23.1
1935	72.5	27.0
1936	82.7	31.0
1937	90.8	29.6
1938	85.2	31.8
1939	91.1	36.2
1940	100.6	42.3
1941	125.8	48.6
1942	159.1	62.9
1943	192.5	79.6
1944	211.4	90.4
1945	213.6	102.3
1946	209.2	110.0
1947	232.2	113.6
1948	257.3	111.6
1949	257.3	111.2
1950	285.1	117.7
1951	328.2	124.5
1952	345.4	129.0
1953	363.2	130.5
1954	360.7	134.4
1955	390.9	138.2
1956	412.4	139.6

Questions

1. Calculate V for each year.
2. Is V constant? If not, how can you account for the variations?

CASE 8-7   Money and national income

"The return in so many countries to the prewar relation between money and national income suggests that in each country the public, in the aggregate, wishes to hold a fairly fixed proportion of its income in the form of money. It would, however, be going too far to say that in a free economy the relation between money and income never varies: there may be not only short-run but also long-run changes. In countries where confi-

---

[7] Economic Report of the President, January 1957.

dence in the currency is severely shaken by a major inflation there may well be a permanent shift, the ratio of money to the national income settling down at a lower level than previously; in France this ratio is still well below the prewar level.

On the other hand, there may be a permanent shift upwards, as seems to have occurred in the United States in the 1930's. [See table below.]

The stability of the ratio of money to national income from 1899 to 1929 is striking: these thirty years included the first world war; population rose from 76 to 123 million and national income (in money terms) increased fivefold. The rise in the ratio during the 1930's was clearly connected with the business crisis: it is hardly surprising that, when the share index fell by 90 per cent. (from 360 in 1929 to 40 in 1932), the American public should have developed a preference for more liquid assets. The relatively high yields on ordinary shares (still about 6 per cent. early in 1951) suggests that this preference has not been eliminated even now that business has revived. Once price and other controls were imposed in 1942 the ratio between money and national income rose again, reaching its peak in 1946; with the subsequent rise in prices it has fallen back a considerable way towards the prewar level (if time deposits are included in the money supply, the ratio is now below the 1935–39 average). . . ." [8]

United States: Money and National Income

YEAR	NATIONAL INCOME (*in billions of dollars*)	MONEY SUPPLY (*in billions of dollars*)	MONEY SUPPLY AS A PERCENTAGE OF NATIONAL INCOME (*percentage*)
1899	15.4	5.3	34
1909	26.5	9.5	36
1913	31.4	11.0	35
1918	57.0	18.1	32
1920	68.4	23.7	35
1929	79.5	26.2	33
1937	69.4	30.7	44
1935–39 average	67.0	31.1	46
1946	180.3	110.0	61
1949	216.8	111.2	51
1950	235.6	118.2	50

Questions

1. What is the relation between money supply as percentage of national income and V as we have defined it?

[8] Bank for International Settlements, *Twenty-first Annual Report*, Basle, 1951, pp. 210–13. The table is included in the source.

2. Convert the figures in the last column of the above table to a form which shows V.

3. What explanations are given above for the fluctuations in V? Can you think of any others?

USE OF THE EQUATION OF EXCHANGE

We are now in a position to examine the use of the equation of exchange in analyzing economic change and determining public economic policy. When our problem is inflation or deflation, our attention is drawn to these phenomena by changes in the gross national product, changes in employment, or changes in the general price level. These changes can be thought of as variations in P, or Q, or both. Since the equation of exchange tells us that any changes in P or Q (unless these exactly offset each other) must be related to changes in M, V, or both, we can see that if we can predict (or control) future values of M and V, we are in a position to predict (or control) future values of P and Q.

The quantity theory of money and the equation of exchange are particularly relevant to the monetary policy of the Federal Reserve System. The Federal Reserve System is charged with the responsibility of helping to maintain both stable prices and stable employment at a high level. Through its control of the banking system, the Federal Reserve System can influence the quantity of money (M), and thereby influence P and Q. But V, which reflects millions of separate decisions by individuals and business firms, is not nearly so amenable to control. Sharp changes in V may therefore weaken, nullify, or perhaps exaggerate the impact of the system's monetary policies.

In this connection we may note that the quantity theory of money, which tells us that the price level (P) is proportional to the quantity of money (M), can satisfy the terms of the equation of exchange only if the relationship Q/V remains constant. Since there are times when the relationship Q/V does not remain constant, the quantity theory cannot solve all our economic problems either of analysis or policy. In spite of this, some economists find it a useful theory; others insist that it be supplemented or perhaps even replaced by other approaches. One of the most important of these other approaches is the Keynesian approach, which we discuss in the next chapter.

CASE 8-8   Use of monetary policy

"PREVENTION OF THE TWIN EVILS OF DEFLATION AND INFLATION IS THE GRAVEST AND MOST URGENT DOMESTIC

ECONOMIC TASK BEFORE THIS COUNTRY TODAY. For a number of recent years the problem before the monetary authorities has been how to use their powers in such a way as to reduce the inflationary impact of rising government outlays for defense. At some time in the future, possibly when the volume of military spending begins to decline, the problem may change from counteracting inflation to preventing deflation and unemployment during the period of transition. The direction of desirable action may be reversed but the underlying principles will remain the same. . . .

Deflation means a rapid decline in prices, curtailment of production, growth of unemployment, depletion of savings, a drop in consumers' purchases, shrinkage of consumption, deterioration of living standards, bankruptcies, and foreclosures. In its early stages deflation is favorable to creditors and holders of money and injurious to debtors and to producers or holders of goods. But as it spirals downward deflation engulfs the entire community—creditors and debtors, holders of money and of goods alike; it disrupts the economic structure, and endangers the social and political fabric of society.

Inflation reverses the sequence, but if carried to the extreme arrives at the same disastrous end as deflation. It means a rise in prices caused by a more rapid increase of spending than of goods. Inflation falls heavily on recipients of fixed incomes and inelastic salaries and cuts down the purchasing power of an ever-widening group of consumers. It disrupts the relationship between costs and prices, results in a shrinkage of the value of money and of confidence in its soundness, damages workers and their families, makes business planning and long-time programs hazardous and undependable, eats up real savings, and destroys incentives to save. In the end, when the bubble bursts, inflation precipitates disastrous liquidation and economic paralysis. Inflation as well as deflation is a threat to our economic organization and to our social and political way of life. . . .

Inflation reflects a demand for goods in excess of the available supply. On the money side this may result from an increase in the amount of money at the disposal of the public or from a more active use of the existing supply of money. Monetary policy can directly affect the amount of money at the disposal of the public and indirectly influence the rate at which the existing supply passes from hand to hand.

More active use of money may be caused by a variety of things: expectation of a rise in prices or of a shrinkage in the supply of goods, contagious business exuberance, reflected in large-scale capital undertakings, or speculation, or a combination of these influences. A restriction of the supply of money that tends to restrain inflation, or is expected to do so, will also moderate the expectations most likely to cause more active use of money. Also, changes in the quantity of money can be used to offset changes in the intensity of use of the existing amount. . . .

No one has been able to determine definitely the extent of the influence of changes in the volume of money on the course of business; the extent of this influence undoubtedly varies, depending on numerous surrounding conditions. But there is agreement that changes in the volume of money at all times exert an influence on the behavior of the economy, and there is agreement on the direction of this influence. Accordingly, it is the function of monetary authorities so to regulate the supply of money, over which they have a substantial degree of control, as to contribute to the maintenance of economic stability. . . ." [9]

Questions

1. Explain how monetary policy can affect M and V.
2. What assurance is there, if any, that a change in M will not be offset by an equal and opposite change in V?
3. Is there any way in which V can increase or decrease without a prior change in M?

CASE 8-9   Policy of the Federal Reserve System

Testifying before the Subcommittee on Economic Stabilization of the Joint Committee on the Economic Report in November 1954, the Chairman of the Board of Governors of the Federal Reserve System (Mr. William McC. Martin, Jr.) submitted the following statement:

"The policy of the Federal Reserve System with respect to the volume of money is to provide as nearly as possible a money supply which is neither so large that it will induce inflationary pressure nor so small that it will stifle initiative and growth. Put another way, the policy is to help maintain a volume of money sufficient to facilitate the consumption and investment outlays necessary to sustain a high level of production and employment, without leading to spending and investing at a rate which would outstrip the supply of available goods at prevailing prices and generate speculative conditions. Judged from this standpoint, the amount of money required varies with such factors as: the productive capacity of the economy; the state of business expectations; economic dislocations of various kinds; seasonal fluctuations; and changes in money turnover or velocity reflecting variations in liquidity and the demand for liquidity on the part of businesses and customers.

---

[9] "Flexible Monetary Policy: What It Is and How It Works," A Statement on National Policy by the Research and Policy Committee of the Committee for Economic Development, New York, N.Y., March 1953, pp. 1–4.

In the past, the monetary supply has shown considerable fluctuation over the course of business cycles. It is the policy of the Federal Reserve System to counteract, insofar as possible, the tendency for excessive cyclical swings in the volume of money.

An economy which is expanding requires an increasing supply of money to facilitate its growing volume of transactions. Additions to population and productive capacity, and a growing complexity of economic organization give rise to increased needs for cash balances. It is the policy of the Federal Reserve System to foster growth in the money supply in accordance with these needs.

Like any other modern monetary system, the monetary system of the United States is complex. In view of its complexities, it is not feasible to rely upon any mechanical formula for the determination of the volume of money appropriate to a given economic situation. This subject is one requiring continuous examination and study—historically, currently, and prospectively—of the various changing forces affecting the economy's need for money. . . ." [10]

Questions

1. Why does an expanding economy require an increasing supply of money?
2. Why is it not feasible to rely upon a mechanical formula to determine the volume of money required at any particular time?
3. What would be the effect of supplying a larger quantity of money than was needed? A smaller quantity? How can the Federal Reserve System determine whether or not the appropriate amount of money has been supplied?

[10] Hearings before the Subcommittee on Economic Stabilization of the Joint Committee on the Economic Report, 83rd Congress, 2nd Session, December 6 and 7, 1954, p. 26.

CHAPTER NINE

Aggregative Analysis: Keynesian Concepts

A DIFFERENT APPROACH

In the previous chapter we saw how the "transactions-velocity" approach can be helpful in analyzing changes in the general level of prices or output. During the 1920's the equation of exchange and the theories associated with it seemed to provide a satisfactory explanatory model and predictive tool for dealing with the economy. When the world was plunged into the great depression, however, many economists became dissatisfied with this approach.

Two main difficulties emerged. First, the usefulness of the equation of exchange seemed to depend to a considerable extent upon the widespread belief that the velocity of money tended to be relatively stable. It is easy to see that if we can assume V to be constant, then PQ can be controlled simply by controlling M. In the 1930's, however, V proved to be highly unstable.

A second problem concerned Q. Prior to 1930 the equation of exchange was used most often and most successfully to explain fluctuations in P. Most economists believed that the economy always *tended* to operate at a full employment level of Q, and that any deviations from that level would be temporary and self-correcting. The 1930's, however, were marked by persistent large-scale unemployment, and the economy did not return to a full employment level of output until World War II.

In 1936 John Maynard Keynes, a British economist who had already achieved an outstanding reputation in the monetary field, published *The General Theory of Employment, Interest, and Money,* which has become the single most influential work on economics of the twentieth century. It suggested a new approach to the analysis of

242

changes in the general level of prices and output, which put the major emphasis on output rather than prices.

The principal objective of Keynes's book was to explain the forces that determine the level of output and employment within a nation, and to provide suggestions for curing or preventing mass unemployment. In developing his ideas, Keynes introduced some new analytical concepts; he also used many of those with which we are already familiar—demand, supply, equilibrium, and the margin—but in special ways. Because of the great influence of his work, every student of economics should become familiar with these Keynesian tools. Probably the best way to achieve this familiarity is by studying the tools as they were used by Keynes in his "system" or theoretical model of the economy. It is important, however, to keep in mind the distinction between the analytical apparatus Keynes developed, and the theories and policy recommendations which he advanced. Many economists who disagree with Keynes and his followers with respect to specific aspects of either theory or policy nevertheless find his concepts and analytical framework extremely useful in studying and theorizing about questions of aggregate economic activity.

BASIC IDENTITIES (TAUTOLOGIES) IN THE KEYNESIAN SYSTEM

The foundation of the Keynesian apparatus is similar to that of the "transactions-velocity" approach. It consists of two tautologies which are established by definition. They are:

$$Y = C + S$$
$$Y = C + I$$

where Y equals national income, i.e., the total output of final commodities and services over a given period of time; C equals aggregate consumption, i.e., total expenditures for consumption commodities and services over the same period; S equals aggregate saving, i.e., the excess of national income over consumption expenditures over the period; and I equals aggregate investment, i.e., total expenditures for additions to capital equipment, together with net changes in inventory, over the period. The first equation says that the national income (Y) [1] is equal to spending for consumption (C) plus saving (S). The second says that national income is equal to spending for consumption plus spending for

[1] Although Keynes calls his analysis a theory of employment, he substitutes national income as being roughly proportional to the volume of employment, and many people now refer to it as "national income theory."

investment (I).[2] These are tautological propositions, which hold true at all times because the terms are defined in such a way that they must be true. They should not be confused with a theory or hypothesis, which may be supported or refuted by looking at the real world. From these two equations we may deduce a third:

$$S = I$$

which says that saving (that which is not spent for consumption) equals investment.

It must be emphasized that Keynes does *not* say that planned or intended saving is always equal to planned or intended investment. Indeed, he stresses the fact that the amounts people would like to save and the amounts people would like to spend for investment may be quite different. As we will see later, it is this very difference that leads to changes in the levels of output and prices. What the above equations tell us is that given our definitions of saving and investment, the actual amounts that are saved and invested must be equal. This equality is achieved by definition, just as MV must equal PQ.

The usefulness of this approach obviously depends upon the explanations of C, S, and I. We turn, therefore, to Keynes's theories and concepts concerning these variables. It is helpful to observe here that unlike the concept of the quantity of money (M), which is measured at a given moment of time (see p. 227), both C, S, and I are "flow" concepts, i.e., they are measured in units over a period of time (e.g., dollars per year). Since the choice of units is an arbitrary one (that is, it depends upon definition), the student must keep in mind the various units in which the concepts are expressed.

CASE 9-1   Y equals PQ

"Keynes's main interest was in monetary theory and policy. The development of his thinking was directed toward 'pushing monetary theory back toward becoming a theory of output as a whole.' His progress can be traced in the transition from $MV = PT$ to $I + C = Y$. . . .

In *The General Theory*, $MV = PT$ is replaced by $I + C = Y$, but one can readily see the old equation underneath. Y is PT. Investment and consumption are the components of income through which monetary changes

---

[2] As set forth above, these equations refer only to the private sector of the economy. If the government is included, the equations should be restated as follows:

$$Y = C + S + G$$

where G refers to tax collections of government; and

$$Y = C + I + G$$

where G refers to government spending.

register their effects. . . . It is the development of the analysis of demand for money which constitutes . . . the chief innovation of *The General Theory,* and upon it, and the use Keynes makes of it, mainly turns the answer to the question whether he has succeeded in 'pushing back the theory of money to becoming a theory of output as a whole.' " [3]

Questions

1. Explain why PT and Y are really the same thing.
2. How does this new formula redirect our attention with respect to the variables we studied when considering the use of the equation of exchange?

THE PROPENSITY TO CONSUME

To explain consumption (i.e., aggregate demand for consumer goods) Keynes introduces the concept of the *consumption function,* or the *propensity to consume.* He points out that while there are many variables which influence consumption, on the whole we may think of it as a fairly stable function of income: $C = f(Y)$. That is, we may think of a schedule which relates various values of C and Y, and we may plot a curve to represent this function, as in Fig. 9-1. This schedule differs from an income demand schedule (see Chapters 2 and 6) in that it refers to demand not for just one good but for all consumer goods, and represents the demand not just of one family but of the entire nation.

From the consumption function we can derive the *average pro-*

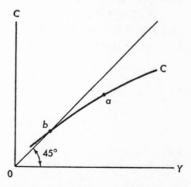

FIG. 9-1
The Propensity to Consume

---

[3] John H. Williams, "An Appraisal of Keynesian Economics," *American Economic Review,* Vol. 38, No. 2, May 1948, pp. 276, 278. © 1948 by the American Economic Association.

You will recall that T is sometimes used in place of Q in the equation of exchange; see footnote 1, p. 226. (Authors' note.)

pensity to consume (*APC*). For any given level of income, *APC* is the ratio of total amount spent for consumption to total income. Since some consumers usually save a part of their income, this ratio is usually smaller than 1; but when the nation's income is depressed to relatively low levels, it may rise to a figure greater than 1, since consumers will tend to spend more than they actually receive in income — the extra spending coming, of course, from previous savings. This is made clear by the 45-degree helping line shown in Fig. 9-1. Since this line is everywhere equidistant from each axis, it represents a continuous series of points at which consumption and income would be precisely equal. In the lower left-hand portion of the chart the propensity-to-consume curve is seen crossing above the 45-degree line, while in the upper right-hand portion it drops away from it.

Economists are even more interested in the relationship between *changes* in income and *changes* in consumption. This relationship Keynes calls the *marginal propensity to consume* (*MPC*). As we saw in Chapter 7, any marginal magnitude is expressed as the ratio of the change in one variable to the change in another variable; in the case of the *MPC*, the ratio is dC/dY. As we also saw in Chapter 7, a marginal magnitude between any two points (or at a single point) on a curve can be expressed in terms of the slope of the curve.[4] A less precise formulation, often encountered in elementary discussions of Keynesian theory, is simply to define the marginal propensity to consume as the amount of extra consumption induced per unit of increase in income. Keynes believed that *MPC* is always less than 1, but greater than zero, meaning that when income changes, consumption will change in the same direction, but not by as great an amount.

We are now ready to discover the relationship between Fig. 9-1 and Fig. 9-2. Since income is defined as consumption plus saving, the concept of the consumption function implies that there must also be a

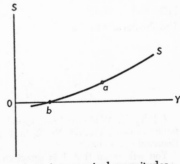

FIG. 9-2
The Propensity to Save

---

[4] See Chapter 7 for a discussion of slope as measuring marginal magnitudes.

saving function, $S = f(Y)$, and a corresponding propensity to save schedule and curve. This schedule is plotted in Fig. 9-2. You will note that at any given level of income, the propensity to consume and the propensity to save must add up to 1. That is, if consumption is 80 per cent of income, saving must be 20 per cent. This is easily verified by examination of the two curves in Figs. 9-1 and 9-2. At any given level of income, the distance from the propensity-to-consume curve (for example at point *a* in Fig. 9-1) to the 45-degree helping line is precisely equal to the height of the propensity-to-save curve at the same level of income (point *a* in Fig. 9-2). The relationship is made even clearer by a glance at point *b* on the two charts. At *b* consumption is precisely equal to income; saving therefore is zero. At still lower income levels, consumption rises *above* income; since the increased consumption can only be financed from savings, the saving curve falls below zero (i.e., becomes negative) by precisely the same amount, and the two propensities still add up to 1. This process of negative saving the economist calls "dissaving."

Just as *MPC* can be derived from the consumption function or propensity-to-consume schedule, so also can *MPS* (the marginal propensity to save) be derived from the saving function. And just as *APC* plus *APS* (the average propensity to save) add up to 1, so also must *MPC* and *MPS* add up to 1. If we know or can estimate the marginal propensity to consume at any level of income, therefore, we can arrive at a figure for the marginal propensity to save, and vice versa. The importance of knowing something about the size of *MPC* will become apparent later in this chapter.

CASE 9-2   Disposable income and consumer demand [5]

YEAR	DISPOSABLE INCOME [*]	CONSUMPTION EXPENDITURES
1929	83.1	79.0
1932	48.7	49.3
1937	71.0	67.3
1938	65.7	64.6
1941	93.0	81.9
1944	146.8	109.8
1947	169.0	165.0
1951	226.1	208.3
1956	287.2	267.2
1957	300.0	280.4

[*] Personal income less personal income taxes.

[5] U.S. Department of Commerce.

Questions

1. Under what assumptions may we regard this table as showing the propensity to consume?
2. On the basis of the above table, draw a curve showing consumption expenditure as a function of disposable income.
3. Using the curve you have just prepared, calculate (a) the average, and (b) the marginal propensity to consume at each of the following levels of disposable income:

$ 50 billion
100 billion
150 billion
200 billion

CASE 9-3   Dishwasher wins sweepstakes

"A 55-year-old dishwasher who won $56,000 last October in the Irish Sweepstakes is already back at dishwashing, because he is broke.

The dishwasher, Peter Zakals, tells readily of going on a spree that included chartering a private airplane on one of his five trips to Florida, living in luxury hotels, and distributing $100 tips. Now living in a $6-a-week hotel room, he still wears his expensive clothes. During his six-month spree Mr. Zakals developed a liver ailment that he blames on his high living. He has $26,000 left in the bank, but it has a lien against it filed by the Internal Revenue Service.

Mr. Zakals told questioners: 'I've had my fling. I want to be a dishwasher again. I got a hunch I'm going to win the sweepstakes again in June.' " [6]

Questions

1. How would you describe Mr. Zakals' marginal propensity to consume? Show it graphically.
2. Do you think this is typical of the nation as a whole? If not, why not?

CASE 9-4   The trend of consumer spending

"For [an] intensive look at the nation's biggest spender—the consumer— the analysts [at the University of Michigan's Fourth Annual Conference on the Economic Outlook, held November 1956] heard a report of studies undertaken by Michigan's pioneering Survey Research Center. The Center carries on a formal program of interviews to plumb individuals' attitudes and intentions. The latest round of interviewing suggested a continuation of underlying optimism, but of the sort that would accompany

[6] New York *Times*, April 17, 1957. © 1957 by The New York Times Company.

a high-level stability in buying rather than a substantial further increase in consumer spending.

In probing for weaknesses in the consumer sector, the Survey Research Center had tried to throw some light on four 'bogey-man' questions about the American consumer: Are his desires for durable goods becoming saturated? Is his interest in new housing on the wane? Is instalment debt currently a burden on borrowing families? Has the trend to 'buying on time,' along with other influences, weakened the will to save? Interviews revealed a set of consumer attitudes, compounded of past experience and innate desires, which suggested a negative answer on the part of the consumer to each of these questions so long as changes in his income flow or the general business picture did not upset his expectations.

On the other hand, the impetus for any major lift to the economy through a new upsurge in consumer spending was difficult to find. Likeliest candidate was judged to be the improvement in consumer asset-to-debt ratios as 1956 progressed, but this is the gradual sort of influence that seldom can trigger a sudden general reaction." [7]

Questions

1. The report suggests stability in consumer spending for 1957. Does this imply absolute or relative stability? If the latter, relative to what?
2. Why in your opinion are the four questions said to be "bogey-man" questions? What would a "yes" reply to these questions imply? Do all of the questions refer to consumer spending?
3. Show how changes in the asset-to-debt ratio can affect consumer spending. In your opinion, would a change in the asset-to-debt ratio affect consumer spending if income remained constant?

CASE 9-5   Savings on the uptrend?

"From late 1953 to early 1955 American consumers showed a marked tendency to spend more and save less. The annual rate of new personal saving declined more than 3 billion dollars even though consumer income was rising steadily. Thus income channeled into savings during this period represented a *declining* portion of a *rising* income stream.

Beginning with the first quarter of 1955, however, personal saving has reversed its downward trend and now is an *increasing* proportion of the *rising* total income. . . .

The question . . . arises as to what form the recent upturn in personal saving has actually taken. . . .

From figures recently published by the Securities and Exchange Com-

[7] Federal Reserve Bank of Chicago, *Business Conditions*, December 1956, pp. 3–4.

mission for the first half of 1956, increases in security holdings of individuals appear to be a major factor in the savings upturn during this period. . . .

A second major factor in the rise in personal saving is the decline in the purchase of automobiles. Inasmuch as credit normally plays a major role in car buying, the effect upon saving has been double-barrelled. With the reduction in spending for automobiles from the peaks reached during 1955, the volume of new consumer borrowing also has declined. Moreover, repayment of such debt contracted in 1955 and prior years has continued to grow. Both factors have resulted in a slowing down in the rate at which consumers add to their outstanding debt, which in turn has increased saving.

Whether or not the apparent revival in personal saving will be sustained depends, as always, on the collective decisions of consumers. Saving is typically a volatile quantity influenced by numerous factors including changing consumer needs, income, assets, indebtedness, and, quite importantly, expectations." [8]

Questions

1. Describe the changes in the marginal propensity to save from 1953 to 1956.
2. What is the relationship of consumer credit to savings? Does repayment of consumer debt constitute spending or saving?
3. Can consumption be a "stable" function of income if "saving is typically a volatile quantity"? Explain.

CASE 9-6 The effect of income changes on the rate of savings

"That in the short run changes in income influence consumption and savings has been dramatically emphasized by Keynes, who called the relationship between the two factors the fundamental psychological law and assigned to it a central place in his theoretical system. . . .

Empirical evidence for the validity of the short-run relationship may be sought, and was usually sought in the past, on the aggregative level, by comparing year-to-year changes in national income, aggregate consumption, and saving. The same relationship that prevails between aggregates may also be found, however, as expressly stated by Keynes, between changes in income and consumption of individual income receivers (or groups of income receivers). It is the latter problem that will be raised here: do recent studies of the financial behavior of families shed light on the relation between changes in income and changes in the amounts saved?

---

[8] Federal Reserve Bank of Chicago, *op. cit.*, pp. 5–9.

1947 Survey of Consumer Finances, Income Change from 1945 to 1946*

	Rate of saving in either 1946 or 1947	Decrease in income (−5% or more)	No change in income (+5% to −5%)	Increase in income (+5% to +25%)	Increase in income (+25% or more)
[SPENDING] UNITS WITH INCOME BETWEEN $1,000–1,999	Negative	40%	22%	21%	36%
	Zero	7	17	7	4
	Positive (1–19% of income)	38	39	47	40
	Positive (20% or more of income)	15	22	25	20
		100	100	100	100
[SPENDING] UNITS WITH INCOME BETWEEN $2,000–2,999	Negative	41	26	23	45
	Zero	2	2	3	4
	Positive (1–19% of income)	38	49	52	27
	Positive (20% or more of income)	19	23	22	24
		100	100	100	100
[SPENDING] UNITS WITH INCOME BETWEEN $3,000–3,999	Negative	21	10	16	21
	Zero	†	2	1	†
	Positive (1–19% of income)	55	60	59	41
	Positive (20% or more of income)	24	28	24	38
		100	100	100	100

* This table shows, for consumers in three income brackets, the rate of saving in 1946 or 1947 that was associated with varying degrees of income change between 1945 and 1946. Thus, if we examine spending units with income between $1,000 and $1,999, we find that of those whose incomes declined 5% or more, 40% had negative saving, 7% had zero saving, 38% saved 1–19% of their incomes, and 15% saved 20% or more of their incomes. (Authors' note.)

† Indicates less than 0.5 per cent.

From the point of view of empirical studies of consumer behavior, the problem presents itself as follows: We consider three groups of families, A, B, and C; in Period 1 families A had a real income of $2,000, B of

$3,000, and C of $4,000; in the subsequent Period 2 all three have the same real income, namely, $3,000. Then we ask: Will families A and C change the amounts they save during Period 2? What will be the relation of such changes (more specifically of ΔS) to the changes in income (ΔY)? We may, however, also ask a second question, although that question has not been emphasized by Keynes: Will the three groups of families save the same amounts of money in Period 2? If not, how will their savings differ (more specifically, what will be the relation between S and ΔY)? Answers to both questions can be derived from the Keynesian thesis. . . .

In the Surveys of Consumer Finances, conducted by the Survey Research Center of the University of Michigan for the Board of Governors of the Federal Reserve System, from which the data presented in this article are taken, it was possible to obtain information relevant to the second but not to the first question." [9]

Questions

1. According to the Keynesian thesis, what answers should we expect to the two questions posed about families A, B, and C?
2. What important Keynesian concept is involved here? What assumptions about it are made to answer the questions?
3. Do the survey results tend to support or refute the Keynesian thesis?
4. Are the results surprising in any respect? How might these "surprises" be explained?

THE MARGINAL EFFICIENCY OF CAPITAL

We have seen that $C + S$ must equal Y in the Keynesian system, and we have also seen that C and S are functions of income. The second basic identity in the Keynesian system is the statement $C + I = Y$, where I stands for investment. It necessarily follows that I must equal S.

But—and this is a crucial point in the Keynesian analysis—it does not follow that I is a function of income. In Keynes's view, the volume of investment, i.e., spending for new productive plant and equipment, depends on two other related variables: the rate of interest (i), and the marginal efficiency of capital (MEC).

Within an economy at any given time there exists a large number of opportunities for investment. Some of these are expected to bring in a high rate of return or "yield"; others to bring in a lower rate of

[9] George Katona, "The Effect of Income Changes on the Rate of Savings," *The Review of Economics and Statistics*, Vol. 31, No. 2, Harvard U. Press, Cambridge, Mass., May 1949, pp. 95–97. Copyright, 1949 by the President and Fellows of Harvard College. Table has been adapted from same source.

return. It is assumed that (such "other things" as the degree of risk being equal) businessmen will prefer those investments which will bring in the largest returns. If, therefore, only a small volume of investment is undertaken, the rate of return on even the least profitable investment will be high. As the most lucrative opportunities are taken up, businessmen will be forced to seek out the lower-paying investments. We can, therefore, think of the various possible levels of investment as a schedule in which the rate of return at the margin (i.e., on the last unit of investment spending) tends to decrease as the volume increases. This is the marginal efficiency of capital schedule plotted in Fig. 9-3. Of course, the schedule itself is subject to shifts with changes in technology, the prices of producer goods, the state of business confidence, and other variables. But *ceteris paribus, MEC* decreases as the volume of investment increases.

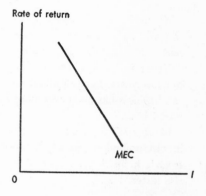

FIG. 9-3
The Marginal Efficiency of Capital Schedule

Given the *MEC* schedule, the actual volume of investment undertaken, i.e., the equilibrium point on the schedule,[10] will depend upon the rate of interest. Keynes argues that as long as the expected return on the use of capital for investment spending is greater than the cost of borrowing (the rate of interest), businessmen will find that it pays to undertake additional investment. But if the cost of borrowing is greater than the expected return, the additional investment will not pay. Given an existing rate of interest, therefore, the actual volume of investment will settle at that point on the schedule where the rate of interest and *MEC* are just equal. This may be seen in Fig. 9-4. By dropping a perpendicular line from the point at which the *i* and *MEC*

[10] The equilibrium concept used here is precisely the same as that discussed in Chapter 4.

curves intersect, we can measure this volume of investment on the horizontal (I) scale.

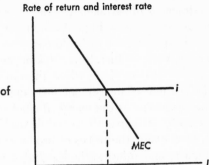

FIG. 9-4
The Determination of the Volume of Investment

CASE 9-7   Demand for capital goods

"In 1957, capital outlays by U.S. business will amount to $48.5 billion, or nearly $4 billion more than they did this year. They will absorb 11.4 per cent of an estimated gross national product of $424 billion. . . .

Never in history has spending on capital goods held so steady over so many years. For just about a decade now, capital spending by American business has been averaging 10.2 per cent of the U.S. gross national product. . . .

Since 1947 . . . outlays for plant have grown much faster than outlays for equipment, mainly because of heavy spending by the gas, oil, and electric industries. . . . From now on, however, equipment outlays will rise faster. . . ."[11]

Questions

1. What factors explain the high level of spending by business for capital goods?
2. What would you expect to happen to capital outlays if there were a sudden drastic rise in interest rates? Why?

CASE 9-8   Investment in the railroad industry

"After crying wolf for nearly ten years about how hard it was to raise money, the nation's railroads are finding now that the wolf is really in among the sheep.

The carriers' one ready source of new capital, the market for equipment trust certificates, shows signs of drying up. This secured, nonrefund-

---

[11] Gilbert Burck and Sanford J. Parker, "Another Big Decade for Capital Goods," *Fortune*, December 1956, pp. 101, 103. © 1956 by Time, Inc.

able lien on new rolling stock, which Wall Street used to regard as a little better than gold because it bore interest over an average eight-year life, now simply can't be sold by the carriers at prices they can afford to pay.

There is hardly a railroad in the East, and very few throughout the country, that can go out today and buy long strings of sorely needed rolling stock without being required to pay more for the mortgage money than the carrier can earn on its capital investment.

When the hard-pressed Boston and Maine Railroad needed $7,080,000 last January to finance 80 per cent of the price of new freight and passenger cars, the best interest rate it could get was 6.11 per cent. The last time a railroad paid more for a loan was in the late Twenties, when the industry had no trouble earning 6 per cent on its net investment.

The Boston and Maine in the last decade earned only 2.22 per cent a year on its net investment. The New York Central Railroad, the nation's second largest rail carrier, after the Pennsylvania, earned only 2.12 per cent on its $2,000,000,000 net investment in road and equipment in the ten years.

Central required a loan of $6,450,000 earlier this month for 80 per cent of the price of 1,000 new freight cars. It went down to Wall Street and learned the bad news—it would cost 5.65 per cent to borrow the money on equipment trust certificates due serially in six months to fifteen years.

Central said: 'No thank you.'

It decided instead to borrow the money 'privately,' although the road's chairman, Robert R. Young, used to fulminate long and loud against railroads that shunned offering securities at competitive bidding to seek more favorable terms in private negotiations.

In fact, Mr. Young's railroad for the past eighteen months has turned less and less to bidding and more and more to 'friendly' banks and institutional investors. Walter Grant, Central's financial vice president, disclosed last week that the Central system had borrowed $129,015,000 since Jan. 1, 1956, and obtained more than $79,000,000 of the total from private offerings.

Central in most of these deals has obtained ten-year money from banks and turned to trust and pension funds for loans of longer maturity. Mr. Grant disclosed that when Central turned down Wall Street's 5.65 per cent offer, the road trimmed its request to $5,000,000 and managed to find lenders willing to accept 4¾ per cent interest.

He added that Central, despite the many private deals it has made, still favors competitive bidding and that 'we don't want to fill up all our sources of funds.' . . .

The giant Pennsylvania has become so alarmed by the increasing cost of money that it wants to turn to the government for help. Evidently it still feels that the issue is a little warm for public hearing, because it hasn't voiced its ideas publicly. But in conversations with the Eastern Railroad Presidents Conference and directors of the Association of American Railroads, representatives of the Pennsylvania are trying to get the industry to ask as a group for federal assistance in financing new equipment.

The Pennsylvania idea is that the government create a new lending agency, somewhat akin to the old Reconstruction Finance Corporation. The agency would use government credit to borrow funds to purchase railroad rolling stock, which the rails would lease at user rates. While the idea has not been formally presented, Congressional committees, the Interstate Commerce Commission, and the President's Cabinet Committee on Transportation all are being dosed with the railroad's prescription.

James M. Symes, president of the Pennsylvania, says he is firmly convinced that normal financing channels are saturated with railroad paper and can no longer be counted upon to absorb much more than $300,000,-000 to $400,000,000 of railroad equipment certificates. This is only about half the amount of funds that the carriers insist that they need to replace worn-out cars. . . ." [12]

Questions

1. Which Keynesian concept is implicit in the above discussion?
2. Can you show the situation graphically?
3. Is the fact that the Boston and Maine earned only 2.22 per cent a year on its net investment sufficient proof that it cannot afford to pay 6.11 per cent per year for a new loan?
4. What justification, if any, is there for the proposal that the government provide funds for the railroads at rates lower than the free market rate of interest?

CASE 9-9   Investment in the electric power industry

"It is a commonly accepted view in economic theory that the flow of capital expenditures depends on the relation between the anticipated productivity of money spent on additions to plant and equipment, and the cost of funds, which is mostly identified with long-term interest rates after some allowance for risk. This view, however, is purely formal and is of doubtful value in a statistical analysis because of the lack of direct information on the anticipated productivity of capital. It has been frequently suggested that the productivity of capital can be approximated by the level of realized profits. This suggestion may have merits in deal-

[12] Robert E. Bedingfield, "Grade's Too Steep for Rail Finances," New York Times, June 23, 1957. © 1957 by The New York Times Company.

ing with competitive industries, although even in this case several assumptions must be made. In a competitive industry a shift to the right of the demand schedule or a reduction in costs should tend initially to increase profits. If the change in cost or demand conditions is regarded as permanent, the initial increase in profits (above the levels prevailing in other industries) would tend to bring about expansion of production and, therefore, investment by the existing firms and/or by new entrants. However, in monopolistic industries a high level of realized profits (i.e., a high *average* productivity of capital) need not be a reliable measure of the marginal productivity of investments, which presumably controls capital outlays; indeed the high level of profits may simply reflect the successful exploitation of the monopoly power which may be 'spoiled' by an expansion. These considerations apply with particular force to regulated industries, such as electric utilities, where firms are usually without direct competition in their service areas and are subject to various controls which greatly affect, directly and indirectly, the level of their profits and the conditions under which the profits are obtained. It is not surprising, therefore, to find that profits and interest rates alone completely fail to account for investment behavior of electrical utilities." [13]

Questions

1. Does the above discussion make use of the concept of *MEC*? Explain.
2. Assuming that (realized) profits are generally a good measure of *MEC* in a competitive industry, why do they not necessarily perform the same role in a monopoly situation?
3. Does the final sentence in the above discussion support the Keynesian views on the determinants of investment spending? Why or why not?

LIQUIDITY PREFERENCE

We have seen that the volume of investment spending depends in part upon the rate of interest. The rate of interest in turn is determined, according to Keynes, by the relationship between the quantity of money (M) and the schedule of liquidity preference (LP). M, in this formulation, is usually defined as in the equation of exchange, i.e., coin and currency held by the public, plus demand deposits in banks. In Keynes's view, the higher the rate of interest, the less willing will people be to hold their assets in a liquid form as money rather than in an income-producing form, such as stocks or bonds. Conversely, the lower the rate of interest, the more they will

[13] Avram Kisselgoff and Franco Modigliani, "Private Investment in the Electric Power Industry and the Acceleration Principle," *The Review of Economics and Statistics,* Vol. 39, No. 4, Harvard U. Press, Cambridge, Mass., November 1957, pp. 363–64. Copyright, 1957 by the President and Fellows of Harvard College.

want to do so. The liquidity preference schedule may thus be plotted
as in Fig. 9-5.

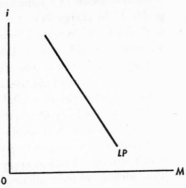

FIG. 9-5
The Liquidity Preference Schedule

This schedule can easily be thought of as the "demand for money,"
directly analogous to the demand schedules and curves we examined
in Chapter 2 and elsewhere. The interest rate i is the "price" of holding money, and therefore the higher the price, the smaller will be the
quantity demanded (*ceteris paribus*). Similarly, the quantity of
money available can be thought of as a supply curve. Since this
quantity at any given time is a fixed amount (and does not depend
upon the rate of interest), we represent it graphically by a vertical
straight line (Fig. 9-6). The equilibrium rate of interest is thus determined by the intersection of the supply and demand curves for
money. If the interest rate is such that the quantity of money people
want to hold is less than the supply of money, the interest rate will
tend to fall. On the other hand, if the interest rate is such that people
want to hold more money than can be supplied, it will tend to rise.
Only at the equilibrium rate of interest will the quantity of money
demanded and supplied be equal.

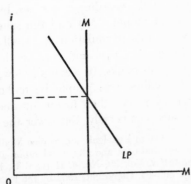

FIG. 9-6
The Determination of the Rate of
Interest

CASE 9-10   Corporate liquidity preference

"Though there is no agreement on the total liquid assets a company needs, there is a growing consensus that it should keep no more cash in the bank than is absolutely necessary to keep its checks from bouncing. Kennecott Copper, for example, still has over $250 million in liquid assets. But whereas $85 million was in the bank in 1949, today all but $25 million is invested in Treasury securities. The sharp rise in short-term interest rates in the past year—ninety-one-day Treasury bills have been yielding upwards of 2.5 per cent—has helped emphasize to many companies the truism that idle money is expensive." [14]

Questions

1. In your opinion, what might account for the "growing consensus" referred to above?
2. Under what circumstances might a corporation want to keep more than the bare minimum on deposit in a bank?
3. To what extent should the above case apply to individuals as well as corporations? Are there any important differences?

AGGREGATE EQUILIBRIUM

To summarize what has gone before, Keynes holds that consumption and saving are functions of income, while investment is a function of the marginal efficiency of capital and the rate of interest (which in turn is dependent upon liquidity preference and the quantity of money). We now have all the concepts necessary to determine the *equilibrium level of national income*—i.e., the level at which income will be stable, tending neither to rise nor fall. This equilibrium level may be shown in either of two ways.

1. One of our basic identities tells us that all income is either spent on consumption or saved $(Y = C + S)$. The other states that all income consists either of spending for consumption or spending for investment $(Y = C + I)$. Therefore, the necessary condition of equilibrium is that saving and investment be equal $(S = I)$.

We saw earlier in the chapter (Fig. 9-2) that S can be plotted as a function of Y. At low levels of income S is small or even negative; at higher levels it increases. In Fig. 9-7 we repeat the S curve from Fig. 9-2. We have also seen that investment is a function, not of income, but of i and MEC. If we assume that the interaction of these two factors has brought about a given level of investment, we can plot this level as a horizontal line above the Y axis in Fig. 9-7, implying

[14] Charles E. Silberman, "The Big Corporate Lenders," *Fortune*, August 1956, p. 113. © 1956 by Time, Inc.

that investment is the same regardless of the level of Y. Where the S and I curves cross is the point (and the only point) where S and I are equal. This point we label E, for reasons that will be apparent shortly.

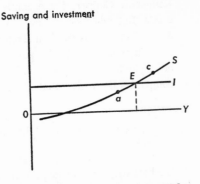

Saving and investment

FIG. 9-7
The Determination of the Level of Income

At any given time, the level of income in an economy can be thought of as having been created by the combined spending within the economy for consumption and for investment (including government expenditures on these items). If income were created only by consumption spending and there were no investment spending, total income would have to shrink whenever consumers or businesses save. In other words, if there is some attempted saving, the only way that the total output of the economy can be sold is if there is spending for investment.

Let us ask what would happen if income were to be at any level other than the one we have described as equilibrium, i.e., the point indicated by the perpendicular line dropped from E in Fig. 9-7. If income were higher, at point c, for example, people would want to save more. Combined spending for consumption and investment would then not be enough to absorb the total output of the economy at prevailing prices. Prices and/or employment therefore would shrink, and income would fall. Only when the level of income (and therefore the level of saving) had moved back to the point where S = I, i.e., point E, would an equilibrium level have been reached in the sense that at this level of income there is no reason for income either to rise or fall. At levels of income below this point, say at point a in Fig. 9-7, those wanting to purchase new plant, equipment, and other investment goods will try to spend more than is available as a result of saving. There will then be an upward pressure on prices and/or employment until income (and saving) move to the point where S = I, i.e., the equilibrium level of income.

2. The analysis just presented may be stated in a slightly different form by using a different set of analytical charts based on the concepts of *aggregate supply* and *aggregate demand*.

We can plot aggregate supply as a function of national income by a line which begins at the origin and rises at a 45-degree angle. This expresses the idea that for each dollar of national income paid out, there is produced or supplied a dollar's worth of final consumption or investment goods. If national income, for example, is at the rate of $300 billion a year, this means that goods are being produced (supplied) at the rate of $300 billion a year (see Fig. 9-8).

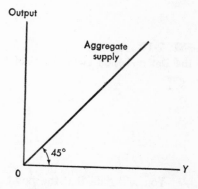

FIG. 9-8
The Aggregate Supply Schedule

When we add the investment demand for goods to the consumption demand, the result is aggregate demand, which may also be plotted as a function of income (see Fig. 9-9). Again, government expenditures for consumption and investment are thought of as included in aggregate demand.

If aggregate demand and aggregate supply are plotted on the same chart, we can find the point at which they are just equal (see

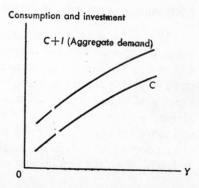

FIG. 9-9
Aggregate Demand

Fig. 9-10). This, according to Keynes, gives us the only equilibrium (stable) level of income for the economy at any given time. For if income were higher, aggregate supply would exceed aggregate demand, and income would tend to fall. If income were below the equilibrium level, aggregate demand would exceed aggregate supply, and income would tend to rise. It is only when aggregate demand and aggregate supply are just equal that there is no tendency for income either to rise or to fall.

FIG. 9-10
The Determination of the Level of Income

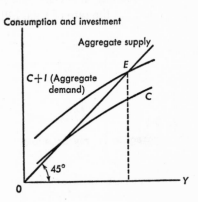

You will note that the point at which the perpendicular dropped from E in Fig. 9-10 intersects the horizontal axis is precisely the same distance from the origin as was true of the perpendicular dropped from E in Fig. 9-7. This is not just coincidence; since both charts are plotted on the same scale, either method must give the same result. For in both cases saving (income minus consumption) must be precisely equal to investment (income minus consumption); and there is only one equilibrium level of income where this condition will be met.

EQUILIBRIUM AND FULL EMPLOYMENT

We are now able to see how changes in investment can bring about changes in national income and employment. As is shown in Fig. 9-11, a shift in the investment schedule either upward or downward will bring about a new position of equilibrium. If we assume that the original equilibrium position is E, an increase in investment (i.e., an upward shift in the investment schedule) to the level shown as I_1 will move the equilibrium point to E_1, while a decrease in investment (i.e., a downward shift in the investment schedule) to the level shown as I_2 will move the equilibrium point to E_2. The level of national income which corresponds to each of these points is found by dropping a perpendicular line from each point to the horizontal (Y) axis.

FIG. 9-11 Alternative Equilibrium Positions

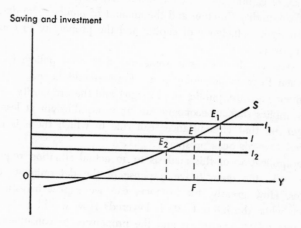

One of the assumptions of classical economics was that the economy would tend to operate at full employment, i.e., that economic forces would tend to bring about an equilibrium level of national income which would enable business to dispose of the whole of its output at prevailing prices. If income were to be either above or below this full-employment level, it was assumed that the appropriate adjustments would take place in prices and/or employment until full employment conditions were restored.[15] The Keynesian analysis requires us to reconsider these conclusions. If we regard point F in Fig. 9-11 as indicating the level of income at which there is full employment, we see that shifts in the investment schedule may result in equilibrium levels of income where there is either less than full employment (i.e., depression) or over-full employment (i.e., inflation). Since investment is based to a large extent upon the individual expectations of businessmen (as indicated in the MEC schedule), such shifts in investment may (and do) easily occur.

---

[15] Classical economics, as we have mentioned previously, placed the greatest stress upon price changes rather than changes in employment. Keynes, however, stresses the point that in our modern economy prices (and wages) tend to be rigid, at least over short periods of time, and that most of the short-run fluctuations in national income would therefore be the result of changes in the level of employment. Keynes agreed that once full employment was reached, all further short-term increases in income could only be the result of higher prices.

CASE 9-11   Application of Keynesian Theory

"The skeleton of the theory is simple: The national income depends upon investment and the income-consumption function. Investment, or more accurately private business investment, depends upon the marginal efficiency of capital and the rate of interest; the rate of interest depends upon the liquidity function and the amount of money. The determinants of the marginal efficiency of capital and the propensity to consume are very numerous. . . .

The skeleton alone gives us some suggestions for policy; for instance, that when there is unemployment, efforts should be made to increase investment (private, public, and foreign) and the propensity to consume. It also implies that an economy can be in equilibrium at less than full employment, that circumstances can rule in which there is no natural tendency towards peak prosperity. . . .

The application of this analysis to an actual situation requires judgments as to the quantitative response of the determinants to various changes. How greatly, for instance, can we expect investment to be affected when the interest rate is lowered? How would a change in the wage rate affect investment and the propensity to consume? Is investment greatly influenced by the rate of growth of population? Would a 50 per cent increase in the stock of capital goods bring about a large reduction in the marginal efficiency of capital, or a small one? These are important questions and the answers put flesh on the skeleton of Keynesian economics. But Keynesian economics does not consist in the answers to these questions. An economist who accepted the Keynesian outline could claim, though most Keynesians would disagree, that private investment could be greatly increased by a minor reduction in the interest rate, and he would then urge a mild expansionist banking policy during depression instead of a policy of, say, public works. Or one might support a wage cut if he believed that it would favor investment and the propensity to consume. Keynesians do not all have to prescribe the same medicine." [16]

Questions

1. What would be the probable effect on the equilibrium level of income of:
   a. an increase in the rate of interest;
   b. a decrease in the quantity of money;
   c. an increase in the propensity to consume;
   d. a shift to the left in the schedule of the marginal efficiency of capital?
2. Show these results graphically.

---

[16] Lorie Tarshis, "An Exposition of Keynesian Economics," *American Economic Review*, Vol. 38, No. 2, May 1948, p. 271. © 1948 by the American Economic Association.

3. How does the Keynesian analysis imply that an economy can be in equilibrium at less than full employment?

4. In the spring of 1958, unemployment in the United States reached 5,000,-000. What measures would you have recommended to bring the economy back to full employment?

CASE 9-12 Aggregate expenditure in selected years [17]

	BILLIONS OF DOLLARS			
	Personal consumption	Private domestic investment	Net foreign investment	Government
1929	79.0	16.2	.8	8.5
1932	49.3	.9	.2	8.1
1937	67.3	11.7	.1	11.7
1938	64.6	6.7	1.1	12.8
1941	81.9	18.1	1.1	24.8
1944	109.8	7.1	−2.1	96.5
1947	165.0	29.7	8.9	28.6
1951	208.3	56.9	.2	62.8
1956	267.2	65.9	1.4	80.2
1957	280.4	63.6	3.3	86.6

Questions

1. The above figures show expenditures. Do these figures also represent aggregate demand?

2. The business and government sectors seem more volatile than the consumer sector. What factors can you suggest to explain this?

CASE 9-13 Shorter work week?

Walter Reuther, president of the United Automobile Workers union, has been quoted as follows: "We must win a shorter work week with increased take-home [pay], for only thus can we create the greater purchasing power needed to balance our greater productive power." [18]

Questions

1. How do each of the following affect aggregate supply or aggregate demand:
   a. shorter work week;
   b. increased productivity;
   c. increased take-home pay?

2. Reuther seems to feel that increased pay will help prevent or cure unemployment and depression. Do you agree? Explain.

[17] U.S. Department of Commerce.

[18] *Business Week*, April 20, 1957, pp. 41–42. Copyright, 1957 by McGraw-Hill Publishing Company, Inc. Reprinted by permission.

3. Would a longer work week and decreased pay be good anti-inflationary moves? Why or why not?

CASE 9-14   Too many jobs

"Booms have their disadvantages, too, and one of these is now being experienced in West Germany, France, and Britain: there just aren't enough people looking for work.

Technically, there is still a smattering of unemployment. The German Labor Ministry lists 479,000 unemployed; Britain, 223,000; France, 108,500. But the statistics represent mostly people taking brief free rides on unemployment compensation, housewives who have decided to relax for a few months, and people shifting jobs.

So far from calling the present period of booming industry the best of all possible times, European economists are deeply concerned. Over-employment is accelerating inflationary cycles in Britain and in France. It also makes for gross inefficiency. During seasonal lulls, businesses hoard their workers. New industries, or expanding ones, find it hard to hire people at anything approaching competitive wage levels—so that overemployment puts a real limit on expansion. Dirty and dull jobs, in the mines and on the farms, find no one to perform them.

The situation has its incongruities. While a half-million French youths have been shipped off to fight in Algeria, 300,000 Algerian youths are taking their places in French factories. And while Northern Europe is frantically looking for workers, Spain, Italy, and Greece are trying to devise jobs for their unemployed.

One obvious solution is to bring the unemployed workers of southern Europe to the mines, mills, and factories of the north. To a very limited degree this is being done. Last winter the German Labor Ministry, with the reluctant approval of the trade unions, announced it would import 30,000 Italian laborers. But half a year later only 8,000 Italians had been persuaded to come. Too many Italians, grumbles the German Labor Ministry, found Switzerland more compatible, or Belgian wages higher, or French subsidies for children more attractive.

Europe's economists have no readier solution for the overemployment of 1956 than they had for the unemployment of a quarter of a century ago. And European politicians can't make up their minds whether to worry or rejoice over the situation. Britain's Conservative government wavers between calling overemployment a 'labor shortage' (when it is grimly warning the country about the dangers of inflation) or 'full employment' (when it is congratulating itself on such piping good times)." [19]

_____
[19] "Too Many Jobs," _Fortune_, September 1956, p. 80. © 1956 by Time, Inc.

Questions

1. Using Keynesian concepts, describe the above situation verbally and graphically.
2. What measures could be taken to change the above situation?

THE MULTIPLIER AND THE ACCELERATOR

The Multiplier

There is one other Keynesian concept which is not basic to the determination of the equilibrium level of income, but which appears very often in discussions using the Keynesian analysis. This is the concept of the multiplier, or more specifically, the multiplier effect of investment spending. Inspection of Fig. 9-7 or 9-10 shows that if there is a change in the volume of investment, there will be a change in the level of income. The multiplier is defined as the change in income divided by the change in investment. Thus, if an increase in investment of $5 billion would lead, *ceteris paribus*, to an increase in income of $10 billion, the multiplier would be 2.

It can easily be shown that the size of the multiplier depends upon the marginal propensity to consume. If the MPC is high, the multiplier will be high, and if it is low, the multiplier will be low. More precisely, the multiplier is equal to:

$$\frac{1}{1 - MPC} \quad \text{or} \quad \frac{1}{MPS}$$

The common sense explanation of this relationship is as follows: An increase in investment spending of $5 billion must create at least an additional $5 billion in income. Whether this increased income will create still more income depends upon whether the recipients of the additional income spend it or save it. To the extent that the new income is spent, it creates additional income for others, and this process continues on and on. Whenever some of the additional income is saved, however, the multiplier effect is reduced, and in any case when income has increased to the point where the rate of saving has increased by $5 billion (the amount of the increase in investment), the expansion stops. If the MPC were 0 (i.e., $MPS = 1$), the increase in income would only be equal to the increase in investment, and the multiplier would be only 1. If the MPC were 1 (i.e., $MPS = 0$), the multiplier and therefore the expansion would be infinitely great.

Since Keynes assumes that the consumption function is stable, the multiplier is not used in the Keynesian analysis in connection with consumption spending. However, we may note that the same effect could be produced if there were to be a shift in the marginal propensity to consume: if people as a whole begin to spend more of their income, additional income will be created for other people, and the final result will be an increase in income greater than the original increase in spending. Moreover, an increase in government spending *over and above any increase in taxes* will have a similar multiplier effect. We will have more to say on this point in the concluding section of this chapter.

The Accelerator

Another concept which is often applied in conjunction with the multiplier is that of the accelerator or acceleration principle. This concept, generally attributed to the American economist, J. M. Clark, was not part of the basic Keynesian apparatus, but in recent years many economists have found it desirable to combine the accelerator with the multiplier when theorizing about fluctuations in the aggregate level of output.

In its simplest form, the acceleration principle states that at least some investment is directly related to income or sales, and especially to rates of change in income or sales. Furthermore, relatively small changes in income may produce relatively large changes in investment. The following hypothetical figures illustrate the nature of this relationship.

Let us assume that $2 worth of capital equipment is required by the automobile industry for every $1 worth of automobiles produced per year, and that this equipment must be replaced, on the average, every 20 years (i.e., at a rate of 5 per cent per year). If automobile sales are stable at a rate of $10 billion per year, the industry will have $20 billion of capital equipment, and will be spending $1 billion for new plant and equipment each year, as shown below.

YEAR	ANNUAL SALES	CAPITAL EQUIPMENT	ANNUAL DEPRECIATION	GROSS NEW INVESTMENT	NET NEW INVESTMENT
1	$10 billion	$20 billion	$1 billion	$1 billion	0
2	10	20	1	1	0
3	10	20	1	1	0

Let us now suppose that demand increases by 20 per cent, to $12 billion of annual sales. This output will require $24 billion of capital equipment. In order to obtain this level of capital equipment, the industry will have to increase its gross new investment to $5 billion, and its net new investment to $4 billion. If sales should then level off at

$12 billion per year, however, investment will not stay at that high level, but will fall back to a level just great enough to cover replacement needs. This is shown in the table below.

YEAR	ANNUAL SALES	CAPITAL EQUIPMENT	ANNUAL DEPRECIATION	GROSS NEW INVESTMENT	NET NEW INVESTMENT
4	$12 billion	$24 billion	$1 billion	$5 billion	$4 billion
5	12	24	1	1	0

If sales should now decrease, back to $11 billion per year, for example, the industry would find that it had excess capacity, and might not even spend for replacement purposes, as shown below.

YEAR	ANNUAL SALES	CAPITAL EQUIPMENT	ANNUAL DEPRECIATION	GROSS NEW INVESTMENT	NET NEW INVESTMENT
6	$11 billion	$23 billion	$1 billion	0	0

Thus we see that the rate of investment is geared to the rate of change of sales, and that small variations in sales can be magnified or "accelerated" into large changes in investment.

Investment spending which depends upon sales or income is referred to as "induced" investment. This may be distinguished from "autonomous" investment, which is supposedly not related to income, but stems from the desire to introduce new processes or new products. The investment spending discussed earlier in this chapter was autonomous; we did not treat it as a function of income. The multiplier principle tells us that changes in autonomous investment may be magnified into much larger changes in income. The accelerator principle tells us that changes in income may induce much larger changes in investment. Most economists agree that there are elements of both autonomous and induced investment present in the economy most of the time, and, therefore, find both the multiplier and the accelerator helpful in analyzing business fluctuations.

CASE 9-15   Interdependence of consumption and investment

"Keynes's law of the propensity to consume is the important novel feature of his theory. . . .

As a first statement, apart from the business cycle or other special circumstances, Keynes's 'law' that as income rises consumption rises by less than unity is a plausible hypothesis; but it does not mean, necessarily, that consumption is the 'passive' factor or that the consumption function is stable. These two assumptions—(1) that consumption is dependent on income, and (2) that there is a 'regular' or 'stable' or 'normal' relation between them, such that the consumption function can be derived as a given datum of the system and used as a basis of policy and prediction—constitute the essence of Keynesian economics. . . .

Historically, there seem to me to be ample grounds for doubting both the assumptions. . . . They do not, for example, account for the effect of the rise of the automobile, a consumption good—or of new products generally—upon the growth of national income, where we have had a dynamic response of consumption and investment, each to the other. The application of an investment 'multiplier' to consumption as a passive, given factor in order to account for such changes seems wholly unrealistic. . . . Keynes's proposition that autonomous changes in investment determine changes in income, and hence in consumption (according to the 'law'), is probably no better than its opposite, that spontaneous changes in consumption determine changes in income, and in investment. The *interdependence* of consumption and investment, each responding to the other—and both responding (spontaneously rather than systematically) to changes in ideas, methods, resources—seems to me to be the essence of economic progress. But it does not lend itself readily to equilibrium analysis. . . .

The rise of consumer durables has been the outstanding economic phenomenon of our times. From the standpoint both of long-run growth and of business cycle behavior, it raises serious questions for Keynesian analysis. Between the two wars, expenditures on such goods were fully as large as those on capital goods, and their fluctuations fully as great; nor can we make any clear generalization as to which played the greater role in initiating cyclical changes. . . ." [20]

Questions

1. Explain how "autonomous changes in investment [can] determine changes in income."

2. Explain how "spontaneous changes in consumption [can] determine changes in income and in investment."

3. Why does the *interdependence* of consumption and investment "not lend itself readily to equilibrium analysis"? Is this a justified criticism of Keynes's equilibrium analysis? Why or why not?

CASE 9-16   Wheels turning on road program

"The wheels have finally begun to turn on a gigantic project that will

---

[20] John H. Williams, *op. cit.*, pp. 280–81.

have a far-reaching impact on the nation's economy this year [1957] and for years to come. It is the new highway building program, which will involve outlays of at least $50,000,000,000 before 1972.

As a whole, the highway program is one of the largest in history. By comparison, it cost $366,700,000 to build the Panama Canal. The total investment in the Tennessee Valley Authority has been about $3,000,-000,000, and the depression-time Works Progress Administration and Public Works Administration together spent about $15,000,000,000 before they went out of existence.

As it gains momentum—and the first big push will come this year—the highway program will constitute a growing and ever more important share of the gross national product. It will affect all types of transportation, the construction industry and scores of others, employment, taxes, commodity prices, marketing, plant location—in fact, about every phase of economic life in this country. . . .

This vast outpouring of funds, increasing yearly, should help to ease any sharp dips in the economy—none of which is now in view. The benefits will spread out in ever-widening circles. . . .

The effect on suppliers of construction materials is significant. For each $1,000,000,000 of new road building above the 1955 rate of $4,600,-000,000 a year, according to the American Road Builders' Association, these added supplies will be needed: 16,564,000 barrels of cement, 76,415,000 tons of aggregates, 510,000 tons of steel, 995,000 tons of bituminous material, and 122,794,000 tons of petroleum products. As the building program hits its peak, the present consumption of 50,000,000 barrels of asphalt is likely to be doubled.

Makers of road-building equipment—the big trucks, bulldozers, and the like—foresee a bonanza. Robert F. Black, president of White Motor Company, says: 'Road construction will require thousands of heavy-duty vehicles.'

It is no coincidence that such spectacular entrepreneurs as Louis E. Wolfson and Leopold D. Silberstein have branched out into the construction field. Merritt-Chapman & Scott Corporation, controlled by Mr. Wolfson and his associates, is engaged directly in construction, including the building of roads, tunnels, and bridges. Quick-Way Truck Shovel, a subsidiary of Mr. Silberstein's diversified Penn-Texas Corporation, makes power shovels and earth-moving equipment.

By 1960, when the highways program is at or near its planned peak, there will be 900,000 or more persons working on the federal-aid roads alone. . . ." [21]

---

[21] "Wheels Turning on Road Program," New York *Times*, January 13, 1957. © 1957 by The New York Times Company.

Questions

1. Does the above discussion involve either the multiplier or the accelerator, or both? Explain.
2. What in your opinion would be the effect of the highway-building program upon national income if it were to be financed by (a) gasoline taxes, (b) income taxes, or (c) government borrowing?

CASE 9-17   The accelerator and investment in the electric power industry

"In this study we have developed and tested a model which appears to provide an acceptable explanation of investment decisions in the electric power industry. The main hypothesis of our model is that investment outlays are primarily determined by the relation between the demand for electricity and the amount of capacity required to satisfy this demand economically. This hypothesis, needless to say, is nothing else but the familiar acceleration principle. If properly understood, this 'principle' is, of course, a broad concept which cannot be applied mechanically, as has sometimes been done in the past. In the present study the acceleration principle was adapted to our specific needs by taking into account a number of characteristics peculiar to the industry studied.

Of primary relevance among these characteristics are (a) the long planning and gestation period for investment; (b) the presence and quantitative importance of indivisibilities in fixed assets; (c) the rapid growth of the demand for electrical energy; (d) the impossibility of storing the product; and last but not least (e) the influence of institutional factors resulting from public regulation of the industry.

The first of these characteristics gives rise to a relatively long lag between capital spending and its principal determinants in our model, and causes year-to-year fluctuations in investment to be influenced not only by the rate of change of demand (as in the classical interpretation of the acceleration principle), but also by the change in the rate of change. The next three characteristics, in conjunction with the first, make it advantageous for utilities to plan their investments so as to provide a normal margin of spare capacity over and above the capacity required to meet immediate needs; this margin in turn makes it possible to take care of the growth of demand which may, and normally does, occur during the long gestation period. . . .

The acceleration principle is also somewhat modified by the influence of profits—probably as a source of funds and a measure of the short-run business outlook. This influence is, however, not very pronounced; it manifests itself not in the planning but in the realization phase of the investment process, tending to stimulate capital expenditures in prosperity and retard them in depression. One may conjecture that the far greater role played by the accelerator mechanism as against profits in explaining investment behavior in the electric utilities industry reflects partly the institutional conditions under which firms operate—their obligation to meet the demand in the geographical regions in which they have a franchise, and the customary support of their capitalization by the regulatory bodies whenever "legitimate" capital outlays are made. It would, therefore, be hazardous to extend our findings to industries having characteristics similar to those of the electric power industry but which are not in a sheltered position. . . ." [22]

Questions

1. Explain how investment in the electric power industry is affected by the characteristics described in the second paragraph above.
2. Why does the acceleration principle, rather than profits, play a greater role in explaining investment behavior in the electric utilities industry? Would this be true in other industries? Why or why not?

USE OF KEYNESIAN CONCEPTS FOR PUBLIC POLICY

The most important conclusion of the Keynesian analysis is that aggregate equilibrium may occur at any one of several levels of national income, and that there is no reason to expect the decisions of individual consumers and investors to lead to a stable level of income at a high level of employment. Sometimes consumers and businessmen will try to spend too much (i.e., more than the economy can produce at full employment at current prices), and inflation will result. At other times, consumers and investors may wish to spend too little (i.e., not enough to absorb the output of the economy at full employment), and deflation or depression will result.

The process whereby consumers and investors spend too much or too little requires some further amplification. Let us assume that the economy is at full employment and the price level is stable. It is easy to see that if consumers should suddenly decide to increase their rate of saving, or if business firms decide that the opportunities for investment seem less promising, spending will be reduced and unemployment will result. (Prices and wages tend to remain "sticky" even in the face of unemployment. Economists are divided as to whether this is desirable or not.) How can there be too much spending? Again part of the answer lies in the consumption function; spending will be in-

---

[22] Avram Kisselgoff and Franco Modigliani, *op. cit.*, pp. 378–79.

creased whenever the propensity to consume increases. Also, business-men may decide to increase their rate of investment while the propensity to save remains constant. If consumers or investors decide to spend more, they probably will resort to borrowing. It is at this point that the Keynesian analysis overlaps with the equation of exchange (see Chapter 8). If additional money is pumped into the economy from the banking system, and if the economy is already at full employment so that Q cannot be increased in the short run, prices will go up (assuming V is constant). Alternatively, an increase in V (M and Q remaining constant) could produce a similar result.

So long as government spending on commodities and services precisely matches the amount of funds it withdraws from consumers and businesses in the form of taxes, government finance has no direct effect on the supply of money or on aggregate demand.[23] When government spends in excess of its tax revenues, however, and finances this spending by borrowing from the banking system, new money is created and pumped into the economy. If, on the other hand, government collects in taxes more than it spends, the money supply will tend to shrink. (This effect of government finance is entirely separate from government influence on the money supply through the Federal Reserve System and the commercial banks; it is quite possible for the Federal Reserve to be stimulating an expansion of the money supply, and therefore an increase in consumption or investment, at a time when government tax and expenditure policies are tending to reduce it. The mechanics of this process, however, lie outside the field of study of the present volume.)

The inference which is most frequently drawn from this analysis is that government can and should play a positive role in helping to avoid the excesses of inflation and depression, and that this can be done most effectively through the influence of the federal budget. If inflation threatens, the government should cut its own spending and/or raise taxes. If unemployment and depression are the problem, the government should increase spending and/or lower taxes.

The above is the essence of the Keynesian policy recommendations in their crudest form. More subtle applications, which space does not permit examining here, involve changes in the kind of taxes and of spending, and other policies which may influence consumption or investment spending independently of the balance between total government receipts and expenditures.

---

[23] This assumes that total private spending will be decreased by the full amount of the tax. At high levels of income this may not be true.

CASE 9-18   The economics of defense spending

"Turning to the problems of economizing on the huge defense budget, which is approaching $40,000,000,000 this year with the added defense support programs, Mr. Cordiner [Ralph J. Cordiner, President of General Electric, and chairman of a special committee appointed by the Secretary of Defense] emphasized the following three points:

1. Although necessary, defense expenditures are a loss and not a contribution to the national economy. He rejected as 'false reasoning' the argument that defense expenditures are a necessary factor in prosperity.

2. Forty billion dollars is so much money to take from the taxpayers that every responsible person must perpetually feel under obligation to save some of it and reduce the tax burden.

3. Inflation caused by defense spending obliges the people to pay twice for their national defense." [24]

Questions

1. Which, if any, of the above points is based on faulty economic analysis?

CASE 9-19   The CED on tax reduction

"This statement deals with the principles that should govern federal tax policy and applies these principles to two questions: Should federal taxes be cut in 1956? If a cut is to be made which taxes should be reduced?

The answer to the first question—should taxes be cut in 1956?—depends upon the state of the economy and upon the state of the budget. The case for cutting taxes would be strong if the prospect were for serious recession, just as there would be a case for raising taxes if the prospect were for serious inflation. Also the case for cutting taxes is much stronger if the prospect is for a large budget surplus than if the prospect is for only a small surplus or deficit.

As this policy statement is written, in May 1956, the economic outlook and the budget outlook are both uncertain. The budget outlook, at least, can be substantially clarified before a tax decision must be made—that is, before the adjournment of Congress this summer. A decision on taxes— and the decision not to cut is a decision—should be deferred, therefore, until the end of the session when as much information as possible can be taken into account.

In this situation we can make only contingent recommendations dependent upon information that will become available later to Congress and the Administration.

[24] New York *Times,* May 19, 1957. © 1957 by The New York Times Company.

1. Under a continuation of existing economic conditions we recommend:
   a. No tax cut should be made unless there is assurance, based on a conservative estimate of the prospective surplus, that a tax cut of reasonable minimum size—say in excess of $2 billion—will not result in a deficit in the cash budget in the fiscal year 1956–57.
   b. If the emerging information about revenues and expenditures should give assurance that a tax cut of reasonable size can be made without causing a deficit, a cut should be enacted to take effect on January 1, 1957.
2. If, between now and the time for decision in Congress, clear signs of a serious recession should appear, a tax cut would be one of the most helpful moves to make, even if there is no significant budget surplus in sight.
3. If inflationary pressures in the economy should build up to a force that is clearly beyond the ability of monetary policy to control, taxes should not be cut, even if there is a large budget surplus in sight. If the inflationary danger was extreme, consideration would have to be given to a tax increase.

When tax reduction becomes possible, whether in 1956, 1957, or a later year, the opportunity should be used to make a balanced move towards a better tax structure. In such a move priority should be given to a reduction of individual income tax rates, especially those that are extremely high, but some reduction in the corporate profits tax, and also, if possible, in selective excises, should be included." [25]

Questions

1. Explain how a tax cut will affect (a) consumption, and (b) the propensity to consume.
2. Why, if there is a large budget surplus, should taxation ever be increased?
3. During a recession government revenues normally decrease. Why should the CED recommend a tax cut if there is a recession?
4. If the federal government should increase spending by $1 billion as an antidepression measure, is it likely that the result would be a rise in national income of (a) $1 billion, (b) less than $1 billion, or (c) more than $1 billion? Explain.

CASE 9-20   Budget deficit versus an increase in taxes

"A budget deficit would be preferable to a tax increase in current economic conditions, President Eisenhower said today.

---

[25] The Committee for Economic Development, *The Budget, the Economy, and Tax Reduction in 1956*, June 1956, pp. 1–2.

The President said that if revenues failed to come up to the expectations expressed in his Budget Message, the economy then would require 'a needle rather than a check rein.'

Shortly after he spoke two government reports portrayed a deepening of the current recession. They revealed notable declines in over-all industrial production and in personal incomes.

The Federal Reserve Board reported that industrial production, seasonally adjusted, dropped three points more in December [1957], bringing it down to 136 (the 1947–49 average is 100). The decline since August [1957] has been 9 points, or 6 per cent. That is roughly the same pace of decline as in the short-lived 1953–54 recession.

The Commerce Department reported that the annual rate of personal income, also seasonally adjusted, fell by $2,500,000,000 in December [1957] to a rate of $343,000,000,000. This was the sharpest monthly drop since incomes began to drift downward in September from their August peak of $346,800,000,000.

The biggest decline was in dividends, which fell at an annual rate of $2,000,000,000, mainly because many companies did not pay year-end extra dividends. However, wages and salaries—much the biggest portion of personal income—dropped by $750,000,000 on an annual basis.

The President was asked several questions about his budget and the economic situation. He made these main points:

[1.] A 'reasonable' deficit—the adjective used by the questioner—would be preferable to a tax increase in current conditions. The President appeared to accept the possibility that either a falling short of revenues or an increase in expenditures above his estimates could produce a deficit.

[2.] He has no plans to ask Congress for any 'specific' measures now to cope with the economic situation. He noted that the Federal Reserve Board 'has a very strong effect on the economy' in its control over the money supply. The Federal Reserve has already switched to a policy of markedly easier money, and some interest rates have declined sharply.

[3.] He based his estimate in the budget of improved business conditions and improved revenues on the 'consensus' of all the people who report to the government, and who work in the government on economic questions. This consensus held that an 'upswing rather than a continuation of any downturn' was likely. The President mentioned reports from a 'whole series of bankers' who confer with the Treasury Department.

[4.] He 'personally' believes that various domestic expenditures of the government 'of lower priority' should be reduced. He invited Congress to 'help the Executive' find ways in which these expenditures could be deferred 'or at least not increased.' " [26]

Questions

1. What did the President mean by "a needle rather than a check rein"? What has this to do with the question of whether or not there should be a tax increase?
2. What measures other than a willingness to incur a deficit might the President have recommended to Congress as a means of coping with the impending recession? Why, in your opinion, did he refrain from making such recommendations?
3. What would be the effect on the economy of reducing some of the domestic expenditures of the government? Is this consistent with the President's desire not to increase taxes? Why or why not?

CASE 9-21   Effects of unemployment compensation

"Industrial Commissioner Isador Lubin said yesterday that unemployment insurance benefits had poured $3,200,000,000 into [New York State's] economy in the last twenty years.

Denying that the benefits were a dole, he said the money was not put into savings accounts or 'hidden away in socks.' Instead, he said, it was 'spent almost immediately after receipt, spent for milk and bread, for light and heat, for rent and installment payments and a pair of shoes.'

'Since this money goes to buy the necessities of life for unemployed workers and their families,' he said, 'it also goes to maintain the business and income of the neighborhood stores, the public utilities, the banks and the department store.

'To people who think of it as a dole, how would the profit and loss statements of these businesses have looked last year without the $214,-000,000 we helped pour into their registers through unemployment insurance?'

Mr. Lubin urged that the present $36 top benefit rate be increased to at least $45 a week. He said this was about half of the average weekly wage. He read a telegram from Governor Harriman, which said in part:

'This year you face a new challenge. With the economic horizon clouded, you will be responsible for getting at least $300,000,000 of purchasing power into the hands of our citizens to cushion the impact of current layoffs and retard what might otherwise be a fast downward spiral.' " [27]

---

[26] Edwin L. Dale, Jr., "President Prefers Deficit to Increase in Taxes Now," New York Times, January 16, 1958. © 1958 by The New York Times Company.

[27] Edmond J. Bartnett, "State Jobless Pay Called Economic Prop," New York Times, January 17, 1958. © 1958 by The New York Times Company.

Questions

1. Which of the concepts set forth in this chapter are helpful in explaining the probable impact upon the nation's economy of the payment of the unemployment insurance benefits described above?
2. Would the probable impact have been different if the same amount had been distributed as a "dole"? Explain your answer.
3. Would the additional expenditure by the State of $300,000,000, as recommended by Governor Harriman, necessarily "retard" the coming of the recession? Why or why not?
4. How are unemployment benefits financed? What effect does the method of financing have upon the economy?

CASE 9-22   Slump in capital goods

1. *Mr. Greenwald.* "My assignment as a member of this panel is to discuss the outlook for private investment in new plants and equipment. My contribution will be based primarily on surveys of business plans for new plants and equipment and of new orders for capital goods carried out by the department of economics of the McGraw-Hill Publishing Co. We have been doing survey work in the capital investment field for over 10 years. . . .

As you know, the capital goods segment is an important area of the economy. Last year it accounted for 60 per cent of gross private domestic investment. In 1956 and 1957, capital spending has set new records, and accounted for 8.5 per cent of the gross national product. In the 7 years prior to 1956, the share averaged 7.5 per cent, and in the 4 years prior to World War II it averaged 6 per cent.

There are three important points which I should like to make about capital investment. The first is that investment is high and will continue high. The second is that the current direction of expenditures on new plants and equipment is down. The third, and final point, is that industry is now spending less on new capacity and more on new cost-saving processes and on research and development of new products. . . .

There is no doubt as to the direction capital investment is taking in 1958. It is going down; but it is down from an extraordinarily high level. The McGraw-Hill preliminary survey of business plans to invest in new plants and equipment was completed late in October. It indicated that total business investment in new facilities will be down about 7 per cent from 1957. Business expects to spend $36.1 billion on new plants and equipment in 1958 compared with $38.6 billion in 1957 and $36.6 billion in 1956. . . .

There will be important variations from the average decline of 7 per cent. Investment in manufacturing is expected to be off by 16 per cent.

The electric-utility industry plans to spend 8 per cent more money on new facilities in 1958 than in 1957. Even in the manufacturing area, where the over-all drop is pronounced, some industries—electrical machinery and petroleum refining—plan to increase spending on new facilities. . . .

The expected decline in investment is confirmed by McGraw-Hill indexes of new orders for machinery and industrial construction. Orders for machinery, except electrical, in the last 3 months of 1957 averaged 11 per cent below the fourth quarter of 1956.

New orders for machinery in the October–December period of last year declined 21 per cent, after seasonal adjustment, from the July–September quarter.

The McGraw-Hill index of new contracts for industrial construction for the fourth quarter of 1957 was off by 52 per cent from the fourth quarter of 1956. And between the third and fourth quarter of 1957, this index declined about one-third. The actual drop in industrial construction will not be so steep as the decline in new contracts would indicate because there is still a relatively large backlog of long-term industrial construction projects already under contract. . . .

Companies plan to spend more on replacement and modernization of plants and equipment in 1958 and 1959 than on new capacity to produce existing products. Since the end of the Korean war, manufacturers have been adding capacity at the rate of about 6 per cent per year, while manufacturing output has increased at less than half that rate. . . ." [28]

2. *Mr. Gainsbrugh.* ". . . My opening comments are confined to what I consider the hard core of this recession, namely, the downward trend in private capital investment. The National Industrial Conference Board, some quarters back began a survey of capital appropriations in large manufacturing industries. And I believe this provides insight in our current and prospective trends. . . .

The seasonally adjusted rate of capital appropriations touched bottom in the first quarter of 1954. In each succeeding quarter of 1954, the adjusted rate of appropriation approvals rose. The rate in the first quarter of 1955 was some 50 per cent above the low point a year earlier. The investment boom was on.

Starting with the fourth quarter of 1954 and continuing through the first half of 1956, unspent appropriation backlogs climbed steadily upwards. It was only in the second and third quarters of 1957 that capital goods spending substantially exceeded the rate of appropriation approv-

---

[28] Statement of Douglas Greenwald, Chief Statistician, Department of Economics, McGraw-Hill Publishing Co., Inc., Hearings on the January 1958 Economic Report of the President, Joint Economic Committee, 85th Congress, 2nd Session, January 27–February 10, 1958, p. 84.

als. During these 6 months over one-fourth of the unspent backlogs accumulated in the previous 10 quarters were used up.

We found in the third quarter of 1957 that capital appropriations of the thousand largest manufacturing corporations had been cut 30 per cent from the figure for the third quarter of 1956.

I now bring you a preliminary result of our findings for the fourth quarter. Mind you, these are for the giants of American industry.

On the basis of returns for about 80 or 90 companies this downward trend in appropriations is still continuing, if not accelerating. Capital appropriations may have been cut back about 40 per cent in the fourth quarter as compared with 30 per cent in the third quarter. It may very well be —I know of no data on which to substantiate it—that you can defend the thesis that excess capacity does not exist in American industry today. I don't see how you can deny the belief that it exists in the psychological feeling of the top men in industry, whether or not it may exist in abstract statistics. . . ."[29]

Questions

1. Are Mr. Greenwald and Mr. Gainsbrugh talking about induced or autonomous investment, or both? Explain.
2. Why would businessmen want to add to capacity at a rate of 6 per cent a year while output was increasing at less than half that rate?
3. If investment spending declined by 7 per cent in 1958, what would be the probable effect on the gross national product?
4. Are there any important differences between Mr. Greenwald's analysis and that of Mr. Gainsbrugh? What might explain these differences?

CASE 9-23   Five economists in search of an anti-recession policy

The following excerpts were taken from testimony before the joint Economic Committee during the hearings cited in Case 9-22.

1. *Mr. Blough.* ". . . I do not believe that we have yet reached the stage in the downward movement when there should be a deliberate expenditure program for the purpose of stimulating the economy. We do not yet know enough about the nature of the present downturn to engage in expenditure programs that are slow in coming into effect and hard to turn off, once they are started. . . .

. . . if further governmental action aside from monetary relaxation is found to be necessary to meet the recession, the next step should be a temporary reduction of individual income taxes. . . . It should be limited to

---

[29] Statement of Martin R. Gainsbrugh, Chief Economist, National Industrial Conference Board, *Ibid.*, p. 133.

the remaining portion of 1958 and 1959, and should expire automatically. . . .

. . . there is no doubt in my mind that dollar for dollar an increase in public expenditures will give a greater stimulus than a decrease in taxes.

The reason I would not at this time rely on increasing public expenditures is the slowness which in our history has marked the carrying out of public expenditure programs. . . ." [30]

2. *Mr. Chandler.* "The principal change in governmental economic policy that I recommend is one whose main purpose is not at all to promote economic stability, but which will have the incidental effect of promoting recovery and perhaps even of creating inflationary pressure before the year is out.

I refer to an immediate and rapid increase in our national security program. I wish to emphasize that the purpose of this step-up in our national security effort should not be to induce recovery. It is to be justified solely on the basis of our national security needs.

. . . such a program would have highly stimulating effects on business activity long before actual Government expenditures rose very much. The very announcement of a sharply expanded program would change business expectations, business attitudes toward inventories, and the willingness of business to undertake investment. And a stepped-up pace of contract letting would immediately lead prime contractors, subcontractors, and suppliers to buy more and to offer more employment. . . .

As to tax policy, I see no justification for any tax cut in the foreseeable future. . . ." [31]

3. *Mr. Galbraith.* ". . . Even the friends of monetary policy have always thought that high interest rates might be more effective in curbing borrowing and investment than low interest rates in stimulating it. Thus, it would be idle to rely on a reduction of interest rates to bring recovery. . . .

Principal reliance in contending with recession will have to be on fiscal measures—on increased public outlays for civilian purposes and on tax reduction. . . .

In the present situation, however, there is a good deal to be said on the choice between lowering taxes and increasing public outlays. And the choice is very strongly in favor of the latter. Tax reduction, as we all recognize, is a rather irrevocable step. Once taxes are reduced, it will be difficult to raise them again. Should the present recession prove temporary, we would want to have them back and fairly promptly. We can't have a deficit in both depression and boom. Life is not yet that wonderful.

---

[30] Statement of Roy Blough (Columbia University), *Ibid.*, pp. 454–55, 473.
[31] Statement of Lester V. Chandler (Princeton University), *Ibid.*, p. 457.

There are other reasons for favoring an increase in expenditures. These have the initial effect of providing jobs and incomes to men who are now unemployed or would become so. Personal tax reduction has the initial effect of providing added income to individuals who already have jobs and incomes and for that reason are taxpayers. . . .

. . . The inevitability of debate over who should benefit from any tax reduction is another reason for avoiding this remedy.

But the most important reason for favoring an increase in civilian public outlays as the principal protective device is that we now have so many things that need doing. . . .

. . . Schools and aid to education, research support and facilities, urban rental housing, urban redevelopment, resource development, metropolitan communications, are all deficient or lagging. . . ." [32]

4. *Mr. Watkins.* ". . . My summary view is that we are undergoing another economic recession roughly comparable with those of 1948–49 and 1953–54; that the recession is on the average already 6 or 7 months old; that there is a good prospect that recovery will be underway before another 6 or 7 months have gone by; that the total output of the economy for the full year 1958 may well equal or slightly exceed the 1957 output. . . .

. . . I believe that public policy must be alert to any evidence of a worsening or lengthening of the recession and prepared for further and stronger remedial action. Among other possible measures, I would lay plans for a tax cut; although as of now I do not see the need or justification for a tax cut, given the present and prospective demands on the Federal budget. . . ." [33]

5. *Mr. Brozen.* "I would suggest that we permit the temporary 5-per cent portion of the 52-per cent corporate income tax to expire and permit the corporate income tax to drop to the 47-per cent level. The reasons for this lie in the fact that if we were to make more funds available for investment and increase the incentives to invest—this would have that double-barreled impact if we permitted the corporate income tax to drop to the 47-per cent level—the result would be that more productive equipment would be put into place more rapidly and high-priced labor would be re-employed more rapidly on this more productive equipment because it would be worth employing on it." [34]

Questions

1. Do you agree that "dollar for dollar an increase in public expenditures will give a greater stimulus than a decrease in taxes"? Why or why not?

---

[32] Statement of John Kenneth Galbraith (Harvard University), *Ibid.*, pp. 463–64.

[33] Statement of Ralph J. Watkins (The Brookings Institute), *Ibid.*, pp. 465–66.

[34] Statement of Yale Brozen (University of Chicago), *Ibid.*, p. 488.

2. In the 1930's, the announcement of large increases in government expenditures did not generally have the beneficial effects which Mr. Chandler now expects. Is the situation different now? Explain.

3. Make a list of Mr. Galbraith's arguments against tax reduction and in favor of increased civilian expenditures. Indicate whether you agree or disagree with each argument and explain your answer.

4. Would an "easy money" policy have the same effect as Mr. Brozen's recommendation of a cut in corporate income tax? Why or why not?

5. Discuss the nature of the disagreements in the policy recommendations of the above quoted economists. In your opinion, what are the reasons for the disagreement?

NOTE: this index is a guide to the topics in *descriptive* and *applied* economics touched on in the cases. Since the Table of Contents serves as a guide to the topics in economic *analysis* illustrated by the cases, no such headings are included here.

Case numbers are given in **boldface,** page references in roman type.